Colors For Your Every Mood

Bold or spare, the colors you choose for a room can set the tone as placid or playful. Imagine this scene as designed by Carl D'Aquino, done in neutral shades of gray, beige, or taupe. The mood would have been very quiet and low energy. But when primary reds, blues, and yellows are used, the mood immediately becomes fun-loving, free spirited, and joyful. Though these are happy hues we associate with childhood, yet as used here, they create a sophisticated "grown-up" setting.

Colors
For Your Every
Mood

Discover Your True
Decorating Colors

Traditional in
architecture and
furnishings, this
entryway in
Alexander Julian's
Connecticut home
took a fresh turn
when it came
to color.
A more predictable
shade of blue might
have been a quiet
midtone.
But this energetic,
vibrant blue with a
touch of purple,
gives a sense of
the dynamic and
dramatic.
The choice
transforms the
interior from
ordinary to
extraordinary!

Leatrice Eiseman

Robert Hickey, Visual Director

CAPITAL BOOKS, INC.

STERLING, VIRGINIA

PHOTO: DON PAULSON

Published by
Capital Books Inc.
22883 Quicksilver Drive, Sterling, Virginia 20166

Reference to PANTONE® Colors displayed in this book
which are printed in four-color process have not been
evaluated by Pantone, Inc. for accuracy and may not
match the PANTONE Color Standards. Pantone, Inc.
assumes no responsibility for color inaccuracy. For the
accurate PANTONE Color Standards, refer to the current
editions of the PANTONE Color Publications.

PANTONE® and PANTONE TEXTILE Color System® are
registered trademarks of Pantone, Inc. ©Pantone, Inc., 1998.

Produced with the permission of Pantone, Inc.

The PANTONE TEXTILE Color System® is a global system
used to select, specify, communicate and control color in the
apparel, home furnishings, architectural and interior design
industries. It currently contains 1,701 fashion-forward textile
colors dyed on fabric, each with its own unique PANTONE
Number and name in six languages, and is continually
updated. Over 200,000 textile professionals around the world
use and rely on the PANTONE TEXTILE Color System® .

LIBRARY OF CONGRESS CATALOGING-IN-PUBLICATION DATA
Eiseman, Leatrice.
Colors for your every mood: discover your true decorating
colors / by Leatrice Eiseman; Robert Hickey, visual director.
    p. cm.
    Included bibliographical references and index.
    ISBN 1-892123-00-2
    1. Color in interior decoration. 2. Color -- Psychological
aspects. 1. Hickey, Robert, 1950- . II. Title.
NK2115.5.C6E48   1998
747'.94--dc21   98-35429
                                      CIP

FIRST EDITION

10 9 8 7 6 5 4 3 2

Printed in Hong Kong through PrintNet.

COLORS
FOR
YOUR
EVERY
MOOD

Contents

Feel the Excitement: Blood and Fire, Power and Strength, Sex
and Seduction, Temptation, Dyes and Pigments, Physiological
Responses, Fertility and New Life, Art, In Bed and Elsewhere,
Personality, If Red Is Your Favorite or Least Favorite Color

The Magic of Color

For as long as there have been people, there have been decorating decisions. I can just imagine Neanderthal Woman asking Neanderthal Man to drag a rather large flattened rock into their cave, thinking it would make a good table, then draping it with an animal skin. She sets the bowl he made her out of bison horn in the center, steps back, and thinks: "It needs something else." Mr. N. picks up his unfinished breakfast berries and plops them into the bowl with a flourish. Just the right touch of color! They both grunt their approval. This rudimentary attempt at interior design must have been just as satisfying eons ago as it is now.

Today we are fortunate to have more decorating guidelines. Bookstores are filled with interior design guides: how-to books by celebrity decorators about celebrated houses we all wish we had. Many of these guides are very helpful. Some look so great sitting on our coffee tables that we wish we could climb right into the picture and take possession.

But let's be honest. Does copying someone else's taste really satisfy your personal need to express who you are and how you feel about your home? Your home is not a decorator showcase. It is the place where you commune with family and friends, relax, and entertain. It is your shelter, replenishment, and comfort— not only to the body, but most importantly, to your psyche.

And that's where color comes in. No matter who you are, where or how you live; what your physical, mental, and spiritual requirements—your environment is essential to your mental balance. Colors are the catalyst for feelings, molding moods, and enhancing our lives. Whether you are conscious of it or not, there is no place where the influence of color is felt more keenly than in the place you call home. The right colors and color combinations will stimulate and relax your senses, release happy memories, reflect how you and your family feel about each room, and how you relate to each other there.

This dining room's subtle and sophisticated mood is created by Lynn Augstein through a harmony of beiges, taupes, tans, browns, and the warm glow of indirect lighting. Monotones calm the atmosphere and slow the pace, but this room is not without a sense of excitement. Why? First, darker and brighter colors have been introduced as accents in the accessories and flowers to electrify the scene.

Then through the windows enters another important color element: the deep blue of the night sky. Blue—both the twilight tones and day time's sky blue— has been used very effectively to complement the golden undertones in the room's earthy hues, adding a drama monotones can't achieve on their own. This is a good example of how to integrate the natural colors surrounding the space to provide a balanced environment of both warm and cool tones.

In these pages, you will find these color combinations. You'll learn which colors will help you create the look and feel you want for each room in your home, which colors will bring peace and beauty to your personal space, harmony and joy. Each color family has a history and a personality of its own (just as yours does). As you read this book, relax and let the colors tell their tale. Then choose the ones that "speak" to you. These will be your true decorating colors.

Throughout the book, the color names in SMALL CAPS are from the PANTONE® TEXTILE Color System®. You'll find a list of all these color names at the back of the book along with their PANTONE Color specification number, so that you can match your color choices exactly at home furnishing and home decorating centers or give the specifications to your interior designer.

May color bring peace, beauty, harmony and joy to your home.

Leatrice Eiseman

PHOTO: HERB EISEMAN

Take a flight of fancy and let your imagination soar as you become more and more aware of your personal connections to color.

Color Wheel Basics

In chapter 15 (page 145) you'll learn more about the basics of color. Here's a brief introduction.

Warm and Cool

Red, yellow and orange radiate warmth. Blue, green and purple cool things down. But sometimes it's more complicated than that. A color's relationship to adjacent colors often determines how warm or cool it appears. In a monochromatic combination of reds, a blue-red may be the coolest color. In a different combination combined with blues, the same blue-red may be the warmest.

It is often the change in undertone that affects the temperature: blue-reds are cooler than yellow-reds. Blue-green is cool, but the more yellow you add to green, the warmer a green gets.

The interplay of warm and cool adds richness and vitality to the color combinations in nature. When you create your color combinations, include both warmer and cooler tones to assure they capture the character of the world around us.

MONOCHROMATIC COMBINATIONS use just one hue in varying intensities, such as three values of red. These schemes create moods that take their cue from the color used and your associations with it. The more contrast between the values, the more energy you will create.

ANALOGOUS OR RELATED COMBINATIONS use colors that are close to one another on the wheel, such as blue, blue-green and yellow. Let one color dominate and use another as an accent, such as a room in blue, with secondary use of blue-green and just a touch of yellow. The intensity of the colors and contrast between their values will establish the mood as calm or kinetic.

COMPLEMENTARY OR CONTRASTING COMBINATIONS use colors located opposite one another on the wheel: red and green or yellow and purple. In proximity they intensify each other, create visual excitement and draw your attention. (Maybe that's why nature put her red roses among green leaves). Lightening or deepening one or both will lower the tension and calm the mood, but complements always add to a room's energy.

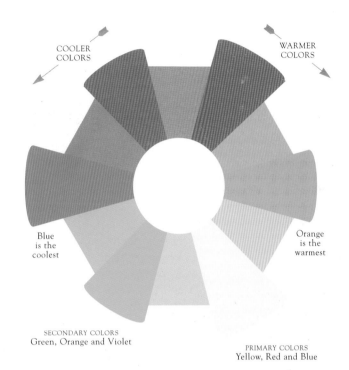

COOLER COLORS — WARMER COLORS

Blue is the coolest

Orange is the warmest

SECONDARY COLORS
Green, Orange and Violet

PRIMARY COLORS
Yellow, Red and Blue

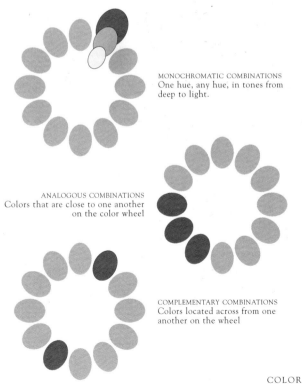

MONOCHROMATIC COMBINATIONS
One hue, any hue, in tones from deep to light.

ANALOGOUS COMBINATIONS
Colors that are close to one another on the color wheel

COMPLEMENTARY COMBINATIONS
Colors located across from one another on the wheel

COLOR
WHEEL

The use of bold color can add an element of surprise and dynamism to areas that serve as entries, such as hallways and foyers—spaces that aren't really lived in but, as passageways, mark a transition from one space to another. In this stairwell designed by Carl D'Aquino the vivid plum-colored wall is a dramatic background to the eclectic artwork as well as an unexpected contrast to the complementary rosey tan and taupe wooden surfaces.

Exploring Your Feelings toward Color

The Color Word Association Quiz provides you with an opportunity to inventory your reactions and associations to a wide variety of hues in every color family: light, medium, dark or bright. This is a vital part of your personal discovery process brought on by your reaction to each color. Get into a quiet place with good daylight and try to avoid any distractions. You may have strong positive or negative reactions to some of the colors and feel indifferent to others. There are no right or wrong answers, only *your* answers. Don't agonize or analyze now (there will be time for that later!). Simply record the first word or words that pop into your mind.

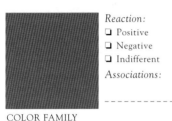

Reaction:
❑ Positive
❑ Negative
❑ Indifferent
Associations:

COLOR FAMILY

Note: If you do not like the color shown as an example but generally like the color family, please treat this sample as the closest representative color. For example, if burgundy red is a color you generally like but the deep blue-red shown here is not the precise shade you like, use the color shown as a representing that family.

Immediately next to the column describing the color, there are three additional columns marked **"P"** (Positive), **"N"** (Negative), **"I"** (Indifferent). Check your **P, N** or **I** reaction immediately after writing the descriptive word next to the color.

Spark Your Imagination

Listed below are words that frequently appear when people define their color associations. You may use these words, but feel free to use your own words and they may give you even more personal insights.

warm	cool	hot	cold	sterile
inviting	masculine	feminine	unisex	sea
earth	sky	ocean	happy	sad
tranquil	exciting	stimulating	dynamic	speedy
restful	fresh	refreshing	sexy	romantic
sunny	hard	soft	loud	subtle
neutral	classic	bland	ugly	beautiful
pretty	disgusting	fun	harsh	insipid
garish	fuzzy	sweet	sour	approachable
nurturing	friendly	juice	sensual	comforting
sensual	classy	peace	quiet	noisy
outgoing	sticky	grief	powerful	nauseating
powerful	basic	strong	passionate	weak
tasteful	elegant	expensive	regal	gregarious
cheap	tacky	rich	robust	dirty
clean	cleansing	serious	heavenly	mysterious
spiritual	serious	secure	rooted	nature
natural	artificial	smooth	tough	traditional

Color Word Association Quiz

Cover all the chips on these pages except the chip you are considering. You may change your attitude about certain colors as you continue to learn more about them or examine your feelings about them. But for now, it's important to record your immediate reaction to each color.

CHIP 12-E

BRIGHT GREEN

Reaction:
- ❏ Positive
- ❏ Negative
- ❏ Indifferent

Associations:

\- - - - - - - - - - - - - - - - - - -

\- - - - - - - - - - - - - - - - - - -

CHIP 12-A

BRIGHT YELLOW

Reaction:
- ❏ Positive
- ❏ Negative
- ☑ Indifferent

Associations:

\- - - - - - - - - - - - - - - - - - -

\- - - - - - - - - - - - - - - - - - -

CHIP 12-F

OLIVE GREEN

Reaction:
- ❏ Positive
- ❏ Negative
- ❏ Indifferent

Associations:

\- - - - - - - - - - - - - - - - - - -

\- - - - - - - - - - - - - - - - - - -

CHIP 12-B

LIGHT YELLOW

Reaction:
- ❏ Positive
- ❏ Negative
- ☑ Indifferent

Associations:

\- - - - - - - - - - - - - - - - - - -

\- - - - - - - - - - - - - - - - - - -

CHIP 12-G

DARK GREEN

Reaction:
- ❏ Positive
- ☑ Negative
- ❏ Indifferent

Associations:

\- - - - - - - - - - - - - - - - - - -

\- - - - - - - - - - - - - - - - - - -

CHIP 12-C

GOLDEN YELLOW

Reaction:
- ☑ Positive
- ❏ Negative
- ❏ Indifferent

Associations:

\- - - - - - - - - - - - - - - - - - -

\- - - - - - - - - - - - - - - - - - -

CHIP 12-H

AQUA

Reaction:
- ☑ Positive
- ❏ Negative
- ❏ Indifferent

Associations:

\- - - - - - - - - - - - - - - - - - -

\- - - - - - - - - - - - - - - - - - -

CHIP 12-D

BRIGHT CHARTREUSE

Reaction:
- ❏ Positive
- ☑ Negative
- ❏ Indifferent

Associations:

\- - - - - - - - - - - - - - - - - - -

\- - - - - - - - - - - - - - - - - - -

CHIP 12-I

TURQUOISE

Reaction:
- ❏ Positive
- ❏ Negative
- ❏ Indifferent

Associations:

\- - - - - - - - - - - - - - - - - - -

\- - - - - - - - - - - - - - - - - - -

CHIP
13-A

Reaction:
❏ Positive
❏ Negative
❏ Indifferent

Associations:

- - - - - - - - - - - - - - - - - -

- - - - - - - - - - - - - - - - - -

TEAL

CHIP
13-F

Reaction:
❏ Positive
❏ Negative
❏ Indifferent

Associations:

- - - - - - - - - - - - - - - - - -

- - - - - - - - - - - - - - - - - -

TERRA COTTA

CHIP
13-B

Reaction:
❏ Positive
❏ Negative
❏ Indifferent

Associations:

- - - - - - - - - - - - - - - - - -

- - - - - - - - - - - - - - - - - -

SKY BLUE

CHIP
13-G

Reaction:
❏ Positive
❏ Negative
❏ Indifferent

Associations:

- - - - - - - - - - - - - - - - - -

- - - - - - - - - - - - - - - - - -

DARK BROWN

CHIP
13-C

Reaction:
❏ Positive
❏ Negative
❏ Indifferent

Associations:

- - - - - - - - - - - - - - - - - -

- - - - - - - - - - - - - - - - - -

CLASSIC BLUE

CHIP
13-H

Reaction:
❏ Positive
❏ Negative
❏ Indifferent

Associations:

- - - - - - - - - - - - - - - - - -

- - - - - - - - - - - - - - - - - -

CREAM

CHIP
13-D

Reaction:
❏ Positive
❏ Negative
❏ Indifferent

Associations:

- - - - - - - - - - - - - - - - - -

- - - - - - - - - - - - - - - - - -

NAVY BLUE

CHIP
13-I

Reaction:
❏ Positive
❏ Negative
❏ Indifferent

Associations:

- - - - - - - - - - - - - - - - - -

- - - - - - - - - - - - - - - - - -

PEACH

CHIP
13-E

Reaction:
❏ Positive
❏ Negative
❏ Indifferent

Associations:

- - - - - - - - - - - - - - - - - -

- - - - - - - - - - - - - - - - - -

BEIGE

CHIP
13-J

Reaction:
❏ Positive
❏ Negative
❏ Indifferent

Associations:

- - - - - - - - - - - - - - - - - -

- - - - - - - - - - - - - - - - - -

ORANGE

CHIP
14-A

LIGHT PINK

Reaction:
❏ Positive
❑ Negative
❏ Indifferent

Associations:

- - - - - - - - - - - - - - - - - -

- - - - - - - - - - - - - - - - - -

CHIP
14-F

BRICK RED

Reaction:
❑ Positive
❏ Negative
❏ Indifferent

Associations:

- - - - - - - - - - - - - - - - - -

- - - - - - - - - - - - - - - - - -

CHIP
14-B

DUSTY PINK

Reaction:
❑ Positive
❏ Negative
❏ Indifferent

Associations:

- - - - - - - - - - - - - - - - - -

- - - - - - - - - - - - - - - - - -

CHIP
14-G

BURGUNDY

Reaction:
❏ Positive
❑ Negative
❏ Indifferent

Associations:

- - - - - - - - - - - - - - - - - -

- - - - - - - - - - - - - - - - - -

CHIP
14-C

BRIGHT PINK

Reaction:
❏ Positive
❑ Negative
❏ Indifferent

Associations:

- - - - - - - - - - - - - - - - - -

- - - - - - - - - - - - - - - - - -

CHIP
14-H

LAVENDER

Reaction:
❑ Positive
❏ Negative
❏ Indifferent

Associations:

- - - - - - - - - - - - - - - - - -

- - - - - - - - - - - - - - - - - -

CHIP
14-D

FUCHSIA

Reaction:
❏ Positive
❑ Negative
❏ Indifferent

Associations:

- - - - - - - - - - - - - - - - - -

- - - - - - - - - - - - - - - - - -

CHIP
14-I

ORCHID

Reaction:
❑ Positive
❏ Negative
❏ Indifferent

Associations:

- - - - - - - - - - - - - - - - - -

- - - - - - - - - - - - - - - - - -

CHIP
14-E

TRUE RED

Reaction:
❏ Positive
❑ Negative
❏ Indifferent

Associations:

- - - - - - - - - - - - - - - - - -

- - - - - - - - - - - - - - - - - -

CHIP
14-J

MAUVE

Reaction:
❏ Positive
❏ Negative
❏ Indifferent

Associations:

- - - - - - - - - - - - - - - - - -

- - - - - - - - - - - - - - - - - -

CHIP
15-A

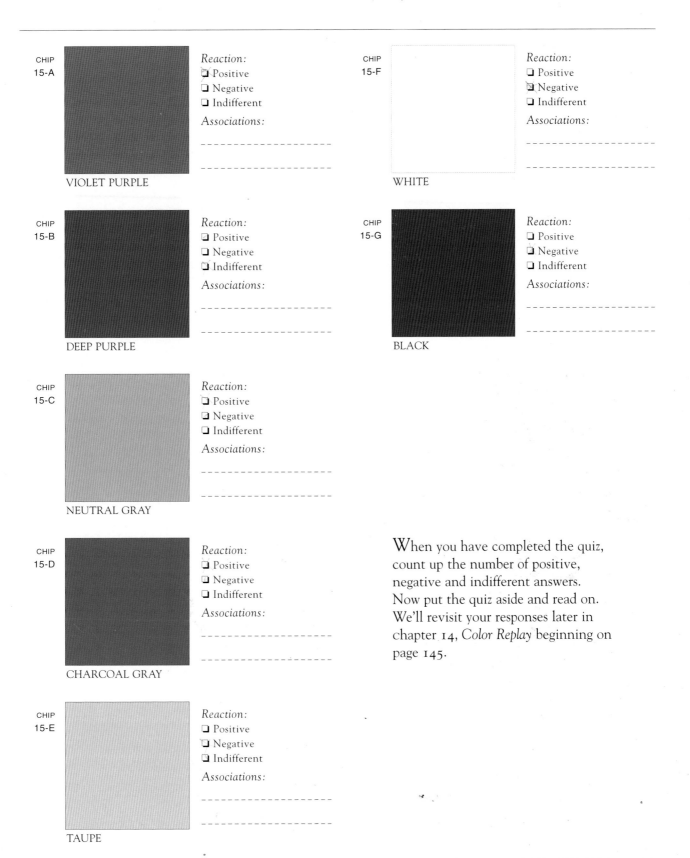

VIOLET PURPLE

Reaction:
☑ Positive
❏ Negative
❏ Indifferent

Associations:

- - - - - - - - - - - - - - - - - -

- - - - - - - - - - - - - - - - - -

CHIP
15-F

Reaction:
❏ Positive
☑ Negative
❏ Indifferent

Associations:

- - - - - - - - - - - - - - - - - -

- - - - - - - - - - - - - - - - - -

WHITE

CHIP
15-B

DEEP PURPLE

Reaction:
❏ Positive
❏ Negative
❏ Indifferent

Associations:

- - - - - - - - - - - - - - - - - -

- - - - - - - - - - - - - - - - - -

CHIP
15-G

Reaction:
❏ Positive
☑ Negative
❏ Indifferent

Associations:

- - - - - - - - - - - - - - - - - -

- - - - - - - - - - - - - - - - - -

BLACK

CHIP
15-C

NEUTRAL GRAY

Reaction:
❏ Positive
❏ Negative
❏ Indifferent

Associations:

- - - - - - - - - - - - - - - - - -

- - - - - - - - - - - - - - - - - -

CHIP
15-D

CHARCOAL GRAY

Reaction:
❏ Positive
❏ Negative
❏ Indifferent

Associations:

- - - - - - - - - - - - - - - - - -

- - - - - - - - - - - - - - - - - -

When you have completed the quiz, count up the number of positive, negative and indifferent answers. Now put the quiz aside and read on. We'll revisit your responses later in chapter 14, *Color Replay* beginning on page 145.

CHIP
15-E

TAUPE

Reaction:
❏ Positive
❏ Negative
❏ Indifferent

Associations:

- - - - - - - - - - - - - - - - - -

- - - - - - - - - - - - - - - - - -

CHAPTER 1

Color and You

Most decorating books tell you how to achieve someone else's notion of how a room should look. This book is different. Our goal is to help you determine how you want yourself, your family, and your friends to feel when they enter and settle into each room in your home. Do you want your living room to be a dynamic, high-energy, party spot, a tranquil retreat for intimate conversation, or a whimsical showcase for your prized folk art collection?

Do you want a dining room where romance flourishes or where the whole family feels comfortable eating and laughing together?

What about your kitchen? Do you want it to be a place where friends feel happy helping you chop the onions, or do you want it to be your own creative space where efficiency prevails? Or do you want it to be the place where you brew the coffee and eat gourmet takeout?

And what about your bedroom? For adults this is usually your room for retreat and intimacy. For children, it is a place to play and begin to develop a sense of personal space.

However you want each room to look and feel, this book will tell you how to use colors alone and in combination to make your own decorating statements and create spaces that are for you and yours to enjoy.

Color is the single most important design element in creating spaces that reflect mood and style. Without color, life would be very bleak. Color surrounds us and defines our world. We are soothed by certain colors and excited by others. We use color to describe our world . . . to attract attention, make a statement, or blend into a team. . . to change a house into our home. Color has forever fascinated people, not only in nature but as a symbol.

When you walk along the beach, what color stones catch your eye? Why are we drawn to the colors we are? What do our preferences reveal about our true nature?

Why do we choose the colors we do? How and when did we come to know which is our favorite color? Do we love only colors that complement us physically? How much are our preferences based on good and bad associations and memories of a certain color at a certain time? Why is color such a personal decision—and what do our choices reveal about our true nature?

Mastering Color Moods

This book is about color and decorating. You'll learn which color combinations create calm and soothing moods . . . which demand drama and excitement . . . which make a place or a person seem whimsical and carefree. You will discover which colors can change a room from formal to romantic, from classic to exotic. You'll find out which colors will stimulate your guests' appetites in the dining room; which will relax (or excite) you in the bedroom; which will trigger creativity in the home office; which will promote a playful mood when the family is together.

Colors for Your Every Mood is about how color can work for you. It will teach you to:

- ❖ Discover your color intuitions and preferences
- ❖ Increase your confidence in color decisions
- ❖ Avoid expensive mistakes
- ❖ Choose colors that take into account not only your own preferences but those of others
- ❖ Select the exact colors that create a special mood or feeling
- ❖ Learn every color's most powerful effect, and how to use it
- ❖ Delve into the history of each color family for some interesting background
- ❖ Understand what your favorite colors say about you!
- ❖ Discover foolproof guidelines for combining colors

. . . and much, much more . . .

This is a practical and insightful book that puts you in touch with your own psychological preferences to decorate your personal space.

Over the past twenty-five years, as founder and director of the Eiseman Center for Color Information and Training as well as the executive director of the Pantone Color Institute, I have delivered thousands of seminars and have been consulted by manufacturers, businesses, and designers on how to make the best and most educated color choices for their new products, packaging, interior and exterior design based primarily on the emotional impact of color. I've appeared on all of the major TV networks and have been quoted in hundreds of publications-- all because of the never ending fascination for color. But I have also spoken to thousands of consumers, like you, and listened to the questions they ask. I know you are fascinated by the mysteries and wonders of color through the ages and in our lives today, but I also know that you want practical solutions to your decorating needs. And that is what *Colors for Your Every Mood* does: It links moods with particular colors to create rooms that are full of your feelings, memories, and style.

Coloring Your Nest

There are limitless tints and tones to calm or excite you, elate or depress you, warm you or cool you, and even stimulate your appetite (more about that later!). There is the irresistible influence of color that tugs at you and appeals to your emotions, often on a very visceral or subliminal level. From infancy through adulthood, the colors in your environment affect and express your deeper impulses, although this is not always readily verbalized or even understood.

We have all walked into someone's home and instantly felt inviting warmth, a sense of greeting before a word was spoken. Although you may not be overtly aware of it, you were responding to the universal, yet silent, language of color.

As you read, you'll discover why each color family can evoke specific emotions and reactions. But before you delve even further into the many moods of color and their recognized associations and effects (and before you can be swayed by what you read), take the quiz that begins on page 11.

The Color Word Association Quiz will demonstrate how your feelings about color are personal, emotional, evocative, and say a lot about you. It will clearly show you that some colors affect you much more than others. By the memories and feelings some colors evoke, they can alter your mood.

The Many Moods of Color

Mood . . . it's such an interesting word. You have silly moods or quiet moods; you can be "in the mood" or not at all. You listen to music with plaintive lyrics about moody blues and moods indigo, and, on your worst days, you're in a foul mood. In the 1970s you may even have worn a ring that changed colors with your moods.

The American Heritage Dictionary defines mood as a general impression produced by a predominant quality or characteristic: "an air, tone, atmosphere, aura . . . a feeling." And feelings are described as "the effective state of consciousness resulting from emotions, sentiments or desires."

Atmosphere is another key word that expresses mood, and it too conveys a dominant emotional effect or appeal. The French have yet another charming word for mood (they usually do): *ambiance*. It is also associated with the feelings that our personal atmosphere engenders.

Color, or the lack of it, is the vital conveyer of color moods and catalyst to creating interior moods. From the moment you enter a space you are inundated with the sense of the colors surrounding you. It is the first thing you notice when you enter and the final message that you take away when you leave. Color is such a powerful presence in your life, the more you learn about it, the more you'll be able to use it to enhance your own sense of comfort and well-being.

Start with Color Moods

The first step in decorating with color is usually the most difficult. Where to begin? It is so much easier to decorate when you start out with a preconceived concept, a definite idea of the mood you want to create and then develop the design of the room around that mood. It simplifies the entire process, gives you a reference point that helps you to define your space and express your personality as well as everyone else's sharing that space. Above all else, color is the key to establishing the mood.

Eight Personal Color Moods

To make your decorating decisions easier, I've defined eight Color Moods:

❖ Whimsical   ❖ Tranquil
❖ Nurturing   ❖ Traditional
❖ Contemplative   ❖ Dynamic
❖ Romantic   ❖ Sensuous

There are three energetic, active moods: Whimsical, Dynamic, and Sensuous. The other five are quiet, soft restful, moods: because most of us want our homes to be places of peace and calm. But each of these eight Color Moods expresses an entirely different feeling.

As you read through the description of each one, think of yourself and the people who live with you. Does one Color Mood pop out at you—does it feel like you and your significant others? Most likely there are two or even three moods that strike your fancy, different ones that would be appropriate for different rooms. That's fine. All the moods are meant to stimulate your own thoughts about color and color combinations. They are not rigid choices, just tried-and-true guidelines for what goes with what. After you've read through all the descriptions, use the chart at the end of the chapter to circle the mood or moods that are the most appealing to you for each room in your home. You'll find many color combinations in later chapters that will reflect that particular mood and help make your decorating choices easier. But first read the descriptions of the Color Moods that follow.

Whimsical

Whimsical (pages 66 and 67) is the fun-loving, free-spirited, joyful set of color combinations, including the primary (red, yellow, and blue) and secondary colors (orange, green, and purple) with lots of brights and contrast between colors. If you want your room to feel lighthearted, playful, capricious, and alive, or you are young at heart, no matter what your age, then these paint-box and jelly bean colors will make you and yours feel happier than any other.

These are the animated color moods that are found where joy prevails, in circuses, theme parks, children's toys, animated cartoons, and primitive art. The dominant colors are bright hues in all the color families—warm reds, cheery oranges, smiling yellows, electric blues, hot purples, and gumdrop greens. These exuberant combinations are great fun in children's rooms, family rooms and kitchens where the entire family or friends you are entertaining gather to cook, but they can be used in any room where you want the spirit of pleasure and activity to come alive.

Some examples of Whimsical combinations are ❖ BRIGHT ROSE, SNOW WHITE and BLARNEY GREEN, or ❖ STRONG BLUE, GRASS GREEN and DAFFODIL.

Tranquil

On a visit to the museum, do you instantly gravitate to seascapes? Do you long to live near the ocean or the sea? Could you gaze at breaking waves forever? If you want a Tranquil room (pages 70 and 71) that evokes the sound and sight of a babbling brook or languidly drifting in a canoe on the lake, sky and water colors are for you. This will be the kind of room that brings you instant solace.

Connected in the mind's eye to the sky and sea, this is the serene, restful, soothing, peaceful, and quiet mood dominated by the cool, clear, light-to-midtone shades of clear greens, misty aquas, soft blues, cool mauves, pristine whites, and vaporous grays. Inspired by what the French call *l'heure bleu*—twilight, when all the world seems to be winding down—an even more quiescent mood is encouraged by the use of deeper dusky blues, blue-greens, and shaded lavenders.

These dominantly cool tones work best if you want to create a quiet place of respite and relaxation, especially in the bedroom. They also invoke a "spa" feeling in the bathroom, creating a place to literally cleanse the soul as well as the body.

Some examples of Tranquil combinations are ❖ SEA BLUE, SEAFOAM GREEN, GRAY VIOLET and STAR WHITE; ❖ SPA BLUE, ORCHID ICE and GRAY MIST; ❖ PURPLE HAZE, DUSK BLUE, CELESTIAL and HUSHED VIOLET.

Nurturing

Nurturing colors (pages 74 and 75) are the snuggly baby blanket colors that take us back to the TLC of infancy when all of our needs were tended to and we hadn't a care in the world. They are the fragile, soft, caring, tender tints that make us feel safe, snug, and loved: pastels and softest yellows, peach, pink, and aqua—perfect for a cozy place that's made for cuddling.

Although typically used in the nursery, these color combinations that call forth delicacy and innocence can be used in any room where we long for an escape from the overanxious grown-up world, particularly in bedrooms and baths. These are approachable, tactile colors that make us want to reach out and touch them. They are so imbued with nurturing feelings that they can instantly transform rough textures like stucco or sturdier wood finishes into a softer look.

The Nurturing mood may seem somewhat similar to the Tranquil environment, but this group of color combinations is lighter, more delicate, and predominantly warm; Tranquil is predominantly cool.

The dominant colors are variations of pale pastels: for example, the lightest warm yellows, peaches, roses, melons, and creams balanced by touches of pastel blues, subtle greens, lavender tints, barely gray, and tinted whites.

Some examples of Nurturing combinations are ❖ MELLOW YELLOW, PEARLBLUSH and ANTIQUE WHITE; ❖ SOFT PINK, SILVER BIRCH, and SEEDLING green.

Traditional

Brooks Brothers button-downs, Burberry raincoats, grandfather's clocks and grandmother's furniture, a venerable library filled with well-used books, this mood (pages 78 and 79) represents exactly what it implies: a sense of history, connectedness, substance and stability. If you are drawn to traditional moods and always have been, the classic colors fit perfectly into your comfort zone with their dependable NAVY, BURGUNDY, and FOREST GREEN in deep, strong, muted tones that evoke strength rather than demanding attention.

The burnished woods and rich patinas of antiques or convincing reproductions express an elegance to you that may reach out to include a touch of another mood, but the dominant theme for you always has been (and probably always will be) Traditional. Given a choice between dark rosewood kitchen cabinets or a Santa Fe sand color, you'll go for the darker, richer tone. You may veer from this direction and experiment with new trends from time to time, but the darker midtones or deeper shades will eventually call you back home.

The colors are those that stand the test of time, from the muted shades of TEAL, CADET, LIGHT TAUPE and ANTIQUE GOLD to deeper tones of WINEBERRY, HUNTER GREEN, INSIGNIA BLUE, BROWN STONE, and PATRICIAN PURPLE. They will always grace dining rooms, living rooms, and dens with a sense of formality and purpose.

Examples of Traditional combinations are ❖ TAPESTRY green, ANTIQUE GOLD, and CLARET RED; ❖ EGGPLANT, SHADED SPRUCE, and PLAZA TAUPE.

Contemplative

If minimal is your middle name and you live by the credo that "less is more," then you will be happiest in a rather stark setting. Monotones may be monotonous by other's standards. But if your longing for utter simplicity in a totally timeless and classically colored environment (pages 82 and 83) is important to you, the neutrals of gray, beige, taupe, ivory, and other off-whites will work best as your background.

Unless you plan on retiring to a monastery, however, a complete lack of color can be less than inspiring, and that is what a Contemplative setting is all about. If we look to inspirational settings for even more inspiration, we see the quiet strength of churches and temples embellished by vibrantly colored stained-glass windows that celebrate high ideals, great museums and galleries hung with awe-inspiring art. In a space that people really live in, this translates, for example, to neutral wall color and floors and a strong focal point centered in the art on the walls, a prized collection of china in a dramatically lit cabinet, or perhaps a special piece of glass or statuary sitting in a prominent niche. Key to this mood are words such as pensive, thought provoking, sacred, and spiritual.

Examples of Contemplative combinations are ❖ COBBLESTONE, FEATHER GRAY, BIRCH, and DEEP PURPLE; ❖ SAUTERNE, WILLOW GREEN, and RUBY WINE; ❖ JADE GREEN, BRIGHT RED VIOLET, and PASTEL ROSE TAN.

Dynamic

Dynamic (pages 86 and 87) is the energetic, electric, dramatic, powerful group of color combinations. It's for those who prefer contemporary sophisticated looks to the traditional, those who want a room to feel vital. No soft colors here. These are the color combinations that evoke flamboyance and sparkle. These are chrome yellows, Ming greens, crimson reds, royal blues, prism violets, ebony blacks, bright whites. Slick surfaces and metallic finishes such as chrome and brass, gold and silver (used in combination), vivid colors, angled geometrics, strong contrasts, or bright accent colors bouncing off combinations of black and white. If this sounds like you or the way you want to feel when you walk into that particular room, the cool sophistication of black glass, granite, stainless steel, and white marble will suit your psyche best. But even the purest, most unadorned combination needs a jolt of color to give it life and spirit.

The multifaceted jewel tones are the perfect accents that keep the black and white from getting too sterile and stark. Everyone has a favorite gemstone. Is yours a sparkling garnet, a radiant ruby or a brilliant peridot? Just as with the jewels themselves, these combinations can be breathtakingly beautiful. But it isn't always necessary to introduce black and white into the picture, especially if you want a really flamboyant mix. Vividly contrasting jewel tones are the head-turners and show stoppers that are bound to invite comments like, "You're always so original. I never would have dared to put those colors together."

If you welcome that kind of response and you're a high-energy, gregarious person drawn to drama and high excitement and want your environment to be the same, the Dynamic mood is made for you.

Examples of Dynamic color combinations include: ❖ AMETHYST, EMPIRE YELLOW, black, and white; ❖ PERIDOT, TOPAZ, and STAR SAPPHIRE; CHARCOAL GRAY, MAGENTA, and SILVER.

Romantic

An herb garden, a delicious whiff of bread baking in the oven, a sense of intimacy—this is the Romantic mood (pages 90 and 91), nostalgic and sentimental but never "cutesy" or contrived. These are the colors of flowers pressed into books as keepsakes, of dried roses and baby's breath, muted colors that delight the senses and soothe the soul. The Romantic mood is not all flourishes and fantasies. It's also for very capable people who truly love making things from scratch, especially for their own homes. They set the Romantic mood right at the front door with a handmade grapevine wreath garnished with flowers or lovingly crafted birdhouses hanging from the trees in the garden. And if they can't make it, or lack the time or the talent, they'll search the flea markets, catalogs and stores until they find just the right thing.

Romantic is weathered pine and wicker combined with damask or lace, of country living or a cottage at the beach, the marriage of rococo Victorian and comfortably casual, all with a loving and thoroughly homey touch.

Romantic mood colors are neither too deep nor too pale, too hot or too cool, but somewhere in between. A more sophisticated take on midtones, these are like the subtle gradations of a fading hydrangea at summer's end, with such Romantic combinations as ❖ DUSTY LAVENDER, TEAL BLUE, and APRICOT CREAM; ❖ TAWNY BIRCH, BRIDAL ROSE, and BASIL.

Sensuous

Rich, dominantly warm and luxurious color combinations (pages 94 and 95) are for those times and places when you want to feel magnetic and, let's admit it, seductive! But your tastes have to lean a bit to the exotic, as this is a room Lawrence of Arabia would have loved. Endangered species are very much alive here in tiger or leopard-like upholstery and faux fur throws. This is a sultry room that tempts you with its opulence and plushy textures; the perfect setting for an Oriental carpet and chaise lounge.

If the sensuous room is (obviously) the master bedroom, the adjoining bathroom might have a jacuzzi built for two surrounded by the flickering flames of scented candles and a collection of bath oils. This is not a setting for the fainthearted—there is a commitment here to robust reds, rich browns, desert camel, burnished gold, indigo blues, hot pinks, orange mango, the spicy tones of curry and paprika and, of course, jet black.

Examples of Sensuous combinations are ❖ CURRY, HOT PINK, and INDIGO; ❖ ITALIAN PLUM, RICH GOLD, and ANTIQUE BRONZE.

Analyzing Your Decisions

At this point, you either have a clear sense of a Color Mood that is most appealing to you for each room, or you're pondering several options. If you are like most people, you've probably circled at least two moods, possibly as many as three or four. Your final decision on the number of moods you use in your home will be based on your living space and your personal history, but the mood you use is strictly your decision. If you were drawn to a Color Mood as soon as you heard its title or immediately after reading its description, it "said" something that made you respond emotionally. You'll learn more in the upcoming chapters about these emotional attachments.

Personal Color Mood Chart

Now consider how you might use Color Moods in room. Choose a mood for each type of room listed. Save it along with the results of the Color Word Association Quiz.

ROOM	INSPIRATION			
Entry Hall	❏ Whimsical ❏ Contemplative	❏ Tranquil ❏ Dynamic	❏ Nurturing ❏ Romantic	❏ Traditional ❏ Sensuous
Living Room	❏ Whimsical ❏ Contemplative	❏ Tranquil ❏ Dynamic	❏ Nurturing ❏ Romantic	❏ Traditional ❏ Sensuous
Dining Room	❏ Whimsical ❏ Contemplative	❏ Tranquil ❏ Dynamic	❏ Nurturing ❏ Romantic	❏ Traditional ❏ Sensuous
Kitchen	❏ Whimsical ❏ Contemplative	❏ Tranquil ❏ Dynamic	❏ Nurturing ❏ Romantic	❏ Traditional ❏ Sensuous
Family Room	❏ Whimsical ❏ Contemplative	❏ Tranquil ❏ Dynamic	❏ Nurturing ❏ Romantic	❏ Traditional ❏ Sensuous
Powder Room	❏ Whimsical ❏ Contemplative	❏ Tranquil ❏ Dynamic	❏ Nurturing ❏ Romantic	❏ Traditional ❏ Sensuous
Master Bedroom	❏ Whimsical ❏ Contemplative	❏ Tranquil ❏ Dynamic	❏ Nurturing ❏ Romantic	❏ Traditional ❏ Sensuous
Master Bathroom	❏ Whimsical ❏ Contemplative	❏ Tranquil ❏ Dynamic	❏ Nurturing ❏ Romantic	❏ Traditional ❏ Sensuous
Guest Bedroom	❏ Whimsical ❏ Contemplative	❏ Tranquil ❏ Dynamic	❏ Nurturing ❏ Romantic	❏ Traditional ❏ Sensuous
Guest Bathroom	❏ Whimsical ❏ Contemplative	❏ Tranquil ❏ Dynamic	❏ Nurturing ❏ Romantic	❏ Traditional ❏ Sensuous
Child's Bedroom 1	❏ Whimsical ❏ Contemplative	❏ Tranquil ❏ Dynamic	❏ Nurturing ❏ Romantic	❏ Traditional ❏ Sensuous
Child's Bedroom 2	❏ Whimsical ❏ Contemplative	❏ Tranquil ❏ Dynamic	❏ Nurturing ❏ Romantic	❏ Traditional ❏ Sensuous
Child's Bathroom	❏ Whimsical ❏ Contemplative	❏ Tranquil ❏ Dynamic	❏ Nurturing ❏ Romantic	❏ Traditional ❏ Sensuous
Home Office	❏ Whimsical ❏ Contemplative	❏ Tranquil ❏ Dynamic	❏ Nurturing ❏ Romantic	❏ Traditional ❏ Sensuous
Outdoor Seating Porch or Gazebo	❏ Whimsical ❏ Contemplative	❏ Tranquil ❏ Dynamic	❏ Nurturing ❏ Romantic	❏ Traditional ❏ Sensuous

COLOR
COMBINATIONS
FOR
PERSONAL
COLOR MOODS

Whimsical 66

Tranquil 70

Nurturing 74

Traditional 78

Contemplative 82

Dynamic 86

Romantic 90

Sensuous 94

Is there mood, not mentioned above, you would like to evoke?

Maybe there are many!

Consider the way the eight described connect color and feelings and let them be an inspiration for a very personal palette, one just for you!

As you read the following pages let this be the beginning of a journey that ends with a better insight into colors and wonderful feelings.

CHAPTER 2

Colorful Memories

It's possible that you are more complicated or more adventurous than one simple mood can express. If so, use more than one. But if you want to explore your emotional reactions to color, let's delve back into your own memory for more meaning.

One of the most fascinating ways of finding your true decorating colors is through a technique called "Guided Imagery." Used primarily to reduce stress, guided imagery simply utilizes your own imagination to lead you gradually into a happy memory that banishes tensions and soothes your nerves. As decorating your home is such an expression of your personality, what better catalyst than your own fertile mind? And if you don't think of yourself as being imaginative, think again. You have a lifetime of experiences from which to draw.

Guided imagery is best done by relaxing in quiet surroundings where you will not be interrupted. Get into a relaxed position. Breathe deeply, slowly, and in a rhythmic pattern, as you pull from your memory a favorite setting where you have truly felt comfortable and happy, energized, joyous, or calm. Immerse yourself in the memory. Think of the scents, the shapes, the sounds, and, most importantly, the colors.

You might be sinking your toes into warm golden sands on a beach in Maui. Or reveling in the sight of the pristine white stucco houses mirrored in the sparkling cool waters of the Greek Islands. Perhaps it's a much simpler vision of mountains undulating into the distance or the nostalgic memory of sitting in Grandma's kitchen with a red-and-white checked tablecloth and matching curtains (can you smell the chocolate chip cookies in the oven?)

These memories still live deep within your heart and brain (in your neocortex, to be exact) stored as millions of neuron impulses, as well as in your amygdala—that section of the brain that gives emotional meaning to those memories of red-and-white gingham curtains and chocolate chip cookies. Now use this same technique to help you pull from your memory the colors you associate with that special scene.

Perhaps your journey will take you back to a sense of one of the eight Personal Color Moods we've just discussed, or it may provide a whole new concept of colors that have given meaning to your life. What you are trying to do is rediscover the colors connected with the guided imagery experience and use them to recreate the mood they inspire in a present-day setting. Allow yourself the luxury of bringing those wonderful places back into your consciousness. They can be relaxing or they can be energizing, whatever you need. This exercise will help you avoid colors that depress or antagonize you. It will also provide moments of quiet introspection.

If you are having trouble visualizing your own memorable scene, here are some very common ones people use in guided imagery.

Nature's Moods

Many people's imaginary excursions take them back to nature where there are several major moods to draw from.

FORAGING THE FOREST

If your mind-tripping has led you directly into the forest, more than likely, you are an outdoor person and need green in your home—lots of it. It's one of nature's great tranquilizers, as anyone addicted to trekking can attest, as well as nature's perfect background color.

If you love shady glades and the most intoxicating scent you can imagine is the smell of pine needles, then you probably can't get enough of green and would be happiest with some variation on the green theme in every room as a pervasive neutral (more about this in the chapter on green). To keep your greens from becoming too cool, and to add a bit more complexity and interest, look at the combinations on pages 98 and 99. Note how green is balanced by accents of complementary reds, russets, roses, wine, and deep plums—exactly the colors you would find on the forest floor. This palette shares some of the same serenity as the Tranquil mood, but the dominant color in the Forest mood will be green, whereas the Tranquil mood leans toward blue as the dominant shade. Sample color combinations for Nature's Forest Mood are ❖ DEEP LICHEN GREEN, TEA GREEN, and BOYSENBERRY; ❖ THYME, CELADON TINT, and ROSE SHADOW; ❖ WOOD VIOLET, DUSTY CEDAR, and REED YELLOW.

RUSTIC REMEMBRANCES

If your flight of fantasy has taken you to the mountains, you're probably the down-to-earth type who prefers weathered wood to stainless steel and could watch the crackling flames of a fireplace for hours. The lodge look is definitely for you: sturdy furniture, exposed beams, and nubby surfaces where Fido is encouraged to sit on the couch and Papa can put his dusty boots on the coffee table without fear of being banished to the woodshed (pages 102 and 103.)

A predominantly warm palette of rustic colors will express your rather no-nonsense nature. The message is rugged and reliable, outdoorsy. Stout-hearted earth tones fit this stalwart scene: honeyed yellows, earthy browns, pebble tans, brick reds, dusty purples, faded denims, light taupes, deep teals, khaki, and the unexpected punch of a vibrant pink cactus flower color.

These colors may be used in any room in the house where you want that earthy message to prevail, particularly family rooms, kitchens, dens, and bedrooms. Sample color combinations for Nature's Rustic Mood are ❖ MALLARD BLUE, KHAKI, and LIGHT TAUPE; ❖ SHEEPSKIN and BRICK RED; ❖ GINGER BREAD, FADED DENIM, and CACTUS FLOWER.

BEACH SCENES

You've never outgrown your childhood love of the beach, spending long hours collecting shells, laboring over dribbles of fanciful sand castles, reveling in the warm sand and cool water. If a day at the beach still brings you that same sense of childlike happiness and it's the first place you think of when planning a vacation (or taking an imaginary trip), then the colors that evoke those childhood scenes are forever a part of your psyche, and you truly need to immerse yourself in them (pages 106 and 107.)

Although somewhat similar to the dominantly cool Tranquil palette, the Beach Scene palette could be inspired by either warm sand or cool sea: the choice of temperature based on your favorite shades. But to get the prevailing mood across, either warm sandy tones or cool sea shades must be dominant. It's your choice, but more about this in the following chapters.

Another difference between this palette and any other is not only the choice of color, but also of finish. Think of the undulating smooth striated tones inside a sea shell or of sparkling underwater creatures that could convert your powder room or bathroom into an iridescent aquarium! Sample color combinations for Nature's Beach Mood are ❖ MAUVE MORN, SCALLOP SHELL, SUN KISS, and OYSTER WHITE; ❖ FAIR AQUA, LIMOGES, and WHITE PEARL.

WINTER FROST

Is heading for the slopes (pages 110 and 111) your absolutely favorite thing to do in winter? Is the silence of the snowfall the very best sound you can imagine? It doesn't matter whether you prefer shushing down the side of a mountain to gazing out on the pristine white landscape from the inside of a cozy condo (or both), there is something about being surrounded by all that cool quiet that is absolutely magical to you.

Recreating that same sense of relaxation is possible. And it's not all about white, although white is an integral part of this mood. Shades of cool Nordic blues or glacier greens are also important. But to keep the atmosphere from getting too icy, some balancing warmth should be introduced, even if the smallest touches.

Think of the colors of the warmer green pine cones and hardy plants that manage to preserve themselves under a coating of frost; think of the sparkle of sunshine that lends some needed warmth; borrow some of the grayed rosy tones of the dawn sky or some of the depth of the purpled sky at dusk. This mood is very similar to the Tranquil mood, but silent white is much more of a presence here. Sample color combinations for Winter Frost are ❖ CRYSTAL BLUE, SNOW WHITE, and GLACIER; ❖ VANILLA ICE, SILVER PINK, GRAY MORN, and LILAC SNOW.

DAWN AND DEW

Is your favorite time of day the quiet dawn (pages 114 and 115) just before the sun peeks over the mountains, when all the world seems enveloped in shades of shrouded blue and grays, hazy greens and the lightest teals and misted mauves?

Mother Nature knows these hues inspire moments of calm preparation as the day quietly begins, when most people are sound asleep, and only a few of us are awake to see the beauty of the world. Think of the moment right before the sun comes up and the wash of tinted color is just lighting the fields and distant mountains with a faint mauve glow. The sky is no longer covered with its shades of intensely deepened blues and blacks, just layers of ethereal grayed shades awash with dew. Sample color combinations for Nature's quiet Dawn and Dew Mood are ❖ DAWN BLUE, HUSHED VIOLET, and MORNING MIST ❖ PINK TINT, CELADON TINT, ALMOST AQUA, SILVER LINING.

SUNSET AND FIRE

Some like it hot, and you are definitely one of them. If you prefer warm, tropical climates to cold and prefer hibernating in front of the fire to shivering on the slopes, combinations inspired by sunset and fire are for you (pages 118 and 119.) The passion and intensity of hot colors doesn't intimidate you in the least, and you could happily surround yourself with the radiant colors of a glowing sunset.

These dramatic combinations make for some of the most spectacular mixtures found in nature. Think of a Santa Fe sunset, a hot Hawaiian sky at sundown, or the Aurora Borealis blazing across the summer sky.

This palette is dominated by hot red, orange, apricot, and yellow tones, often offset with somewhat cooler shades to keep the fire from getting too hot: magnificent purples, a sudden splash of midnight blue. The difference between this palette and the Dynamic palette is that the latter often shares some space with black, white, or charcoal while Sunset and Fire prefers to blaze brilliantly on its own. Sample color combinations for Sunset and Fire Mood are ❖ AUTUMN SUNSET, EMBERGLOW and RADIANT ORCHID; ❖ SUNSET GOLD, WARM APRICOT, AURORA RED and MIDNIGHT BLUE.

Floral Bouquets

If nothing makes you happier than rooting around in the garden, and your idea of heaven is planting seeds or pulling weeds, then floral bouquets are definitely your source of inspiration. If you can't possibly imagine a home without a garden (or at least a few potted plants on the window ledge and scattered abundantly throughout the apartment), then this pastoral palette is for you.

There are two paths you can take. The first path (pages 122 and 123) will lead to ebullient **VIVID WILDFLOWERS** — bright and irrepressible. This palette shares many colors, and feelings, with the Whimsical and Dynamic palettes Examples of Vivid Wildflowers color combinations are ❖ PERIWINKLE, PRIMROSE YELLOW and IVY; ❖ BLUE IRIS, VIVID GREEN, and AZALEA accented with a brilliant FREESIA.

The second path (pages 126 and 127) leads to **SUMMER'S GENTLE PETALS.** It includes color combinations such as ❖ ALMOND BLOSSOM, SACHET LILAC and SAP GREEN; ❖ FLAX and LAVENDER ❖ IMPATIENS PINK, GOLDEN FLEECE, and SWEET PEA. Look back at those Romantic and Nurturing palettes and think of your particular color favorites—wherever you find them, you will feel most at home.

Travel Color Moods

Your flight of fancy may land you even farther away from your point of departure. If you're the intrepid traveler (or a wannabe) then memories or memorabilia from a favorite country you've visited may inspire your guided imagery and your new color combinations.

Or perhaps you love history and are inspired by some scene in another time or country. It could be your ethnic or cultural heritage that is calling you and offers you a special group of colors. They may be there in the furnishings, fabrics, and art work of that part of your world or in something you've inherited whose colors can help you recreate your roots in a new personal space. Celebrating your cultural origins can make you feel truly at home.

If you've done a lot of traveling, you can't help but come away with wonderful memories of the colors that express the personality of each area. These can inspire you. And if you haven't had the chance to travel very much, you've probably fantasized about the places that you would love to visit. There are certainly colorful books, travelogues, and videotapes, not to mention films and TV shows that beckon you to visit. For instance, you no longer have to visit Africa to emulate that continent's colors. African-inspired color can help you make it the next best thing to reality! The colors mentioned here may not be the same as you might recall or even as typical as you might expect, but, that's not the point -- it's your imagination and personal "take" on the colors whether it be the color in a treasured snapshot or the colors that exist in your mind. Here are some places that evoke colors in my mind.

CALYPSO BEAT

Awash with uninhibited Calypso colors (page 130), Caribbean culture defines what vivid color is all about. Underscored by the rollicking rhythm of steel drums, shades of hot pink, coral, bold turquoise, vibrant violets, blues, mynah bird greens, and sunny yellows are all a celebration of tropical contrasts. Examples of Calypso Beat color combinations are ❖ SKIPPER BLUE, TROPICAL GREEN, PURPLE ORCHID and LIME GREEN; ❖ CALYPSO CORAL, SUNDANCE and SCUBA BLUE.

AFRICAN HERITAGE

Rich in native crafts and wildlife, the colors of the great African continent display the diversity of its people through the variety of hues available in their textile dyeing and ornamental beadwork, which reflect the vibrant colors of forest birds and flowers, and the warm rich colors of the wide grass plains, dotted with wildlife (page 131.) The color spectrum is well represented in vibrant reds, blues, greens, oranges and yellow, but it is the marriage of these brights with the ever present ivory, earthen brown and ebony black that produces the intriguing combinations. Examples of African Heritage color combinations are ❖ IVORY, EBONY, RED CLAY and JUNIPER; ❖ GOLDEN GLOW, INDIGO, TIGER LILY and SUDAN BROWN.

MAINE LIGHTHOUSE

This is pure Americana—the "Down East" colors of Maine (page 134): quaint fishing villages with their nautical clear blues, sturdy barns in traditional reds, the shining beacon of flashing amber light on the white lighthouse, a patch of green in summer's vegetable garden, the solid browns and grays of the craggy coastline. Examples of Maine's color combinations are ❖ PATRIOT BLUE, STAR WHITE, AMERICAN BEAUTY and BUTTERCUP; ❖ REGATTA, GARDEN GREEN and BARBERRY.

NEW ENGLAND FOLIAGE

Whether you live in central Vermont or overlooking Central Park, it doesn't take much to conjure up pictures of autumn colors (page 135.) How many leaves did we collect on our way to or from school to share with the teacher or take home to Mother? And we still continue our pilgrimages to see the autumn leaves, no matter where we live. No simple uncomplicated greens or golds here: They're burnished gold, bronze green, pale green-yellow. They're red, orange, purple and brown, magenta, red-violet, burnt ochre, crabapple, and chestnut—a feast of fall hues. Examples of New England Foliage color combinations are ❖ BUTTERUM, HEDGE GREEN and TAWNY ORANGE; ❖ MAPLE SUGAR, WILLOW GREEN, RED VIOLET and SUNSET GOLD.

PARISIAN CAFE

One of the world's most beautiful and elegant cities, Paris (page 138) is a melange of the colors of its timeworn limestone and granite, stone grays, and greige outlined with wrought-iron blacks; the sidewalk cafes with their green-trimmed awnings, the ubiquitous rattan chairs and geranium flower boxes. Examples of Paris's color combinations are ❖ DEEP CLARET, PARISIAN BLUE, DEAUVILLE MAUVE and WROUGHT IRON; ❖ FRENCH VANILLA, OMBRE BLUE, DRY ROSE and GARGOYLE.

SAN MIGUEL DE ALLENDE

Colonial Mexico is rich with traditional arts and crafts (page 139.) Silver jewelry shining from shop windows, old facades peeling away to show yesterday's earthen hues, the sun-baked, clay-colored brick, the gray of the cobblestones, weathered blue doors opening into colorful foliage-filled courtyards. Examples of San Miguel's colors are ❖ PEACH BEIGE, PROVINCIAL BLUE and BRICK DUST; ❖ PASTEL PARCHMENT, LIGHT TAUPE and BLUE SHADOW.

MARRAKECH

This warm pastel traditional capital of Morocco (page 142) is full of pink clay mosques and buildings, parks and gardens washed by sunlight, peaceful arcades of remarkably subtle shades that are appropriate for reflection and prayer such as teal, taupe, and lavender. Examples of Marrakech's color combinations are ❖ DESERT MIST, DUSTY LAVENDER, ALMOST APRICOT and BISQUE; ❖ ANTIQUE WHITE, PALE BLUSH, LAVENDER and PINK SAND.

HONG KONG COURTYARD

It's a bustling city that entices us with all of its colorful and glittering array of goods displayed in store windows and shopping arcades. but there is another view of Hong Kong worthy of exploration (page 143)—the quiet courtyards and ancient shrines in midtone colors that are as subdued as their environments: TEAK, BAMBOO, ASH ROSE, COCOON, CARNELIAN, JADE and CHINESE YELLOW. Examples of Hong Kong color combinations include; ❖ CINNABAR, CHINESE YELLOW and ORIENTAL BLUE; ❖ OPAL GRAY, ROSE GRAY, COCOON and ROSE DUST.

Examples of More Inspiration—Your Favorite Things

Like the song says: "Raindrops on roses and whiskers on kittens . . ." your favorite things can be an inspiration for color combinations. Unlike guided imagery, this exercise needs to be done with your eyes open. Look around at some of your favorite objects. It could be a treasured piece of celadon pottery, a paisley piano shawl, an art book celebrating Picasso, traditional Wedgwood blue dishes in the china cabinet, a brilliantly colored silk tie, or a faded plaid flannel shirt from L.L. Bean!

All of these things say something special to you, if only subliminally—providing the emotional tug that can inspire the colors and moods of your personal space and comfort level. They will fit into one of the Color Moods, and even though the colors may not be exactly the same as those mentioned, you can use these shades as your starting point.

Use this chart to record your choices among the Nature and Travel Color Moods for each room in your home. Now you may find that one of these is a better choice than the Personal Color Mood you selected at the end of chapter 1. If not, keep the original mood you selected and fill it in here again.

Nature's & Travel Color Moods Chart

ROOM	COLOR INSPIRATION
Entry Hall	❏ Natural Environment: ❏ Travel Destination:
Living Room	❏ Natural Environment: ❏ Travel Destination:
Dining Room	❏ Natural Environment: ❏ Travel Destination:
Kitchen	❏ Natural Environment: ❏ Travel Destination:
Family Room	❏ Natural Environment: ❏ Travel Destination:
Powder Room	❏ Natural Environment: ❏ Travel Destination:
Master Bedroom	❏ Natural Environment: ❏ Travel Destination:
Master Bathroom	❏ Natural Environment: ❏ Travel Destination:
Guest Bedroom	❏ Natural Environment: ❏ Travel Destination:
Guest Bathroom	❏ Natural Environment: ❏ Travel Destination:
Children's Bedroom 1	❏ Natural Environment: ❏ Travel Destination:
Children's Bedroom 2	❏ Natural Environment: ❏ Travel Destination:
Children's Bathroom	❏ Natural Environment: ❏ Travel Destination:
Home Office	❏ Natural Environment: ❏ Travel Destination:

In the next chapters we'll delve into the history, culture and psychology of each color family. Now you'll discover what it means if you love a particular color—or hate it; and what color preferences say about where you came from, and maybe, where you are going.

CHAPTER 3

Red
Feel the Excitement

Throughout history, red has signaled excitement, dynamism, danger and sex. It elicits the strongest of emotions in every culture: love and the pulsating heart; anarchy and the waving war banner; Satan and the martyred saint. It is the color of life and the color of evil, the color of danger and the color of excitement. Red's message is ardent and impassioned, never insipid.

Red is the highest arc of the rainbow and the longest wavelength of color. It is the never-to-be ignored hue that instantly commands our attention—from early infancy on. In fact, red is believed to be the first color that a baby sees. In the most primitive languages it is the first color named after black and white. It is the beginning of the color spectrum, and along with it comes all the implications of mankind's beginnings.

From the gentlest of shell pink to the deepest vibrant ruby red; at its warmest, it's romantic or passionate; at its coolest, it's mature, authoritative, regal. Red is commanding, whatever its shade.

Red's Message: Blood and Fire

From primitive times, red has been associated with fire and flame—hot, dangerous, exciting, provocative, and fascinating, capable of stirring emotions to the boiling point. The most ancient association with red is the color of blood: the elemental, life-giving force that brings forth birth, vitality, activity, strength.

Throughout the world, the word for red is typically derived from the word for blood. In the ancient Indo-European language, Sanskrit, *rudhire* meant blood. The root of the English word is found in the Greek and Latin words for red (*erythos* and *rutilus*), as well as in many modern languages. In Italian, red is *rosso*, in Spanish it's *rojo*, *rouge* in French, *rood* in Dutch, *rot* in German, and even the Eskimo word for red, *aupaluktak*, is derived from the word for blood, which is *auk*.

Red is the most visceral of colors because of its associations with blood and fire, birth and renewal, destruction and evil. Red meanings are never timid and often express opposite passions. To wave a red flag is to incite riot. Red marks the revolutionary or the martyr. The red heart of Valentine's Day is love; but we also "see red" if we are in a terrible fury or in anguish.

To be caught "red-handed" means clear evidence of guilt. Originating in ancient Britain, the bloodied red hand belonged to the man guilty of killing the king's deer. The cheap "red-eye" whiskey served in saloons of the Old West got its name from alcohol-produced dilation of the blood vessels in the eye.

Red Is Power and Strength

The fiery, strong tones of MARS RED, CRIMSON, CARDINAL, and SCARLET are majestic and imperious, commanding. To be "red-blooded" is to be patriotic and macho. For the brave, there is the "red badge of courage." Exciting news is "red hot," and the most urgent warning is a "red alert." Special days are "red-letter days" (originally commemorating martyred saints). Important dignitaries are often accorded the "red carpet" treatment. But if too much "painting the town red" leaves us broke, without a "red cent to our names," the bookkeeper marks the bad news with red ink and informs us that we are "in the red." To be entangled in "red tape" is to be mired in bureaucratic regulations and officialdom—an expression stemming from the red tape that really does bind and seal official documents. Red is not subtle.

Red Is Sex and Seduction

True reds and hot reds have always symbolized sexual energy and stimulation. CHERRY, POPPY, and LOLLIPOP are used to create a sense of youth, vivacity, ebullience and energy. Indeed cosmetics were invented to simulate erotic arousal—reddened lips and blushing cheeks. There's even a perfume called Red, and it's not one you would wear to Sunday school.

Many consider a red sports car to be the ultimate sex symbol. To drive one is to feel empowered, independent, adventurous, and impetuous. Notice how many ads for sport cars are red, how many middle-aged men drive them, and how many traffic tickets red car drivers "win." Statistics show that not all reds get the same attention though: it's the hot-orange reds, not the cooler, more dignified reds that attract the sharp-eyed highway patrol.

But red has its more serious side. The jeweled tone of RUBY WINE is considered very elegant; the refined tones of blue-red, such as ROSE WINE and CLARET RED, denote more dignity than desire—a sumptuous suggestion of richness, power, and tradition. The excitement of red still exists as an undertone, but the added depth tempers the fiery nature of primary red.

Reds that tend to orange, such as VERMILION ORANGE, TOMATO, FIESTA, and MANDARIN ORANGE are seen as outgoing and filled with a sensuous inner warmth. GRENADINE and CRANBERRY are delicious and inviting.

Red in Nature—Temptation

Red is nature's sexual "signal" color because it provides strong contrast against green foliage or blue sky. In the animal kingdom (including humans), red can signal approach as in sexual display. The male cardinal is red to catch the attention of the gray female. Red berries tempt birds to eat them and spread their seed. Red flowers attract hummingbirds, and bees seek their nectar and carry their pollen elsewhere, spreading them in other places. Red is the sexual symbol in nature.

Throughout history red has been used to evoke love and passion. Some women have gone to great lengths with it: Rouge was made from the pulverized cochineal (a red insect), Indians of the Amazon colored their lips with red hot chili peppers, the ancient Egyptians made lip balms of red henna and fat, and when Cleopatra prepared a romantic dinner for Marc Anthony, she had the floor covered with bright red roses eighteen inches deep.

Dyeing for Red

Many red dyes came from the dried bodies of insects. Scarlet (from the Persian *sakirlat*) was made from the lowly louse. Crimson, which comes from the Sanskrit root *krmi* (meaning worm), actually comes from the Kermes insect found in the Mediterranean oak tree. In French, it is *cramoise*, in Italian *cremesine*, in German *karmin*, and in Arabic *al-quirmiz*. The prestigious senators of Venice wore deep crimson robes, and the expense records of King Henry VIII showed the purchase of taffeta *crymsin*. Legend has it that under the light of the moon, women with extremely long nails (and good eyesight) harvested the insects.

The Aztecs and Peruvians discovered a red dye made from the scale insect called the cochineal. Seventy thousand insects had to be collected, dried, and crushed to make just one pound of dye. The Spanish conquerors dominated the cochineal trade through the 1700s when they exported the dye to Europe.

Madder, a hardy herbaceous plant, was widely cultivated for its roots, which yield a ruby red dye. The top of the plant was also fed to the cattle and caused the cows to give pink milk. Thomas Jefferson urged growers in the colonies to cultivate the plant—originally cultivated in India and Egypt, and widely exported from Turkey—but to no avail. Perhaps the deterrent to producing this glorious "turkey red" was a presoaking in oil, oak leaves, sheep's blood intestines, alum, and cow dung! By the middle of the 19th century, the madder plant was grown in various places throughout the world. When madder was mixed with woad, a purple tint was produced.

During the early Kamakura period, about A.D. 1200, Japanese artist Jigoku Soshi painted his *Hell Scroll* with frightening red demons chasing tormented victims; while to Persians and Turks, as reflected in their magnificent carpets, red symbolizes happiness and joy. The red bat means good luck to the Chinese.

Physiological Responses to Red

To better understand how red affects you in your environments, we must explore its physical effects, as well as its psychological effects. The human reaction to red is actually more rooted physiologically than psychologically. Because of its earliest associations to fire and bloodshed, red can provoke a "fight or flight" response. With the constant threat to life and limb in prehistoric times, red was the color that instantly signaled attention. And that attention response remains with us today, indelibly imprinted in the human psyche, where it is passed on from generation to generation.

Physiologically, red causes an increased frequency of eye blinking and a rise in the blood pressure, respiration, heartbeat, and pulse rate; increases galvanic skin response (GSR or perspiration); releases adrenaline into the bloodstream, and prepares us to take sudden physical action. We may literally "see red" as the blood rushes to our brain, especially if we become enraged. It is difficult to hide our emotions of anger, fear, or embarrassment, when we literally wear red on our faces!

The pituitary gland is affected when we are exposed to red—a chemical signal is sent from the pituitary to the adrenal glands, and adrenaline (epinephrine) is released. The adrenaline flows into the bloodstream and produces physiological alterations that affect the metabolism. In turn, this can affect our homeostasis—the body's attempt to maintain equilibrium. Our reactions become more automatic as the autonomic nervous system takes over.

In addition, the sense of smell improves, the taste buds can become sensitive, and appetite improves. It wouldn't be a good idea to use too much red in the kitchen or dining room if you're perpetually on a diet; but if you own a restaurant, touches of red help rev up the appetites of your highly suggestible patrons.

The presence of red can also increase hormonal and sexual activity. The physical intensity of passion is also associated with red—the face becomes "flushed with excitement." The obvious response to that fact could cause a run on red paint for the bedroom. But in reality, most people are too timid to paint the bedroom red and justifiably find it too aggressive a color for a romantic setting. Needless to say, many of the color combinations in the Sensuous Color Mood (pages 22 and 94) include red.

In addition, lengths seem longer and weight seems heavier under a red light. A chair that seems a bit lightweight under cool fluorescent light will seem more substantial under a red-based and warmer incandescent. The vertically striped wallpaper will make the room look even longer when bathed in a reddish light.

Studies have also found that brain function, as measured by electrical responses, is more affected by red than any other color of equal intensity. Some researchers maintain that this is not because of conditioning, but because red is inherently exciting to the human brain. People will actually gamble more under red lights than under blue. So when you go to Las Vegas or any other gambling spot, notice how may red lights there are!

The passage of time can be overestimated or underestimated, depending on the color of a room. Although we associate red with speed and quick movement, paradoxically, time seems to pass more slowly in a red environment. So you may not want to use red in a guest room (especially if the guest is someone whose visit you hope will be short)!

Red and Culture: Fertility and New Life

In Hebrew, the name Adam, the first man on earth, means "red clay." Red's association with fertility, birth, and beginnings is common to many cultures. Xipe T'tec, the Aztec's red-clad god of spring, dwelt in the eastern sky, the place of sunrise, the dawning of a new day.

To the Hindu, red symbolizes joy, life, energy, and creativity. The great god Brahma was red or golden-hued. His name meant "The Ground of all Existence." In folklore, red was the color of the sacred cloth of Lakshmi, the goddess who imparted beauty and wealth.

To the native American Indian of the Pawnee tribe, red represents the color of life. The Hopi bride wears a wedding garment trimmed in red as a talisman to bring forth new life. In the Aztec world, red stood for the heart, feeling, and fertility. The Aztec bride wore red feathers on her arms and legs during the wedding ceremony.

When the young Bantu boy is initiated into manhood, his whole body is painted red to represent the energy of life that awaits him as an adult. In Nigeria, red was used in female puberty rites to symbolize the important rite of passage. Young women were sent to a "fattening house" where they were fed on a high-calorie diet to make them plump, fertile brides. Their bodies were covered with a red palm oil and red clay to prevent weight loss through perspiration. Compare that custom to the current ritual of going to a "fat farm" to be oiled, massaged, and exercised on a low-calorie diet to make slim, independent brides!

Red is still used ritualistically in ceremonies related to sustaining or creating life. It was the color of choice for European wedding dresses in the Middle Ages and is still worn by Islamic, Hindu, and Chinese brides. In pre-revolutionary China, red was used to commemorate a blood tie, marriage. The bride wore red garments embroidered with dragons. Her nuptial carriage, lanterns, and parasol were all red. Red firecrackers were exploded in her honor, and the bride and bridegroom drank from two cups held together by a red cord. Ribbons of red cloth were tied to children's pigtails to promote long life.

Many young brides in countries like Taiwan and Korea are now opting to do two wedding ceremonies. They wear red for a traditional service and a Westernized white wedding dress, complete with a white veil, for the second ceremony. It is fortunate that the traditional wedding gift is money: those changes of costumes can get very expensive.

Healing and Health

To the ancient Greeks red also represented life. Pliny the Elder suggested a treatment for headache far less appealing than modern aspirin: the snout and ear tips of a mouse wrapped in a red cloth (but he was not specific about what to do with it). For a headache, it was far more complicated. He recommended wrapping the head in a red garment filled with a plant that grew on the head of a statue (which one he didn't say) and tied on with a red thread.

In countries as diverse as Russia and Ireland the same cure was used as a remedy for scarlet fever: a symbolically red flannel cloth wrapped around the throat. Often the cure seems far worse than the disease, such as the red-colored potion suggested for the treatment of epilepsy, which consisted of pomegranate juice and blood. Pomegranate juice or tortoise blood was also used as a treatment for epilepsy in ancient Rome.

In the second century, Galen, a much-respected Greek physician and writer, urged that all males eat red food and drink red liquid to become more sanguine: full-blooded, optimistic, cheerful, confident, and, most importantly, ardent.

Red amulets were worn in many cultures to prolong life and drive away disease: the garnet in India and Persia, the red jasper in Egypt, and the ruby in China. Gemstones were believed to imbue the wearer with the qualities of the color. The ancients believed that the glowing red light that came from the ruby was an eternal flame burning in the stone, making the wearer invulnerable to harm, as long as the stones were worn on the left side over the heart. Legend stated that should the ruby appear to lighten or darken, a terrible tragedy would befall the wearer.

In the 13th century Hindu physicians prescribed an elixir made of rubies for burping and biliousness. Obviously, because of the expense, this early antacid had a very limited market!

Magic and Beauty

Throughout Asia, red has always been the traditional color of magic and sorcery. In Japan red clay was dabbed on the lips to ward off evil spirits. The Japanese still celebrate the use of red and white as symbols of happiness: red and black for religious festivals, kabuki plays, martial accomplishment, the national flag, as well as stylized accents in works of art. It is considered sensuous and mysterious.

 Ikko Tanaka and Kazuko Koife describe the importance of red in Japanese culture as " . . . perhaps the color most rich in the associations of the climate and the culture where it is used . . .the color of fire and blood . . . the most sensual and psychological. Among other colors, most are abstractions from nature . . . they are somehow self-explanatory, unlike red, which seems to resound from the deepest recesses of the human soul." (*Japan Color*, Chronicle Books, 1982).

Young Greek women believed in the magic of red to lure back a wayward lover. In early Greek writings, an anxious maiden bids her servant to bring her red "magic stuffs" in a bowl so that she can "bind a spell upon my love . . . for eleven days he has not visited me!" We are not told what the magic stuff was, or if it actually worked!

Medieval magicians celebrated Tuesdays as a special day of vengeance, and on this day, they wore red. It is ironic that a color may represent both extremes—the color of life as well as the flames of hell. But blood and fire are both red, so to the ancients the symbolism was logical. The Egyptians originated the idea of red fiends or red devils, the origin of the Christian image of a red Satan. In later dynasties, words with evil connotations were written in papyri in red ink.

Not surprisingly, vampires are said to shed red tears.

Artful Red

Red was the first of the spectral colors to be used by artists and artisans, the red pigments made from the dust of the earth. From the cave drawings at Lescaux to contemporary fashions, artists have long understood the psychological significance of red in their work. Red can represent such disparate moods as love, joy, sex or hell (is there a connection here!).

In Jan Van Eyck's painting, *Wedding Portrait*, the solemn groom clad in brown holds the hand of the equally solemn bride wearing green. The bed in the background is a very obvious red.

Henri Matisse once stated that the purpose of his pictures was to evoke pleasure. He joyously celebrated the blazing hue in his *Harmony in Red (Red Room)*. It does take self-assured and extroverted individuals to paint their world in red.

Colorful New York writer Dorothy Parker so loved red that she did her living room in nine shades of the hue during the 1920s, including SCARLET, VERMILION, CRIMSON, MAROON and various shades of pink. The great fashion designer Elsa Schiaparelli combined reds brazenly in her apartment in Paris with varying shades of CRANBERRY, CLARET RED, SCARLET, AND MANDARIN RED.

Philippe Starck, internationally acclaimed product, furniture, and interior designer, says that red is his favorite color because it was the color of his mother's lipstick, what he calls, "kiss red, indelible red, a balanced red."

Diana Vreeland, fashion doyenne, former editor of *Vogue* and *Harper's Bazaar*, creator of fashion-as-wearable art shows for the Metropolitan Museum, literally lived and worked in scarlet surroundings. From the time she was a teenager and painted her nails a fiery red, the color was her trademark. As she stated in her autobiography: "All my life, I've pursued the perfect red. I can never get painters to mix it for me. It's exactly as if I'd said, 'I want rococo with a spot of Gothic in it and a bit of Buddhist temple'—they have no idea what I'm talking about. About the best red is to copy the color of a child's cap in any Renaissance portrait."

She also said: "Red is the great clarifier—bright, cleansing, and revealing. It makes all other colors look beautiful. I can't imagine getting bored with red—it would be like getting bored with the person you love" (*DV*, Diana Vreeland, Vintage Books, 1985).

In his book *Mark Hampton: On Decorating* (Conde Nast, 1989) the renowned interior designer states: "The ability to communicate mood is a characteristic of many colors and red, I think, has more connotations than any other. These connotations have a great influence on personal taste in interior decoration." He goes on to mention that some people see red as restricted to children's rooms or public spaces like hotel lobbies or first-class airline lounges, perhaps a Victorian vicarage or the church. But the most interesting dichotomy of decorating with red is, as he points out, that it can represent the sacredness of the church or the profanity of the brothel. Saint or sinner, red will not be ignored.

Red in Bed and Elsewhere

Conventional wisdom about any color is just that—conventional (and boring)! Forget the old cliché about using red only in children's rooms or dens. Red can be used sensationally in any room in the home, and it will be just that, sensational. It's not so much where it's used, but how much. Let's look at some of the possibilities.

Children's Rooms: Of course. Red wagons, red balloons, the big nose on the funny clown, Santa and Mrs. Claus, not to mention Rudolph—what would childhood memories be without the ebullience of red? Infants see the contrast of black and white before they see color. But when they mature to the point of actually seeing color, red is the first hue that captures their attention. It's the most stimulating of colors, but too much red in a child's room can overstimulate. If the kid is bouncing off the walls, those walls are probably in the more intense shades of red. Remember that many of the child's toys and other paraphernalia are bound to be red, not to mention the bed linens and/or accents in wall coverings. This is all part of the general landscape of kids' rooms and should be taken into consideration. Check out the Whimsical mood (page 67) combinations for the appropriate amounts of red to be used as well as the most pleasing mixtures.

The Kitchen: The kitchen and other dining areas are other places where red walls can rev up the "appestat," and we don't want to do that when we're trying to keep the appetite down to a dull roar. But they are wonderful places for using red as an accent. It's the perfect time to use red if you are timid about using color in other areas of the home. Here you will find a variety of reds are so connected to many healthy and delectable fruits, veggies, and salsas, that it seems quite natural for those shades to feel deliciously right in the kitchen or dining areas. Think tomatoes, pomegranates, watermelons, strawberries, raspberries and cranberries, and you'll get the picture.

The Den: Long thought of as the pipe and slippers "masculine" refuge, this is the most traditional room for red to feel at home; the usual place for tartan plaid upholstery or carpet, cordovan leather, paintings, prints or posters of hunting coats, riding to the hounds, and little foxes. Of course they're all in some shade of red. Some of the best reds for this hideaway are dark and rich, like CARDINAL, CRIMSON, DEEP CLARET, BARBERRY, and MAROON.

The Bedroom: Bright red is thought of as the sexiest color, after all, so why not in the bedroom? A good case could be made for the stimulation factor here, but the only problem is that many people do not use the bedroom solely for recreation or rest these days. It can double as home office or for TV viewing, and dominant areas of bright red walls, carpet, and bed coverings could simply be tiring in a bedroom. Again, accents or prints are fine, but large areas of solid red might make your rest uneasy in the bedroom. Try soft reddish-pinks such as SILVER PEONY, CHINTZ ROSE or PALE BLUSH or deep reds like GARNET, BURGUNDY, and AMERICAN BEAUTY.

Hallways, Entries, and Powder Rooms: The place where red can really radiate in all its glory is in entryways, passageways, or small spaces that aren't really "lived in" for any prolonged time. The use of red in these spaces is dramatic and unexpected. People will often react by saying, "I wouldn't have the nerve to do this, but it's wonderful!"

A small space with no windows can be lightened with paint or wall covering, of course, but it's still small (and bland). But a small space with POMPEIAN RED or ROCOCO RED walls (or any other vivid color) can be spectacular.

Red as Background: Because of its ability to attract the eye, red is a terrific background color in niches, the inside of cabinets, or armoires, especially when combined with rich, dark woods. And if you have an Oriental carpet with any red in it at all, one wall in red or an upholstered piece done in red can really make the carpet come to life.

Red on the Front Door: A really cheery red on the front door is a great way to greet your guests. It instantly engages them as only red can. In the ancient art of Chinese feng shui (the art of balance and harmony), red is recommended as a color for the front door because it is believed to invite prosperity to the owners of the house. That certainly makes a case for painting the front door red!

Personality and Red

If red is your favorite color, you are very self-confident. A preference for red is directly linked to society's most secure individuals—the wealthiest and most economically stable segments and/or achievers unafraid to take risks and set trends. Red is the hottest hue, the sexiest, most exciting, loudest, strongest, most fun, most revitalizing, and most delicious.

Word association tests ascribe additional consumer associations to bright red: intense, passionate, dramatic, energetic, stimulating, happy, dynamic, daring, provocative. It is the second most powerful color, following black. And those who view red as the most powerful are themselves high powered, active, and more often, women.

Just as a child is drawn to candy, we are irresistibly drawn to red. A physiological reaction, it simply is beyond our control. Advancing forward in our line of vision and commanding our attention, red imposes itself on us. But in spite of its ardent and demanding presence, it overflows with characteristics that are inevitably appealing . . . warm, lively, and energetic.

If Red Is Your Favorite Color: People don't just like red—they love it. People whose favorite color is red have a zest for life; they are, quite literally "movers and shakers." They need to be well informed, involved. Because of its psychological associations with fire, heat, blood, and danger, red is impossible to ignore and so is the person who prefers this most exciting of colors. They are passionate in their pursuits, ardent, and extroverted. Red lovers are achievers, intense, impulsive, competitive, energetic, daring, and aggressive. They are exciting, optimistic, animated people, leaders who like to be the center of attention. Desire is a strong motivator as they hunger for the fullness of the experience of living. Lovers of red have a strong sex drive and entertain stimulating fantasies!

Red people can also be restless and driven. Routine drives them crazy. They crave new things and new experiences. Because they are assertive, they can be opinionated and overbearing as well. They can be moody, bossy, and fickle in the pursuit of new challenges. But what would the world be like without these exciting people?

If Red Is Your Least Favorite Color: Since red is primarily associated with excitement and passionate pursuits, a dislike of this hue could mean that this active intensity is too hot to handle at this point in your life. Perhaps you are bothered by the aggressiveness that red signifies. You might long for more fulfillment but are afraid to get involved. People who are ill, stressed out, exhausted, or beset by what seem to be overwhelming problems turn to the calmer colors for rest and relaxation. Red is not a color of peace and retreat.

CHAPTER 4

Pink
Soft and Innocent

Red is the matriarch and all the pink offspring emanate from her. Where red is an obvious "flush," pinks are a modest "blush." Pink is red with much of the passion removed, a watered-down red. So when we are pleased, but not necessarily ecstatic, we are "tickled pink" (the tint some people's complexions take on when they are pleased). When we are happy, we look at the world through "rose-colored glasses," and when fair-skinned people are healthy, we say they are "in the pink," meaning their skin looks pink and fresh rather than pale. Pink tempers passion with purity; it elicits an aura of innocent romance. It is the most gentle, blissful, and acquiescent of reds.

Pink is a garden of soft spring flowers. It is the flower of the species dianthus whose name in Old English is *pynke*. Synonymous with rose in the romance languages, variations of pink are given floral names like WILD ROSE, GERANIUM PINK, and AZALEA PINK.

Light pink is innocence and babyhood—POWDER PINK, HEAVENLY PINK, CANDY PINK. These connote sweetness, tenderness, intimacy, softness, and baby girls. Pinks such as CLOUD PINK, CHALK PINK, PEARL, and LOTUS are perceived as sweet-smelling and lighthearted. Muted, dusty roses and pinks, such as SEA PINK, MAUVEGLOW, BLUSH, SILVER PINK, DUSTY ROSE, and ASH ROSE, are the most sophisticated and upscale tints in the pink family. Brighter, clearer pinks such as STRAWBERRY PINK, CONFETTI, BUBBLEGUM, CANDY PINK, AURORA PINK, and PRISM PINK are youthful and fun.

Sexy Pink

The brightest variations of the color, such as SHOCKING PINK, HOT PINK, PHLOX PINK, and FUCHSIA PINK, have much the same dynamism as vibrant reds. They are more aggressive and assertive than softer pinks, more blatantly sexual. The fashion designer Schiaparelli startled the fashion world in the 1930s when she introduced shocking pink into her designs. She was fascinated by the vivid Peruvian pinks of the Incas, and it became her signature color. Yves St. Laurent, who worked for her briefly, felt that only Schiaparelli could have created this new color with the verve of red, this neon, "unreal" pink that had the ability to shock and was appropriately christened "shocking pink."

Brilliant pinks are whimsical, trendy, and "unignorable." For the introvert, such pink is tacky. For the extrovert, it can be tantalizing.

Pink and Culture

While we may think that fox-hunting jackets are red, to be entirely proper, you must call them "pink." The British upper classes sported "pink" only for hunting, but never at other times. Anyone of the upper classes would never wear SHOCKING PINK in the country, as it is considered very declassé.

The lighter, softer pinks have long been considered a pleasing color to live with and to use in interiors. The great hall of Glamis Castle in northern Scotland was painted an exacting shade of pastel pink, obtained by mixing white paint with pig's blood.

In the early days of the American colonies, pastel pink paint was obtained by mixing sour milk with deeper shades of red pigment. The resulting pink tint was beautiful; the scent was not!

In some cultures, pink is a basic color. It has been said that bright pink is the navy blue of India. In Indian folklore, pink was one of the favorite colors of the ladies of the harem. On the night of the full moon, they danced in gossamer pink gowns, casting delicate shadows against the glistening white marbled palace walls. The maharajah of Jaipur was so enamored with the color pink that he constructed an entire pink city, miles and miles of pink palaces, bazaars, temples, and towers shimmering in the sunlight. The single note of contrast came from the splash of brilliant green doors on the buildings. Did the clever maharajah know that by decreeing complementary green accents, his pink city appeared to be even pinker?

In ancient Japan, pink signified a poor income. Red dye was so expensive that only the wealthy could afford it. The masses were forbidden to use red and had to settle for the faintest reddish-pink tint made from a cheap dye.

As William Wrigley learned in the 1940s, pink is considered a lucky color in China. Spearmint gum was introduced into the country in the usual green package, and nobody bought it. When the packaging was changed to pink, sales soared!

The Fashion for Pink

Magenta, the deepest and most luxuriant of pinks, was developed in 1859 as one of the first synthetic dyes. It became enormously popular with the Victorians who loved the hue in heavy velvets, sumptuous damasks, and taffetas. But it wasn't until the period preceding World War I that magenta really burst forth on the scene, when the Russian Ballet was the rage of Paris and the rich regal colors of Imperial Russia became fashionable. Stylish visionaries like Isadora Duncan were way ahead of their time when they combined the gorgeous deep blue-red with brilliant orange and vibrant violet. Unfortunately, the descending gloom of wartime replaced these dazzling colors with muddied tones.

By the time the 1920s arrived, the use of makeup was openly acceptable. Lips were red: It was estimated that 50 million American women used 3,000 miles of lipstick in 1924, and cheeks were obviously pink. The daring flappers didn't stop there—rouge was brazenly daubed on the knees to highlight the new short skirts.

Pink made its way into interior decor in limited usage in the 1920s, 1930s and 1940s, but it wasn't until the 1950s that pink reigned supreme. It was called the color of the decade. Advertisements advised women to "think pink" and Audrey Hepburn captivated moviegoers in her pink taffeta gown in the film *Funny Face*. Women all over the world recognized that they looked pretty in pink and when surrounded by pink. The renowned hotelier Madame Ritz of the famous Ritz Hotel in Paris decreed that lampshades should always be lined in pink. The flattering glow emanating from the pink lamps brought her clientele back again and again.

Christian Dior designed fabulous jewels in coordinating colors, among them pink tourmaline for his misty pink ensembles. He also introduced color-coordinated stiletto heels. In this same era, pink made its modern-day debut in men's shirts.

Physiological Responses to Pink

The color pink has been shown to influence all growing things, plants and people. Dr. Bernard Jensen, a natural health scientist, conducted studies where he demonstrated that plants growing in a pink-glassed hothouse will grow twice as fast and sturdier than those grown in blue hothouses (*Health and Light,* by John Ott, Pocket Books, 1973).

John Ott also said that different shades of pink may have completely different effects. He cited the case of a radio station in Florida (where FLAMINGO PINK is pervasive) that changed its lighting from regular fluorescent tubes to a deep pink. Tempers flared, performers were irritable, and everyone was generally disagreeable. Someone finally remembered that the bad behavior commenced with the deep pink lighting and had it removed. Within a week, harmony was restored.

Alexander Schauss, of the American Institute for Biosocial Research in Tacoma, Washington, developed the concept of using a bright Pepto Bismol pink environment to calm subjects after he noted that his own blood pressure, pulse, and heart beat lowered more rapidly after a period of hyperexcitement when he viewed that vivid shade of pink. He felt that it might have an effect on human aggression and tested the theory at the Naval Correctional Center in Seattle. An admission cell was painted the vibrant Baker-Miller pink. Newly confined prisoners were admitted to the cell and observed for fifteen minutes during which no incidents of erratic behavior were recorded. The effects of the color lingered on for at least 30 minutes after their removal from the cell. Interestingly color-blind subjects at Bryce Hospital in Tuscaloosa exhibited the same physiological responses to Baker-Miller pink as those who were not colorblind. Schauss states that "the effect of Baker-Miller pink is physical, not psychological or cultural." Although a person may not be able to differentiate color, transmitters in the eyes pick up information from visible radiant energy sources and transmit that energy to the hypothalamus, and the pineal and pituitary glands. So it may be possible to "see" with your glands. (*The International Journal for Biosocial Research,* vol. 2, 1981).

In word association studies, light pinks are described as soft, tender, romantic, and cute. These tints also conjure up sweet tastes and sweet scents. Dusty pinks are perceived as soft, soothing, cozy, romantic, rosy, subtle, yet sophisticated; while bright pinks are seen as exciting, happy, hot, trendy, attention-getting, energetic, youthful, fun, and spirited.

Decorating with Pink

Bedrooms: Because of its soft, cozy, and romantic nature, pink is perfect for the bedroom. It makes the skin glow with health, and what better place to make use of those flattering reflections?

Bathrooms: The warm and flattering effect of pink works well in a bathroom, especially in a windowless space or a room facing north. It's another place where pink can bring a healthy glow to exposed complexions.

Girls' Rooms: This is a natural place for pink, especially if you're a traditional "pink-is-for-girls" person, but more importantly, if it's the child's choice.

Living and Dining Rooms: As it's perceived as sweet tasting, too much pink can get a little cloying. How much is "too much"—that's in the eye of the beholder. But imagine pink on major areas such as the walls and upholstery fabrics or carpeting! It can be too much, unless you just utilize pink in prints and patterns or choose rosy, clay, or mauve tones for rooms where lots of different types of people gather. Pink is pretty personal.

The Kitchen: This is where pink can be the most fun—not the sweet bedroom pinks, but the active ebullient hotter pinks, especially in placemats, ceramics and glassware where they create cheerful tabletop accessories. And if your kitchen is an extension of your family room, all the better, as this happy color spills its cheer into the family's activity center.

Pink and Personality

If You Love Pink: Tempering passion with purity, pink is a softened red. A pink person is less showy than a red person, but that does not mean there is less substance there. Pink's personality is variable. In its softer tints, it is demure and romantic—still related to red, but not as ardent. People who prefer pink are the soft, tender friends. Romantic and refined, they are upset by violence of any kind. If you love pink, you are talented but not overambitious.

People are drawn to you by your charm and warmth, but you don't expose your feelings to everyone. While red is assertive, pink is gentle and innocent: more subtle, more contemplative, more cautious. You can't hide behind red, but you can conceal yourself with pink.

Dazzling hot pinks are more closely related to bright red with all the same passion and dynamism. So your personality is more closely akin to the lovers of red . . . more tempestuous and energetic.

If You Dislike Pink: If you dislike pink, the naivete, innocence, and sweetness strike you as cloying, even a bit "wimpish." You long for the passion that was removed from red.

CHAPTER 5

Yellow
Energy and Life

Give any child a piece of paper and a yellow crayon. Immediately there appears a drawing of the sun, complete with little yellow rays sparkling optimistically around a big vibrant yellow circle. Child and adult alike feel cheered and comforted when enveloped in sunshine. We instinctively lift our faces to the sun, just as the buttercups and daffodils do.

From the beginning of time, humans have worshiped the golden glow of the sun. The association of yellow to the sun is universal. For many ancient civilizations, yellow and its glimmering sister of gold were deified and sacred. Because of their proximity to the heavens, these colors signified divine love and enlightened human understanding.

The Golden Glow

In most cultures gold also expresses status and prestige. It is the most precious of all metals. The pursuit of turning baser metals into gold (a process known as alchemy) may have been practiced as far back as 3,000 B.C. with the Egyptians, who first developed the technique of gilding. In medieval times this chemistry flourished, but it died out with the arrival of Descartes and the Age of Rationalism in the 17th century.

Because of the ancient associations of sun and gold to the gods, this most perfect of metals was equated to the perfect spirit. The golden-yellow aura that meant power for the Egyptians came to mean glory in the Christian world. In Western Christian civilizations, gold-leaf backgrounds of sacred paintings and altar covers signify salvation and divine glory.

In classical times, yellow was the color of the sun god Apollo. It stood for generosity, nobility, wisdom, and divinity. In ancient Greek and Roman civilizations, the brides and priests wore yellow because it was considered sacred.

In most languages, it is almost impossible to separate the meaning of gold from yellow. The English word for yellow is derived primarily from the Indo-European *ghelwo*, "related to gold" or "to gleam." Additional inspiration for yellow names comes from less lofty sources: flowers, animals, vegetables, fruits, and minerals: LEMONADE, DANDELION, PRIMROSE YELLOW, NUGGET GOLD, CANARY YELLOW and POPCORN.

Yellow's Uses

Almost as coveted as purple were the yellow dyes—especially those made from saffron, the world's most expensive spice, which comes from the late-blooming crocus plant. Ounce for ounce saffron often rivals the cost of gold, and secrecy has shrouded the manufacturing process. It was a valuable commodity in ancient and medieval trade throughout Asia and was mentioned in the early medical documents of India, England, and Egypt, where tiny bits of stigma were found in mummies. Cleopatra used saffron in her cosmetics. Greek poets extolled the beauty of saffron yellow garments. The Phoenicians dedicated saffron cakes to their goddesses. Nero required that the streets of Rome be sprinkled before him with saffron. The Arabs introduced zafarin to Spain, and returning crusaders brought the precious powder to Europe.

During the Middle Ages Edward III of England encouraged the farmers of Essex to cultivate the crocus plant. Perhaps Edward knew that saffron had been used not only as a flavoring, dye, digestive, sedative, and hangover cure but even as an exhilarant and aphrodisiac, which caused Sir Francis Bacon to observe that "the English are rendered sprightly by a liberal use of saffron in sweet meats and broth." The old English expression "to sleep on a bag of saffron" meant to be happy, giddy, and in today's language, more than a little high.

The Medical Companion published in America in 1838 claimed that saffron "exhilarates the spirits when taken in small doses but if used in too large portions it produces immoderate mirth."

More thrifty American pioneers made a yellow from the buckwheat family, such as a prickly plant appropriately named "arsesmart." Safflower blossoms steeped in water were also used as a yellow dye, often combined with the more expensive saffron. Pomegranate skin, turmeric root, onion skins, crab apple, pear and plum leaves, tree sap, bark, twigs, lichens, and sulphur yielded various shades of yellow.

Yellow dyes were especially important because they could be used to create additional colors. Many greens were produced by using yellow over the initial dye of woad or indigo blue; and orange was obtained by using yellow dye over a foundation of madder red.

An herb known as weld *(Reseda luteola)* was a primary source of yellow dye. The earliest wool fabrics found in the 6th century B.C. were dyed with red from madder, blue from woad or indigo and yellow from weld.

Yellow in Cultures

In ancient Jewish weddings, a marriage was performed under a golden silk prayer shawl called a talis supported by four posts that formed a canopy, or chupal, for the ceremony. This is still a traditional part of modern-day weddings, but the color of the canopy may vary. In the ancient mystical Hebrew Kabbalism, a yellow emanation of light from the magical Sephiroth tree stood for beauty, the child of sensibilities.

Rulers of countries as diverse as Ireland and Africa chose yellow as their regal color. Even today to the Akans of Africa, yellow means royalty. Their symbols of authority and prestige are traditionally golden. Ceremonial weapons are gilded, and as in many other cultures, items of personal adornment are solid gold. Gold-colored threads are woven into kente cloth designs to express the status and wealth of the wearer. To the Bambaras of Mali in West Africa, yellow is the color of change or transformation. It is worn for specific purposes: embarking on a journey, farming, or performing sacrifices.

In Indonesia yellow has special significance because, as symbolic of the sun, it nurtures all living things and causes them to grow.

In Japan, gold is considered the color of heaven. The statues of Buddha glitter in gold, and an amber light is thought to emanate from Buddha. Gold was said to be the son of the sun, and ripened stalks of life-sustaining rice are called *kogane no nami* (golden waves).

The Hindu god of universal understanding, Vishnu and the priests are depicted in spectral yellow garments. It was customary for the Hindu bride to wear frayed old yellow clothing for six days prior to the ceremony to keep the evil spirits away. After marriage, the faithful wife wore yellow when her husband returned home from a long journey.

In ancient China, it was a sacred hue designating nobility and holiness, solely reserved for the emperor and his retinue but banned for use by the common man. For the Chinese, yellow is symbolic of wisdom, civilization, and bright prospects. It is the color of Buddha and his followers. They chose yellow for their monasteries and dyed their robes saffron.

In the Korean culture it is believed that happiness (*poke*) is preserved inside the pojagi cloth used for transporting or storing goods and gift wrapping. Beautifully embellished works of art are inspired by mythology and nature and often feature subtle shades of yellow or more glamorous paper-thin sheets of gold.

Artful Yellow

Medieval painters' palettes relied on the use of brown-yellow pigment called sienna after the Italian city of the same name. During the Renaissance the Italian earthenware called majolica became very popular because of the ocher and clear bright yellows of allegorical or biblical scenes decorating the pottery.

In Britain during the Regency Period (1811 to 1820) sumptuous yellow silk became very popular for upholstered furnishings. Between 1890 and 1900 the hue was so favored that the period was known as the "Yellow Nineties." Oscar Wilde popularized it and Aubrey Beardsley, the creator of exotic illustrations, loved yellow and used it lavishly. Beardsley accessorized his outfits with yellow gloves that, just as he hoped, caused quite a stir in English society. Always the nonconformist, he also painted his studio a deep rich yellow with contrasting black trim, an entirely new look in interior color schemes. Evening dresses of shiny yellow satin were the rage and *The Yellow Book* was the literary sensation of the day.

In France during that same period Henri de Toulouse-Lautrec lavishly splashed yellow on his posters, and many popular French novels were covered in the same hue. The world of art, fashion, and interior and stage design sparkled in yellows.

Goethe spoke of yellow as the color closest to light. He saw its purity as symbolizing brightness, cheer, and a stimulating character. "Experience teaches us that yellow makes a thoroughly warm and comforting impression. With yellow the eye rejoices, the heart expands, the spirit is cheered and we immediately feel warmed. Many people feel an inclination to laugh when looking through a yellow glass" (*Theory of Colors*, Wolfgang von Goethe, John Murray, London, 1840).

The artist Wassily Kandinsky was greatly affected by the emotional aspects of all colors. He observed in his book, *The Art of Spiritual Harmony:*

Yellow tends so greatly toward lightness (white), that there can be no such thing as very dark yellow. If one looks at a circle filled with yellow, one notices that the yellow radiates, a motion comes from the center and approaches us almost visibly . . . the first motion of yellow, the striving toward the person, which can be intensified to a point of obtrusiveness . . . and also the second motion of the yellow, the leap across the border, the dispersal of energy in the environment . . . streaming out aimlessly on all sides.

Hans Hoffman, the renowned art teacher who taught first in Munich and then in America, felt that there were many painters who could depict the sun with a spot of yellow paint, but that only an artist could "make a spot of yellow paint become the sun." And utilizing yellow magnificently in his work, Vincent Van Gogh felt that yellow was "capable of charming God."

We all know that the yellow brick road takes us to the Emerald City, but in L. Frank Baum's classic *Oz*, if we traveled a bit farther west, we'd find Winkie Country, where most everything is colored a dazzling yellow.

In the classic Cary Grant film entitled *Mr. Blandings Builds His Dreamhouse*, Mrs. Blandings (Myrna Loy) is a stickler for precisely the "right shade" of yellow. She instructs her decorator to "have the painter go to the store for a pound of butter" to give him the exactly delicious yellow she wants in her kitchen. It has been said that chefs perform more creatively in a yellow kitchen because this buttery hue brings joy to the food. Obviously, master colorist Claude Monet understood the value of yellow and filled his kitchen in Giverny with this radiant color.

The ebullient American-born decorator Nancy Lancaster started the craze for yellow in her adopted country of England in the 1950s with a color she christened (in her very Southern manner) "buttah yellah."

Yellow's Messages

Throughout history, there are people who have claimed to see auras or an astral light that emanates from all living creatures. When yellow is seen radiating from the body, especially a golden yellow, it is thought to indicate an intellectual mind. In Jungian psychology, yellow stands for intuition, for "comprehension in a flash of light." People who are drawn to yellow are often insightful and intuitive (*Man and His Symbols*, Carl Jung, Anchor Press, Doubleday, New York, 1964).

Yellow is thought of as joyful, outgoing, open, and friendly. In color-mood association studies, yellow is associated with comedy, a happy mood, and playfulness. Dr. Max Luscher states in his *The Luscher Color Test* (Test-Verlag, Basel, Switzerland, 1969): "After white, yellow is the color that most strongly reflects the light hitting it . . . (it) always triggers a gay, light, free, open feeling. . .a liberating, loosening effect. Therefore it corresponds to a definite sense of freedom and self-development."

Yellow ribbons have been used as a sign of hope and optimism since the 19th century when they were worn by American women waiting for their men to come home from the wartime cavalry. But in 1876, yellow ribbons took on new meaning when women donned them as emblems of their struggle for women's rights. Still seen as a symbol of hope in more recent years, yellow has been used decoratively to symbolize a safe return, especially in the campaign to support America's hostages in Lebanon in the 1970s.

Light pastel yellows are seen as childlike. CANARY YELLOW is delicate and feather soft. Ambered yellows are perceived as mellow and warm. Vivid yellows are seen as active, ebullient, sparkling with enthusiasm and youthful vigor. Consistent favorites are LEMON CHROME and BANANA. Generally any shade of yellow that can be described with a delicious name such as BANANA CUSTARD or DOUBLE CREAM are among the most popular.

Studies show that yellow is most often associated with words like "cheerful," "jovial," "joyful," and "sunny," somewhat associated with "exciting" and "stimulating" and almost never associated with "despondent," "dejected," "melancholy," or "unhappy." In short, a wonderful color for lifting the spirits and letting the sunshine in.

As with the neighboring shades of red and orange, yellow increases respiration rates, heartbeat, and blood pressure (although not as consistently as with red). By being associated with the light of day, yellow incites expectation and preparation for activity.

Because of its association with cheerful optimism and its connection to the sun, yellow is the perfect color to use in dreary climates, north-facing rooms, and windowless spaces. It would be an excellent hue to use in alleviating the depression of the seasonal affective disorder (SAD syndrome). For those who literally suffer through the dismal days of winter, what could be better than painting the walls with sunshine where it doesn't exist. It's Prozac in a paint can (and a lot less expensive)!

Many people do not link their depression to dreary surroundings, much less understand how to counteract it. It is so simple and so effective and illustrates how very important it is to keep our environments in tune with our psyches.

Yellow in Nature

With its luminating heat and high reflection, yellow advances to the eye so that it appears to be the largest of all colors. Nature has made good use of this phenomenon by using yellow as a warning signal. Exotic fish, stinging insects, and other predators often announce that they are dangerous or unpalatable by their vivid yellow colorations, especially in the combination of yellow and black stripes. This instantaneous message of possible danger has been imprinted on the human mind over eons, making the combination unignorable wherever and however it is used.

Some insects have the same warning coloration of bees, hornets, and wasps but are actually devoid of sting. The deception cleverly keeps predators away. Because of its yellow and black coloration, the hoverfly looks just like a wasp, protecting it from attack by unsuspecting birds.

Yellow flowers are abundant in nature. Humans find sunflowers as irresistible as birds do, while daffodils trumpet the early sounds of spring. Every season brings forth its special variation of yellow flowers or foliage so spectacular or cheerful that we are instantly drawn to them. In a field of wildflowers it is the first color we notice; and how many of us nervously pulled yellow daisy petals of to see if "he loves me, he loves me not?"

The Sullied Side of Yellow

In spite of all the cheery, smiling, and exuberant connotations of yellow, there are also some negatives, particularly in greenish or muddied sulfuric undertones. It carries a heavy guilt trip—but it's guilt by association and truly not deserved. Judas, the betrayer, was invariably pictured in yellow robes. This message of deceit and treachery carried through to many cultures.

In 10th-century France, the doors on the houses of traitors and criminals were painted yellow. In ecclesiastical color symbolism, saffron yellow represents the confessors. Yellow was considered unsuitable for wedding decorations in France, where it symbolized the cuckold.

In 16th-century Spain, heretics were burned at the stake in yellow. In more recent times, the Nazis made it mandatory for Jews to wear yellow armbands and a yellow star of David. But the negative connotation turned into a positive one when many courageous Dutch non-Jews in World War II wore a yellow star of David inscribed with the words: "Jew and non-Jew are one in their struggle."

The negative attributes of a color may come from an event that has little to do with the real meaning of the color. For example: the "yellow" press got its name from the publication, in 1895, of an illustration of a little girl in a yellow coat on the cover of the *New York World*, a newspaper that sensationalized and exploited its often lurid and graphic stories (not unlike today's tabloids!).

A jaundiced complexion appears to be yellow, so from medieval times a quarantine ship flies a yellow flag. Throughout history, however, there have been many interesting initiations and rites involving the use of yellow as a cure. Among the most fascinating (and gross!) are the cures for yellow jaundice. The Germans ate yellow turnips, saffron, gold coins, or other yellow objects. The English ate yellow spiders rolled in butter. It is debatable as to which was worse—the disease or the cure!

Yellow was the color of the medieval fool. At the Lord Mayor's banquet in London every November, the fool was summoned to jump into a huge bowl of custard. The term "fool" is still used today in England to describe a yellowish custard or cream-based dessert.

The fool carried a staff with yellow baubles on the tip—a symbol of fertility. The use of baubles in fertility rites can be traced back to ancient totem ceremonies. The medieval Germans saw yellow as lusty, and "ladies of pleasure" wore yellow as a sign of their profession. William Shakespeare saw the exuberance of yellow as a sign of love. In *Twelfth Night* Malvalio shows his love by donning yellow stockings.

But inevitably yellow takes us back to sunshine, smiles, hope, and promise—just as Dorothy, Toto, the Tin Man, the Scarecrow, and the Cowardly Lion knew that the only way to get to the Emerald City was to follow the yellow brick road.

Mellow Yellow

Where other colors darken with saturation, yellow is the one color that becomes brighter with greater saturation. It is an excellent color to draw the eye to areas where attention is needed or to highlight a focal point—a special piece of furniture, a nook or a niche or object d'art.

The Kitchen, Dining, and Family Rooms: Until recent years, yellow had been held captive in the kitchen almost as long as women were. While it is true that in its golden, buttery, or custard tones it is highly suggestive of deliciousness, it should not be confined to the kitchen. With its expansive and sunny personality, it is a natural for the gathering, greeting, and eating areas for family and friends.

Exteriors, Interiors, and Front Doors: Yellow wraps itself around a home, inviting us into its instant warmth, an ideal color for exterior as well as interior and especially friendly on the front door. Eye-arresting and offering instantaneous warmth, yellow gives a house "curb appeal," drawing people into looking further.

Children's Rooms: Yellow is a fun color for kids' rooms. Several years ago there was the unfounded rumor that children cried more in yellow rooms and anxiety was increased in yellow surroundings. This was not based on any credible research and was probably started by someone who simply did not understand or appreciate this luminous and happy hue (or had an unhappy childhood)!

Hallways and Small Spaces: Yellow is ideal for opening up cramped and dark spaces such as hallways; the suggestion of sunshine casts a luminous glow that draws people in and through the space.

Personality and Yellow

A preference for yellow is a preference for sunshine. Like a cat, you will seek out the warmest, sunniest spots and lap it up. Of all of the emotions, yellow evokes good cheer. It is seen by most people as the happiest of all colors. It's summer flowers and autumn harvest, abundance in nature.

If Yellow Is Your Favorite Color: Yellow is luminous and warm, and so are the people who prefer it. It sparkles with optimism and activity. Yellow people are very original, imaginative, idealistic, creative, artistic, often spiritual, and highly intuitive. They thrive on novelty and challenge and have inquiring minds. They are reliable friends and confidants and usually have sunny dispositions—how could they not? Their sense of curiosity is often rewarded with accomplishments. Lovers of yellow are often perfectionists, but their sense of joy can override their perfectionist tendencies.

If Yellow Is Your Least Favorite Color: You're a realist—a practical, no pie-in-the-sky kind of person, generally skeptical of new ideas. Rather than trying something innovative, you prefer to concentrate on things that you know you can accomplish. Guaranteed results are important to you because you like to protect yourself from disappointment.

CHAPTER 6

Orange
Radiant and Hot

Ask anyone to name the color of a sunset and invariably the answer is "orange." The meaning of orange is inexorably linked to the sensations of radiant energy, heat and the glowing presence of the setting sun. The link between red and yellow, orange takes its traits from both. It is less passionate and intense than red, incorporating the sunny disposition of yellow.

The brightest tones of orange are seen as gregarious, fun-loving, high-energy. Cool orange simply does not exist. Everything about orange is luminous and hot. It is perceived as the hottest of all colors—even more so than red because it takes its heat from two radiant sources, yellow and red.

Ancient Orange

In ancient times, orange was a color reflective of love, both earthly and heavenly. The Greek muses wore orange, as did Bacchus, the pagan Roman god. The Greek messiah was called "Orient" (of gold) and was covered by an orange veil. Orange flowers were often sprinkled on tombs to placate the vengeful gods. In ancient Rome, the wives of the priests of Jupiter wore a *flammeum*, an orange and yellow veil. The young Roman women betrothed in marriage copied this style as a symbol of hope for a long and fruitful marriage. At the marriage ceremony the bride wore not only the flaming veil, but orange shoes as well.

Oranges and orange blossoms have historically been symbols of love. Pomegranate seeds were eaten as an aphrodisiac. In the 14th century, lovers bathed in orange flower water and courtesans sprinkled their sheets with orange perfume. German suitors were far more practical. They sent oranges instead of flowers, and when a lover came to call, rather than dropping a handkerchief from the balcony as the romantic Spanish *señoritas* did, the *frauleins* dropped oranges on their suitors (perhaps they should have sent flowers!).

Believed to be the symbol of fruitfulness, orange blossoms were shipped to Paris from Provence because all French brides wore them in their hair, carried them in bouquets, and sprinkled them under the bed linens. And in 1556, the sensual power of oranges and orange blossoms was felt to be so strong that a how-to book (probably the first) was published on the preparation of orange-scented cosmetics.

The notorious Medicis of Florence were very much into orange decor, as are many present day Italians. The ceilings of the Medicis' gorgeous Pitti Palace were painted in orange, and oranges were part of their coat of arms.

Red hair was popular in Rome, and many women dyed their hair to please their spouses. Henna was the earliest hair dye used not only for women's hair but also to dye horses' manes and the beards of prophets. Eventually the garish orange henna tints were darkened with indigo or lightened with a yellow dye from the chamomile

Continues on page 52

Creating a Mood with Color

Are elaborate furnishings and expensive accessories what you need to create the room of your dreams? Not necessarily. Wonderful furniture, wall and floor coverings, accessories, and architectural features are important. But no matter what you want to put into that dream space, you need color to pull it all together into a cohesive whole. It is color that warms, cools, energizes, pacifies, defines, blurs edges, and completes the effect.

Whether you are starting from scratch or freshening up what you already have, start with color. Color evokes moods and memories.

In this book, you'll discover how Color Moods will help you organize your decorating decisions around color combinations that will lift your spirits, your comfort level, and your confidence.

Using color does not always mean *bold*. Less color is also an option. This elegant room is dominated by yellow in all it's many variations. The happiest color in the spectrum, yellow brings its touch of sun, warmth, and welcome to what might otherwise be a stiff and very formal setting. Gilded metallics, first cousins to yellow, contribute to the sense of opulence and dancing light. Note, too, how small accents of apricot, coral and blue (in low contrast) add richness and depth.

plant. In 16th-century England, during the reign of Elizabeth I, many women imitated her flaming red tresses.

In Greece, orange symbolized avenged infidelity. The poet Homer wrote about Helen of Troy having to wear orange garments because of her adultery with Paris. The marigold became the symbolic flower of deceived husbands.

During the Middle Ages bright orange became the symbol for false love, deceit, and disloyalty. Lusty medieval orange was as intense as fire. It was closely akin to flaming red. The brilliant hue was made from a poisonous red oxide of lead, which was treacherous business to pound into pigment. Inhaling the dust was deadly. No doubt medieval man was fascinated by the glimmering hue, but very wary of its dangers.

During the time of the Restoration, orange as a slang word had certain naughty connotations. At one point in time, orange featured prominently in erotic art.

The vibrant deep red-orange lacquers called cinnabar are as ancient as Chinese civilization. Believed to symbolize life's joys, this warm, earthy tone made from the vermilion mineral was thought to have magical properties. Elixirs made of cinnabar were believed to make drinkers wise and blissful. Birthdays and marriages were made more auspicious when surrounded by this magical shade. Palaces and temples, the ornate doors of magnificent mansions, opulent furnishings, and delicate jewelry were sheathed in cinnabar lacquers over intricate designs.

The wearing of warm carnelian gemstones was believed to imbue the wearer with courage, especially recommended to those with weak voices who were nervous about public speaking, considered the most fearful terror of all.

Orange has also symbolized war. The Knights of the Order of the Holy Spirit founded by Henry III of England wore orange crosses on their cloaks. Since 1795 the Orangemen have been a secret society organized in northern Ireland supporting Protestantism and fighting Catholicism.

Orange Messages

Of all the colors in the spectrum, orange is probably the least understood and the most maligned. Long-standing attitudes are slow to change, so it is easy to see why some people might find this flamboyant, vivacious, extroverted sibling of red too offensive, obvious, or blatant. For the subdued soul, vibrant orange is simply overwhelming, and firecracker orange is too noisy.

Deeper shades of orange brown are looked upon more favorably, representing strength and endurance. Bright upbeat oranges pop out in the fashion world every few years, heartily embraced by the youth, the young-at-heart, and the trendies.

A wonderfully theatrical color, orange is often linked to warmth and earth. For example, the lush blazing tropical shades of TIGERLILY, MANGO, FLAMINGO, SUN ORANGE, and GOLD EARTH; the exotic shadings of ARABESQUE and AMBERGLOW, or JAFFA ORANGE and CARNELIAN, PAPRIKA, GRENADINE, CORAL SANDS, and ORANGE OCHRE—all reminiscent of paisley and musk, the pungent spices of the East, desert tents, and Arabian Nights.

There is the inevitable association to the time of harvest: the flaming oranges and burnt oranges of falling autumn leaves; jolly pumpkins, and Halloween trick or treat.

Stimulating the Appetites

Orange is a known appetite stimulant. Closely related to red, it has been shown to exert a measurable effect on the autonomic nervous system to stimulate the appetite. If you are on a diet, don't use vivid orange in the kitchen!

Why do you see so much orange in the food-packaging business? It is an instant attention-getter on the shelf. The inherent personality traits of orange—fun, active, energetic, stimulating, appealing to the appetite, make it the perfect color choice for fast food and takeout. It is not coincidental that many chains have used the color to great advantage, if not in the decor, then for sure in the signage. The message is: "Eat fast, eat a lot, get out to make room for the next victim!" Some day in the distant future when archaeologists uncover the ruins of our civilization, they will wonder about what manner of gods were served under the red-orange signs and golden arches.

The appealing tints of PEACH BLOSSOM, PEACH PINK, PEACHBEIGE, and PEACH FUZZ; APRICOT ICE, SALMON, SALMON ROSE, SHRIMP, CAMELLIA, and CORAL PINK create a gentler form of appetite-persuasion, more appealing to aesthetic tastes than fast-food orange. The restaurateur charging premium prices to an up-scale clientele would be well advised to paint the walls a delectable peachy color.

The Language of Orange

The origin of the word "orange" is similar in many languages. From the ancient Sanskrit *naranga*; Persian *naranj*, Spanish *naranja*; French *orenge*, Latin *aurangia*—meaning golden apple or the fruit of gold.

The tomato, which can be either an orange-red or yellow-orange, was considered an aphrodisiac called *pomme d'amour* or "apple of love" (which may have prompted the Puritans to declare tomatoes poisonous!).

Orange is strongly identified with delicious fruits and juices; the tang and taste of PERSIMMON, MUSKMELLON, TANGERINE, MANDARIN ORANGE, APRICOT, and CRABAPPLE.

In many European languages, there was no word for orange until the fruit was imported from Asia in the 10th century. The Greeks had one word for all fruits, melon, and later included citron for lemon and lime. The Romans had two additional words: *malum* (from the Greek melon) and *pomum* (apple). The early Anglo-Saxons classified all fruits as apples or berries. Interestingly, in most early languages, all fruits including citrus were called apples.

So it is not surprising that peach comes from the Latin *persicum*, meaning Persian apple. Actually the peach is a member of the rose family. The most beautiful and best loved of the orange tints, peach has an instant association to the sense of taste, delicious and sweet, or to the sense of touch, soft and fuzzy. Peach is highly recommended for dining rooms, restaurants, hospitals, and nursing homes—wherever the mood calls for a receptive, warm, welcoming, tender, and nurturing ambiance.

As modern as the word sounds, "peachy" is an old slang expression for excellent, beautiful, any person or thing well liked. To be called "a peach" is a lovely compliment. It is the perfect shade to reflect on skin, projecting a healthy glow to the complexion.

Continues on page 56

Putting Your Furnishings and Your Colors Together

Outside of a museum it's rare to see a truly accurate period room. More often we mix furnishings, not only from different periods and materials, but also from different cultures. When you introduce your own color scheme to this eclectic mix, what happens?

While certain colors are traditionally linked with specific decorating styles—such as Southwestern furniture with desert pastels, or Colonial furniture with Williamsburg blue and white—understanding the Color Moods allows you to break with tradition and make your own personal statement. How about a warm infusion of Santa Fe desert colors mixed with the cool, clean lines of Scandinavian furnishings? Or a bold red, white, and blue antique American quilt displayed in a formal mahoghany English armoire? The soft peaceful greens and taupes of a Bonsai tree and touches of azalea pink from a Japanese rock garden contrasted with a sleek contemporary look? The result is an expression of you—an eclectic mix of styles linked by color.

In cool blue, blue-green, and lavender, this eclectic mix of European classicism and Asian antiquities would have suggested calm tradition. Instead, the designer chose to be daring and used red and yellow to create a Dynamic mood. Red creates a feeling of drama and excitement. Yellow brings the warmth and power of the sun. Together these bold colors provide a striking background for the Asian artifacts.

Children and Orange

Studies show that children who like to use orange crayons or paints in their drawings are outgoing, sympathetic, and friendly, rather than intense and emotional. They also turn more to fantasy and imagination than to deep intellectual research.

Children respond happily to orange. To them, orange is as friendly as a freckle, as giddy as a giggle. It is, after all, the color of lollipops, gumdrops, and juicy popsicles; the first goldfish won at a carnival game, the funny clown with the carrot-top hair. It is especially appealing to the three- to six-year-old age group as the first of the secondary colors they discover after their initial and infantile attraction to the bright primaries.

Decorating with Orange

In his book, *Mark Hampton on Decorating*, the famous decorator says:

> Peach or some other shade of it will go with absolutely any other color . . .
> dining rooms always look great with any shade of this inviting color . . .
> Bedrooms and bathrooms are warm and soothing painted in peach tones.
> What better color for any place where bare skin is a factor?

I heartily support him.

Entry Areas: From the palest peach tones to deeper apricot, some variation of light to midtone orange works extremely well in entry areas because of its warm and welcoming presence. An entry mirror that reflects the inviting and flattering color can't help but make your guests both feel and look good!

Dining Room: A dining room is both delectable and dramatic in many shades of orange, such as CANTALOUPE, APRICOT NECTAR, PAPAYA PUNCH and BRANDIED MELON. These shades subtly stimulate the appetite, and your guests will think you're a great cook!

The Kitchen: This is a room that can handle the brighter shades of orange, but not too much of it on the walls if you are dieting. Orange is best kept to accessories or accents like ceramics, glassware, or tabletop. Its cheerful good nature brings a sense of fun to this family gathering place.

Bedrooms: Specific shades of orange like peach and apricot are wonderful in the bedroom because they are so warm, nurturing, and inviting. It provides the perfect setting for reading the Sunday funnies or cuddling with the kids (or significant others).

The Family Room: Its happy associations make orange an appropriate color family for this room that serves as a gathering place. The deeper orange tones work best here, not only because of the wear-and-tear factor, but as the oranges start to approach brown, the more secure and rooted they feel, both good-reassuring messages for family living.

The Bath: The lighter peachy tones are not only flattering to the skin, but they also provide a great backdrop for applying makeup.

Kids' Rooms: Its ebullient nature makes the brighter oranges fun in a kid's room (especially for those between the ages of three to six or adolescents). And, just as with yellow, the lighter shades of peach are an excellent compromise color when the sex of the expected baby is not known.

Orange and Personality

As orange is a combination of red and yellow, it takes on many of the characteristics of both colors. Vibrant and warm, orange has the physical force of red, but is less frenetic, intense and passionate.

If You Like Orange: Lovers of this color work and play hard, are adventurous and enthusiastic. They are good-natured, expansive, and extroverted with a disposition as bright as their favorite color. They like to be with people, their ideas are original, and they have strong determination. However, they are more agreeable than aggressive.

Orange people can be fickle. Their newest friend is often their best friend (until the next friend comes along). Orange lovers aren't always the best mates, as they are always looking for new worlds and challenges to conquer. Success in business can come easily to this gregarious, charming person.

If your preferences tend to the peach tones, you have all of the same traits as the orange person, but you are much less assertive about it. You work hard, but your play activities (especially sports activities) are more as an observer than as a participant. You are friendly and charming as well, but in a much more subtle way.

If You Dislike Orange: Life is definitely not all fun and games to the rejecter of orange. Nothing flamboyant appeals to you. You dislike too much partying, hilarity, loud laughter, showing off, and obvious intimacy. As a result, you may be difficult to get to know, if not a loner. You prefer a few genuine close friends to a large circle of acquaintances; and once you've made a friend, you've made a friend for life.

Balance In All Things: Seeking Equilibrium

Throughout our lives, we seek balance on many levels: physically, aesthetically, emotionally and spiritually. The ancient Chinese understood this as the balance of yang and yin. Today our lifestyles and attitudes require a perpetual balancing act between work and play; practicality and fantasy; technology and humanism; seeking what is new while treasuring the old.

Above all, our homes are critical to our sense of equilibrium. For increasing numbers of people, it is both work place and living space. Now, more than ever, there is a need for home to be a safe haven: a place where we can feel secure, nurtured, connected and comfortable; a place to re-group, refresh and replenish. Color can be an instant equalizer and a "quick fix" in helping us to achieve that ever-important balance in our busy, often hectic lives.

Although we have no conscious awareness of this, our eyes search for color balance in our immediate environments. Our innate longing for balance welcomes the soothing touch of green plants in a warm-colored room, while a large vase of red tulips brings a cheering warmth to a too-cool interior. Look at all of the photographs in this book. See how while there are major colors, certain accessories and details add to the balance and success of each interior. To find out more about this very important balancing act, turn to Chapter 15 beginning on page 151.

Imagine how the cool blue-green waters of an oasis bring the desert's sandy colors into balance. In this powder room by designers Lynn Augstein and Gail Woolaway, toasted brown, umber, terra cotta, and brass create a feeling of earthy warmth. It's the cool blue-green of the glass countertop and the contrasting spot of colored lighting on the wall that add balance and sophistication to this intimate space.

The Crossovers

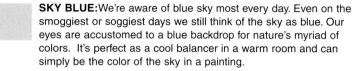

Nature's most versatile colors: In nature's grand design, these hues appear everywhere. They can work in every palette.

SKY BLUE: We're aware of blue sky most every day. Even on the smoggiest or soggiest days we still think of the sky as blue. Our eyes are accustomed to a blue backdrop for nature's myriad of colors. It's perfect as a cool balancer in a warm room and can simply be the color of the sky in a painting.

SUNSHINE: We always think of yellow as the color of sunlight that permeates our atmosphere. It works well as a neutral and is a wonderful way to bring warmth to a cool room.

DARK EARTH: This French call it *terre brun* which is far more elegant than dirt brown. They just understand how wonderful a neutral it can be as it is an integral part of nature's basic color scheme.

DARK RED BROWN: A brother to brown and the first cousin to wine and aubergine, this slightly purpled brown has a complexity that makes it a beautiful blending shade.

PINE NEEDLE: You wouldn't think twice about bring in a beautiful green plant into any room because it clashed with the colors. Just as nature arranges flowers with green in just about every combination, this green works with all other colors.

AUBERGINE: Aubergine is French for Eggplant, but Aubergine is so much more elegant (that French touch again). They understand that this deep purpled-maroon is truly a classic and so will you.

DEEP CLARET: One of the most deliciously useful colors, this hue had excitement of red, the mystery of purple and the warmth of brown making it work with everything.

LIGHT TAUPE AND BLEACHED SAND: Ideal neutrals, there is no end to the versatility of these taupe colors. Wonderful "when-in-doubt" choices that work equally well with warm or cool tones.

NEUTRAL GRAY AND PEWTER: Two more ideal neutrals, these are the gray shades that are the best blenders. If you think of grays in the context of nature, they appear, very subtly, at dawn and dusk, often as undertone to the blue sky. They're in rocks, stone and pebbles we encounter on a hike or the cement, concrete and steel of the city.

MIDNIGHT NAVY: The most useful of all basic colors, the midnight blues give us the strength and power of black but with a lighter tough.

TRUE RED: Although it may seem odd to include a color with such a distinctive personality in the list of Crossovers, think about the frequency of red in nature and how it blends with so many other shades. This particular shade is very special because it is a true red that gives life to both warm and cool colors.

DUSKY BLUE GREEN: This shade of teal is another great background or foreground color that is so very adaptable. It combines the best of blue and green and every other color can be used with it.

RAVEN: The inevitable basic. In nature it is most identified with night. Powerful, classic, fundamental and sophisticated -- the quintessential background color.

CHAPTER 7

Blue
Eternal Blue

Blue is the color of constancy and truth. It is the color of the sky—as ephemeral and transparent as it may be, it is always there. Even on a cloudy or gray day there is the hope that the clarity of azure blue will eventually break through. The true blue of the daylight sky is associated with the continuity of yet another day, dependable and consoling. Survival was difficult in primitive times, so the dawning of a new day, in any shade of blue, must have been comforting.

Because of the enormous expanse of sky, we see blue as distant and receding into outer space. It suggests the ancient past or faraway future. As Goethe wrote in his *Theory of Colors*:

> A blue surface seems to return from us . . . but as we readily follow an
> agreeable object that flies from us, so we love to contemplate blue, not
> because it advances to us, but because it draws us after it.

In fact, gazing at the blue sky brings a sense of peace and tranquillity to the human spirit. It is imprinted in our psyches as a retiring, quiescent color.

Beyond the blue sky lies the promise of heaven. Early Christians saw hope in blue: It implied love of divine works, piety, and a spiritual quality of faith, humility, and devotion. Christ is frequently pictured in a blue mantle, and the Virgin Mary (often called the Blue Lady) is invariably depicted in blue. Blue is regarded universally as the color of the spirit, of the sublime upper world.

It was the hue that predominated in the traditional vestments of the Hebrew high priests: their long blue robes were an allusion to the sky. The miter that the revered men carried was blue, and a huge breastplate supporting twelve magnificent stones was attached to their chests with blue ribbons. The Hebrew tribes of Issachar and Napaali carried blue emblems and related blue to glory. The important symbolism of blue to the Jewish people is shown in the Bible, where the Lord commands Moses to have the Israelites put a blue ribbon on the fringes of the borders of their garments as a reminder to keep his commandments.

Just as blue symbolizes the sky above, it also evokes the sea below. The cleansing waters of blue surf; the serenity of quiet streams and babbling brooks. Deep blue softly speaks of the silent depths of an ink-blue ocean. Because of its association with endless skies and tranquil seas, blue is universally beloved. My wise color-theory professor at UCLA once advised: "Study the blues carefully . . . somewhere in there is the precise shade of heaven."

Protective Blue

In many cultures blue is used for protection against evil forces. In Morocco, a blue spot is painted behind the groom's ear to ward off evil (evidently the bride has to fend for herself!). In Jerusalem a blue hand is painted on the doors or walls of the dwellings. In ancient times, the blue star sapphire was believed to be protection from witchcraft, the three crossbars radiating from the stone representing faith, hope, and destiny. It was believed to be unique and so potent that it continued its protective influence over the previous owner even when it had passed into other hands.

In the American Southwest many native Americans paint the doors of their adobe houses a bright blue to keep the evil spirits away. In many areas of the American Southeast, the ceilings of porches are painted blue to prevent ghosts from entering the house. In Greece a piece of blue cloth is pinned to babies' undergarments to protect them from harm.

In ancient Japan the shade was recommended for travel and work clothes, as well as for protection against poisonous snakes (which evidently did not care for the color).

Blue and Culture

It was not until 4500 B.C. in Mesopotamia that blue emerged as a decorative hue. Brilliant blue threads were used in ancient Peruvian embroideries circa 800 B.C. While thousands of miles away, blue was used in linen fabrics found in the caves of the Dead Sea Scrolls.

Indigo replaced woad in importance as a dye in the Middle Ages because it proved to be more hardy and reliable. It also made blue a more available color. Marco Polo was fascinated by the production of indigo in India where it was produced in great quantities and its quality was desired. The color was extracted by plucking out a species of the herb by the roots, putting it into tubs of water and other ingredients and leaving it to rot. The reality of this glamorous color, admired by all the world, was some very labor and animal-intensive effort. The tubs of water contained the dye were also filled with a mixture of fruits, wood ash, or putrefied urine (camel urine was especially effective!). The dye-bath was actually a pale yellow, but oxidation eventually turned the textiles to blue.

Additional blues came from a mineral that was difficult to mine. Lapis lazuli, a semi-precious stone of rich azure, was the primary source of ultramarine blue. It was so expensive to obtain that it was reserved for special symbolic uses, such as the color of the Madonna's robes. Artists charged extra for its use and it became a status symbol for wealthy art patrons.

Variations on blue were obtained by mixing indigo with white substances. A typical 12th-century recipe called for taking a piece of white marble and putting it into hot dung for a day and night, taking it out (very carefully!), and grinding it on another marble to produce a fine powder.

"And then take the foam which is found in the cauldron in which cloths are dyed the color of indigo, and put it on this powder . . . when it is dry, add more of the foam until it acquires a good azure color." (*The Materials and Techniques of Medieval Painting*, Daniel V. Thompson, Dover Publications, New York, 1956)

After it was thoroughly dried, the powdering, washing, and drying were repeated and yet another powdering with marble. This was a laborious, tedious (not to mention odiferous!) task but evidently worth the time and trouble to obtain the blue shadings so loved and admired in the Middle Ages.

Still another recipe from the 14th century gave instructions for making ultramarine. Lapis lazuli in powdered form was combined with lye. The formula called for keeping the hands coated with linseed oil while kneading the extremely caustic lye with sticks. The procedure continued for days, until eighteen containers of the mixture could be divided into various grades of blue. After very long,

Continues on page 64

Seeking and finding. When your mind wanders, do you seek exotic places? Or find pristine natural preserves? Do you think of wild tropical nights? Or do imagine sitting by a silvery brook sheltered by the deep forest whose magical leaves are caught in the water flashing by?

Each of us has special feelings, places, or memories of the past that bring us happiness. Why not use these memories—and the colors of those places—to infuse your home with some of the magic?

If you are in touch with places you dream to be then you are halfway there. If not, take your imagination off to a quiet place for some moments of silent reflection to see where you go when you don't have an itinerary. See page 24 for step-by-step instructions on taking a guided imagery voyage that will take you to your memories and fantasies.

And, if your mental image is not exactly the same as mine (and it may not be), not to worry The Color Moods described in these pages, are based on inspiration from the beauty of nature and the riches of the world's ports of call. Let these moods help you capture that special feeling, place, or moment in time in your own personal space.

63

detailed directions, readers were admonished to keep the recipe to themselves "For it is an unusual ability to know how to make it properly." And in keeping with the chauvinistic attitude of the Middle Ages, a further warning was given: "Know too, that making it (the dye or pigment) is an occupation for pretty girls rather than men; for they are always at home and reliable, and they have more dainty hands. Just beware of old women!"

To the Japanese, blue represents the productive world of the sea as an eternal and spiritually calming source. Blue not only represented the beauty of springtime, but was also believed to bring victory in battle—a curious dichotomy.

Visitors to Japan in the 19th century came away with an abiding sense of omnipresent blue houses under blue roofs, shop fronts hung with blue cloth, and people clothed in blue. One of the early writers on Japan, Lafacadio Hearn, saw Yokohama as an atmosphere with a faint suggestion of blue in it because of the fluttering blue flags and banners.

Blue symbolized immortality to the ancient Chinese. The emperor rode in a blue sedan chair (lesser officials rode in green chairs), and even today it is the conventional color of clothing in mainland China.

To the Druids, blue was truth and harmony. To the ancient Greeks and Egyptians it was the sign of truth, goodness, and faith. Egyptians especially loved blue. As early as 4500 B.C. they used indigo dyes, and their mummies were often wrapped in blue cloth. The interiors of the temples were all in blue, to imitate the sky and the Nile. Nut, the goddess of the night sky, as well as Amen, the god of reproduction and life, were depicted in blue. To ward off evil and ill health, mystic priests prescribed certain charms, amulets, talismans, and medicines (such as ground-up sapphires to use as an eyewash). They wore breastplates of blue to demonstrate the sacredness of their tasks. The pharaohs wore a blue leather crown, an ancient symbol of their supremacy and descent from the gods.

Brilliant blue threads were used in ancient Peruvian embroideries circa 800 B.C. while thousands of miles away blue linen was found in the caves where the Dead Sea scrolls were discovered.

To the ancient Briton, blue was considered the color of "good standing." When Julius Caesar arrived in Britain in 58 B.C., he found his adversaries, the Picts, had painted themselves blue, which no doubt inspired George Bernard Shaw to state in *Caesar and Cleopatra*: "In war we stain our bodies blue so that though our enemies may strip us of our clothes and our lives, they cannot strip us of our respectability." In Britain today, it still implies conservative political views, a respect and acceptance of the status quo.

In Roman temples, blue stood for the great god Jupiter; in Greece it was symbolic of Zeus. The Yorubas of Nigeria so love the color that they decorate sculptured house posts and doors of prestigious homes with indigo blue, wear blue clothing, and tattoo their bodies with that venerable shade.

In India, it was believed that blue was the color of supreme wisdom and that the true color of the sun was blue. Sapphire brings peace of mind to the Buddhist. Ancient Indians and Tibetans often used indigo blue in prayer scrolls. They believed that the hue was the color of the "third Eye," and intensified the powers of meditation and heightened intuition. Indigo blue and deep midnight blue have long been associated with the calming quality of night. It is often recommended to create a restful environment for periods of study and contemplation.

The *Cordon-bleu* was a blue ribbon badge originally worn by knights under the Bourbon dynasty of France. Today it denotes individuals distinguished in their fields, especially a notable chef. Blue ribbons still proclaim the highest award in many fields of endeavor.

In the 18th century, the sapphire gemstone was used as a test of female virtue—a change of the true color showed the lady to be unfaithful.

When a Frenchman has a baby boy, he wears a blue bachelor button (an interesting choice of flowers!) in his buttonhole. In many cultures, blue is symbolic of baby boys. But in the United States, this was not always so. From a 1918 publication called "The Infants' Department" and quoted in *Men and Women*, Claudia Brush Kidwell and Valerie Steele (Smithsonian Institution Press, 1989):

> There has been a great deal of diversity on the subject, but the generally accepted rule is pink for the boys and blue for the girls. The reason is that pink being a more decided and stronger color is more suitable for the boy; while blue, which is more delicate and dainty, is prettier for the girl.

The change took place in the 1920s with the proliferation of pretty pinks identified with feminine cosmetics, and blue became the stronger, more masculine color.

Some cultures take a very practical approach to blue. American farmers often paint their barnstalls blue because it keeps the flies away (flies have an aversion to blue), while a gate painted blue in an Amish community signals that there is a marriageable daughter in the house.

There is one culture that does not revere the color. The Yezidis in Armenia curse their enemies by saying, "May you die in blue garments!" But they are in the minority, for in much of the world, blue symbolizes fair skies, loyalty, and constancy.

Healing Blue

Clairvoyants and mystics have long believed in the healing qualities of blue rays. Edgar Cayce in his book *Auras* (Association for Research and Enlightenment, 1945) saw a blue aura as a natural emanation of the soul. He believed that deep blue and indigo implied a comprehension of the purpose in life.

S. G. J. Ousley, the English chromotherapist, described his meditation techniques in his book *Color Meditations* (Grosvenor Press, Portsmouth England, 1949). He suggested that students and those in pursuit of knowledge will be greatly helped by visualizing the ray of indigo blue: "This produces a receptivity of the mind which is most helpful to students of all classes." Ousely saw indigo, exactly the same way as the ancient Indian mystics: the hue that heightened intuition.

Physiologically, the viewing of blue reduces blood pressure and heartbeat, and respiration rate, and creates a calming effect. Studies have shown that there is a strong tendency for red to create abnormal convulsive responses in epileptics and that blue glasses will filter out long wavelength radiation.

Dr. Max Luscher, the noted Swiss psychologist, in his book, *Four Color Person* (Pocket Books, Simon & Schuster, 1979) says:

> Just sit down in front of a dark blue color and see what kind of mood it produces in you. You will feel a motionless calm, a relaxed satisfaction, an endless sense of harmony and contentment will come over you.

Continues on page 68

66   COLORS FOR YOUR EVERY MOOD

COMBO 67-A

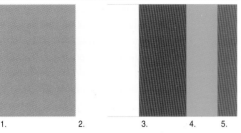

1. Jade
   Lime
2. Sunshine
3. Grenadine
4. Peacock
   Blue
5. Burnt
   Orange

1.　　2.　　3.　　4.　　5.

Whimsical

Freed from the shackles of the ordinary, the spirited, joyful, energetic combinations of the Whimsical mood are not just for kids. Contrast is key. Many of the colors are as bright as you would see in a child's room. But the room at left is whimsical despite the fact that not all the hues are blatantly bright because the accent colors are. Throw a few basics into the mix and play with the possibilities.

COMBO 67-B

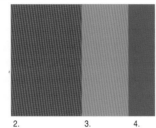

1. Bluewash
2. Bright
   Red
   Violet
3. Leprechaun
4. Bright
   Cobalt

1.　　2.　　3.　　4.

COMBO 67-C

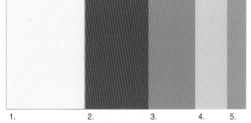

1. Bone
   White
2. Clover
3. Ultramarine
4. Spectra
   Yellow
5. Shocking
   Pink

1.　　2.　　3.　　4.　　5.

COMBO 67-D

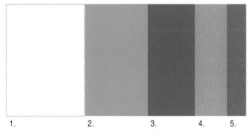

1. Snow
   White
2. Deep
   Peacock
   Blue
3. Bright
   Cobalt
4. Living Coral
5. Chocolate
   Chip

1.　　2.　　3.　　4.　　5.

COMBO 67-E

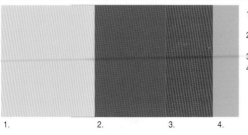

1. Aspen
   Gold
2. Reddish
   Blue
3. Lollipop
4. Billiard
   Green

1.　　2.　　3.　　4.

COMBO 67-F

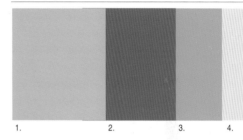

1. Poison
   Green
2. Nautical
   Blue
3. Vivid
   Blue
4. Lemon
   Chrome

1.　　2.　　3.　　4.

COMBO 67-G

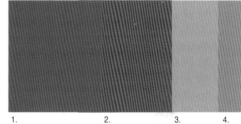

1. Bluish
   Lavender
2. Fandango
   Pink
3. Honey
   Gold
4. Firecracker

1.　　2.　　3.　　4.

COMBO 67-H

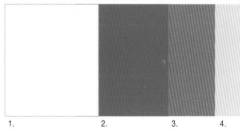

1. Bright
   White
2. Princess
   Blue
3. Calypso
   Coral
4. Super
   Lemon

1.　　2.　　3.　　4.

COMBO 67-I

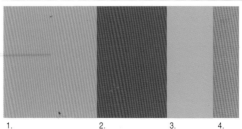

1. Jacaranda
2. Mahogany
3. Kelly
   Green
4. Hot
   Pink

1.　　2.　　3.　　4.

Under hypnotic suggestion, Dr. Arthur Ellis has told me, subjects concentrating on blue report a sense of calm and relaxation and, given the suggestion of blue surroundings on a very hot day, actually became cool. The pace of all things seemed slower, and all subjects felt very much in control. In fact, gazing at the blue sky brings a restful and serene tranquillity. With the exception of the brightest blues, these associations imprint blue on our psyches as a retiring, quieting color.

In their book *Insomnia*, researchers Gay Gaer Luce and Dr. Julius Segal state:

A combination of meditation and yoga, plus concentration on an inward image of a deep blue light for three minutes can bring on a state of relaxation called the alpha rhythm.

Barbara Brown, a pioneer in biofeedback research, says in her book *New Mind, New Body* (Harper and Row, 1974) that color affects brain waves, thus supporting the theory that "color induces emotional states which are specific to difference hues." Her research concludes that the: ". . .brain electrical response to red is one of alerting or arousal, whereas the brain electrical response to blue is one of relaxation."

Blue is an excellent color on ceilings in small, cramped, or windowless spaces to alleviate claustrophobia. Simply painting the ceiling blue or utilizing skylights can open the space and soothe the mind into imagining the vast openness of the outdoors. Blue would be an inspired and humane color to use for patients undergoing traumatic treatments or who are enclosed in what they perceive as frightening and tightly constricted spaces.

Blue's Messages

From early childhood, blue skies bring memories of picnics in the park and the freedom to play outdoors. Somehow, if we pressed our noses against the window long enough (even if it took days), the blue sky would appear eventually. If blue is anything, it is ultimately dependable and faithful.

From the blue tunic worn by the faithful servant, the tradesmen's apron, or apprentice of the Middle Ages, to the blue jeans of today's working man or woman, whether they are construction workers or investment bankers on weekend, their hardy blue serves the same earnest, straightforward, reliable purpose. Medium and grayed-blues in particular, such as QUARRY, SLATE, and ALPINE are seen as sincere.

As blue moves toward black, it becomes more serious and authoritative, a tradition started by the guardians of the Roman senate who were clothed in blue. Dark blue uniforms carry the message of leadership—whether a naval officer, airline pilot, or policeman—any "civilian" clothing colored in dark blue carries the same suggestion of trustworthy power, dignity, poise and reserve. Deep blue-violets, navy, and almost black midnight blue have the same weighty importance of black, yet they lack the darker and more sinister implications and retain an air of credible importance.

The light pastel blues such as CHALK, MURMUR, CELESTIAL, and POWDER BLUE create a rather delicate, detached ethereal ambiance.

Dr. Hans and Shulamith Kreitler, authors of *Psychology of the Arts* (Duke University Press, 1972), state:

In modern studies, blue emerges as tender, soothing, cool, passive, secure and comfortable—which inspires calm, confidence and harmony, a sense of control and responsibility.

Too much blue, however, can seem mildly depressing and melancholy. The authors caution that the restraint and coolness may not only be soothing, but could also be taken as "hard, cold and calmly hostile, while the distance it implies may turn into withdrawal." In interiors, it is especially important to balance blue with touches of warmth. A too-blue room can seem cold and sterile.

Not all blues are quiet, retiring, or classic. In nature there exists a cosmic or atmospheric energy that is seen as blue. The phenomenon known as St. Elmo's Fire, a discharge of atmospheric electricity (as seen on the masts of ships and other tall objects), casts a gleaming blue light. The luminous tails of glittering glow worms are blue. The base of a gaseous flame burns a brilliant blue.

The vivid, strong, brilliant, and spectrum blues are thought of as electric. They are active rather than acquiescent; more playful than passive. Because of their neon quality, they are energizing and youthful. These shades are preferred by the young, as well as the young at heart.

Most connections to blue—those things with which we associate most readily—are derived from a nonturbulent sky and sea; clear, clean, calm, composed, and consoling. Coolness is also associated with heights, the upper atmosphere, and bodies of water. The surface of water reflects the image of sky, and deep clear water appears blue-green. So it is not surprising that most names describing blue remind us of sea and sky: ICE FLOW, MARINE BLUE, NILE BLUE, MORNING MIST, DEEP WATER, and GLACIER; the lofty heights of SKY BLUE, AIR BLUE, CRYSTAL BLUE, CLOUD BLUE, and STRATOSPHERE.

Bizarre Blue

For much of the population, (35 percent in the United States) blue is the favorite color. Blue as a skin tone, however, is seen as abnormal or unhealthy. Anoxia, a condition caused by insufficient oxygen to the tissues, causes the skin to turn blue. Blue lips signify extreme color or fright; blue is the color of bruising; dark-blue toe nails indicate a fungus is afoot.

There are rare instances of people having blue skin. In the Ozarks there are people who, due to a recessive gene causing the lack of an enzyme, have pastel blue skin. There are blue people in the Sahara who have skin the same color as the blue robes they dye.

Living at 20,000 feet in the Andes are blue people whose skin has adapted to the low level of oxygen at those heights. Undoubtedly for the same reason, Tibetan priests in the Himalayas have skin with a bluish cast.

The eyeball color of psychics can turn blue when they are in altered states of consciousness. Some experts feel that this might be due less to supernatural talents than to the delay of blood to the optic nerve caused by holding the breath for one or two minutes (not recommended!).

The Language of Blue

In spite of the general universal appeal of the color blue, it is apparent that in every country the words for the colors at the warm end of the spectrum were developed at an earlier time than those at the cool end. Latin was much richer in synonyms for warm colors than those for the cool colors. The Latin language, usually so full and comprehensive borrowed a word for blue, *caeruleus* (cerulean), from Teutonic speech.

Continues on page 72

COMBO 71-A

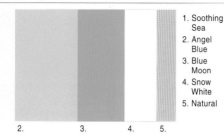

1. Soothing Sea
2. Angel Blue
3. Blue Moon
4. Snow White
5. Natural

Tranquil

The Tranquil mood calls forth the blues, blue-greens, and greens, used in subtle harmony, with a subtle touch of warmth, to create a peaceful and calming atmosphere—forever associated with sea and sky. If serenity is what you long for these are the colors that will help you relax, refresh and replenish both body and soul.

COMBO 71-B

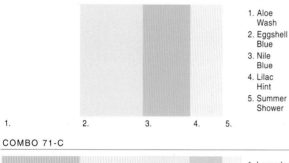

1. Aloe Wash
2. Eggshell Blue
3. Nile Blue
4. Lilac Hint
5. Summer Shower

COMBO 71-F

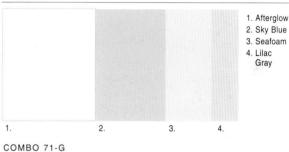

1. Afterglow
2. Sky Blue
3. Seafoam
4. Lilac Gray

COMBO 71-C

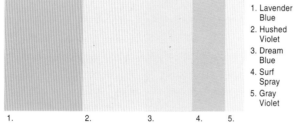

1. Lavender Blue
2. Hushed Violet
3. Dream Blue
4. Surf Spray
5. Gray Violet

COMBO 71-G

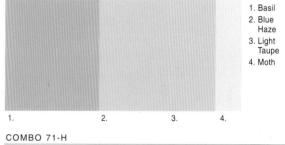

1. Basil
2. Blue Haze
3. Light Taupe
4. Moth

COMBO 71-D

1. Spa Blue
2. Aqua Sky
3. Air Blue
4. Murmur
5. Transparent Yellow

COMBO 71-H

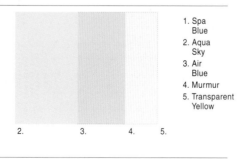

1. Celadon
2. Aqua
3. Pussywillow Gray
4. Apricot Illusion

COMBO 71-E

1. Whisper White
2. Garden Glade
3. Starlight Blue
4. Cream Pearl

COMBO 71-I

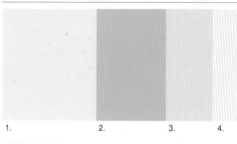

1. Bone White
2. Dusk
3. Wild Dove
4. Vapor Blue
5. Twilight Blue

Researchers have concluded that the earlier development of words for warm colors is not because primitive peoples lacked perception of blue, green and violet, but because of the stronger emotional appeal of colors at the red end of the spectrum. Ancient humans simply saw the warm advancing colors first, just as nature had intended.

Artful Blue

Various distinctive and classic shadings of blue have developed with the art of ceramics, porcelains, earthenware, and bone china. Colors such as FAIENCE, DRESDEN, CHINA BLUE, LIMOGES, and WEDGWOOD, have become a vital part of the blue family. The first known examples of blue ceramic decoration were found in Mesopotamian tin-glass wares of the 9th century. The Persians and ultimately the Chinese in the 14th century established the popularity of blue china which has lasted to the present.

The Chinese craftsmen used a cobalt ore to paint their beautiful blues. These naturalistic and rococo-like blue ceramics were imitated throughout Europe. The Dutch developed the particularly handsome Delft tin-glass pottery, which derived its color from being taken out of the kiln prematurely—a practice these frugal people may have invented because they wanted to use the same fire to smoke their herrings!

It took approximately 10,000 experiments for Englishman Josiah Wedgwood to develop just the right blue—a color so successful that for 200 years it was the only blue used in continuous production by the Wedgwood Company. When it comes to color, the English truly are perfectionists.

Grimsthorpe Castle in Bourne, Lincolnshire, England, was given a modern facelift by John Fowler, the famous English decorator with an assist from the owner, Lady Nancy Lancaster, an outgoing Anglo-American. They were an exceptional team and managed to transform a rather grim Grimsthorpe into a cheerful family home with lovely colors. In spite of some very basic personality differences, they were both perfectionists and held strong views. As so often happens with creative partners, an element of tension produces the best results. Fowler wanted to repaint the Chinese drawing room ceiling in its authentically bright Georgian Blue, and Lady Lancaster wanted something more subtle. "It takes 200 years for the right colors to fade," Fowler said. "I don't have that much time," she replied.

The popularity of blue in the bedroom was originated by the famous 18th-century lady of dubious reputation, Madame de Pompadour. She had a passion for pastels, particularly powder blue. Fascinated by her notorious (and highly successful) lifestyle, many elegant French ladies decorated their *boudoirs* in blue.

If you are a collector of anything blue, you can relate to the sentiments of the French writer Colette, who adored blue and felt that, just as there are connoisseurs of good French wine, there are also connoisseurs of blue.

Perhaps in a child's rhyme, the oldest and most simple symbolism of blue remains:

If you love me (but not quite)
Send me a ribbon, A ribbon of white.
If you love me, love me true
Send me a ribbon, a ribbon of blue.

Blue in Bed and Elsewhere

Children's Rooms: Of course little boys' rooms are often blue, but there is really no law that says it must be so. If your little girl loves blue, then why deprive her of her favorite color? Forget the stereotypical pink for girls and blue for boys, and think instead of the inherent message of the color. As blue is quiet and serene, if you have a daughter who is bouncing off walls with nonstop energy, blue might be just the shade to calm her down. And if she resists an all-blue bedroom, at least include some touches of blue in accessories or bed linens in order to achieve the necessary balance.

Adult Bedrooms: Blue has long been a favorite choice for bedrooms because of its relaxing feel. If your bedroom is a favorite place to unwind, blue is a good choice. If your bedroom also serves as a home office, then think twice about blue—you don't want to be too relaxed, especially if you have deadlines to meet. The best blues for that purpose would be brighter, higher energy blues, but again, in moderation. You will also have to unwind in this room as well, and too many stimulating bright tones won't lull you to sleep.

Bathrooms: Blue is a natural in an area where water is present. The bathroom is often the last stronghold of privacy, especially when there are kids around. If this is your favorite place to regroup as well as refresh, blue is a good choice. But the blue needs to be balanced with some warm colors. If not, you'll start feeling chilled and uncomfortable—not a good feeling when you wearing nothing but a towel!

Family Rooms: As this is the gathering place for the family and blue is such a pervasive favorite, there's a good chance it will be a good compromise color. But choose a blue that leans a bit to periwinkle as that shade has a warmer undertone. The same is true for greenish blues—they are usually crowd pleasers and seem more hospitable than solid blue.

Dens and Libraries: These are the rooms that are perfect for deeper blues, as they encourage meditative thinking and contemplation. If dark colors seem depressing to you, remember that complementary warm tones can help to brighten up the deep tones, as will good lighting.

Kitchens and Dining Areas: Every so often, the notion that blue depresses appetites makes its way into the tabloids. The only people who benefit from this news are the paint manufacturers, as it simply isn't so. No studies support this claim. If it were so, with so many people choosing blue plates as background to their food (it's the number one color for tableware internationally), there would be a lot of slim people all over the world benefiting from this quick and easy method of weight loss.

My favorite claim for blue's fictitious appetite-suppressing quality was made by a person selling blue light bulbs to place inside the refrigerator. Were you supposed to climb inside the fridge and eat, or did your appetite disappear in that split-second glance at the food under blue light?

Blue china is a special favorite in everything from traditional Willoware to Pottery Barn blue. And there are collectors of blue china who never tire of the color. If you are one of them, your affinity to the collection, the history of where it came from, or special memories will be evoked every time you look at the color.

BLUE

Continues on page 76

74   COLORS FOR YOUR EVERY MOOD

COMBO 75-A

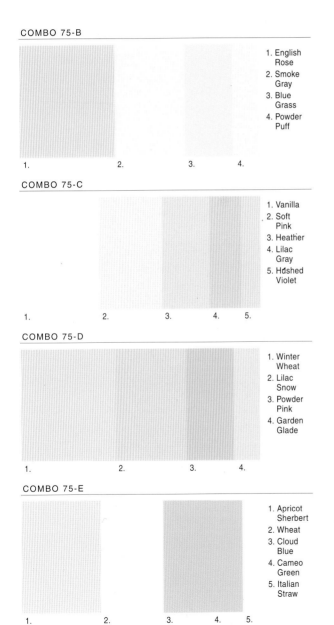

1. Bisque
2. Double Cream
3. Whisper White
4. Moonlight
5. Gobelin Blue

1.   2.   3.   4.   5.

Nurturing

The soft, warm colors of the Nurturing mood invite us to sit down and relax and feel comfortable. Inspired by fragile pastels, these tender tints—used in subtle combinations—are not just perfect for babies' rooms, but also for adult spaces where a sense of care, protection, safety, and love is needed or wanted.

COMBO 75-B

1. English Rose
2. Smoke Gray
3. Blue Grass
4. Powder Puff

1.   2.   3.   4.

COMBO 75-C

1. Vanilla
2. Soft Pink
3. Heather
4. Lilac Gray
5. Hushed Violet

1.   2.   3.   4.   5.

COMBO 75-D

1. Winter Wheat
2. Lilac Snow
3. Powder Pink
4. Garden Glade

1.   2.   3.   4.

COMBO 75-E

1. Apricot Sherbert
2. Wheat
3. Cloud Blue
4. Cameo Green
5. Italian Straw

1.   2.   3.   4.   5.

COMBO 75-F

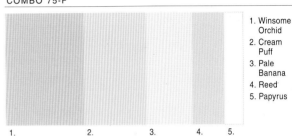

1. Winsome Orchid
2. Cream Puff
3. Pale Banana
4. Reed
5. Papyrus

1.   2.   3.   4.   5.

PHOTO: DON PAULSON

Personality and Blue

Blue is not only America's favorite color, but it appears to be a universal favorite. Studies show that designers from all the major countries select a shade of blue as their first choice. It is, after all, all over the world, the color of blue sky, blue sea, blue jeans, and all other things dependable and consoling. In this wired age of the digital revolution and technology racing ahead of the human ability to process it all, it is easy to understand why people would want to retreat into a place of quiet blue calm.

A Preference for Blue: People who prefer blue are absolutely mesmerized by it. They have loved the color all their lives and will probably never sway from their devotion to it. Perhaps they have blue eyes, and from the time they were infants they were praised every time they wore blue (blue-eyed people invariably choose it as their favorite color). They might have lived near the water (or longed to) and blue feels very natural to them, or it might have been those picnics under blue skies or Sundays at the beach that speak to them of happy family times and the freedom to run and play.

Most people will respond to dark blues as credible, authoritative, basic, classic, conservative, strong, dependable, traditional, serviceable, confident, nautical, professional, serene and quiet, while sky blues are calm, clean, cool, wet, sky, sea, peaceful, restful, constant, fresh, happy, soft, heavenly, faithful, and true. Teal blues are thought of as classy, cool, expensive, sophisticated, pleasing, rich, and unique.

If Blue is Your Favorite Color: Blue people are trusting and need to be trusted. Although cool and confident (or always striving to be), blue-lovers can be vulnerable. They are sensitive to the needs of others and form strong attachments, and they are deeply hurt if their trust is betrayed.

They aspire to harmony, serenity, patience, perseverance, and peace. They are somewhat social but prefer sticking to their own close circle of friends. They think twice before acting out, are generally conservative, even-tempered, and reliable.

Because of their highly developed sense of responsibility, blue personalities must be careful of perfectionist tendencies that may make them unrealistically demanding. Their gentleness, however, will win out.

If Blue Is Your Least Favorite Color: People who dislike blue may just be restless and need to break away from monotony. Perhaps they would like to change their jobs, or even their lives, and long for more excitement. They might be tired of being "depended on," but their highly developed conscience makes them stick to it. They wish that they were either wealthy or brilliant (or both) because that would enable them to have all the good things in life without working so hard or being so conscientious. Deeper blues may mean sadness and melancholy to them—blue just gives them the blues.

CHAPTER 8

Green
Deep Forests and Wide Meadows

If you were playing a word association game, what would be your immediate response to the word "green?" Would you visualize the brilliant blue-green of a tropical ocean, a verdant bed of velvety moss, silver-green willow branches, the lush deep green of a pine scented arbor, the sophisticated sparkle of emeralds, or the sickly yellow-green associated with nausea and mold or slimy, scary creatures? As the range of green is enormous, so are the possibilities of positive or negative associations.

The Gamut of Greens

Perhaps it was Kermit the Frog who best understood this complex color when he so aptly stated: "It's not easy being green!"

Responses to green run from high praise to pure disgust. Why the extreme divergence of opinion on greens? Perhaps it's because, of the 8 million to 10 million colors discernible to the human eye, the widest range distinguishable is in the vast variety of greens. The color of many edible plants (or at least their leaves), green was the first color to appear on earth and very necessary to human survival.

Slimy Green

To see the green in the world around us is quite natural and pleasant, but to be green is perceived of as eerie, supernatural, or sick. Humans come in assorted shades of red, yellow, black, brown, or white (and occasionally blue), but never green, which is simply alien as a skin tone.

Green creatures are slimy and skulking, creepy or cadaverous. Insects and snakes, lizards and alligators, dinosaurs and dragons are seen as scary. Childhood fears associated with icky green things are difficult to overcome as an adult. The frightening memories of childhood may conjure up images of scaly green creatures silently slithering out from beneath the bed and under the sheets ready to attack the moment the lights go out!

Weird aberrations from outer space (like Martians) are invariably green. In Britain folklore tells of green men—a "green knight" and fairies with green eyes, green skin and green hair.

When we are ill, have overindulged, or are seasick, our complexions take on a bilious yellow-green tinge. There is a form of anemia called chlorosis that actually does make the skin green. Fortunately, it is rare and easily controllable today. The oozy yellow-greens that emanate from infections are downright disgusting. John Ruskin, the 19th-century British art critic, said yellow-green had "the worst general character a color can have!" (*Savage Ruskin*, Patrick Conner, Wayne State University Press, 1979).

Being ill as a child is a particularly restrictive and unhappy time. We had to eat bland food (if we could eat at all), stay in bed, and miss the fun that we knew all our friends were enjoying. And to top it off, we saw this awful yellow-green face staring back at us in the mirror on our all-too-frequent trips to the bathroom. These lingering unpleasant associations are often hard to erase.

Continues on page 80

COMBO 79-A

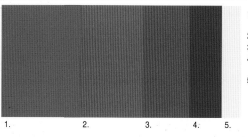

1. Hunter Green
2. Cranberry
3. Mahogany
4. Patriot Blue
5. Pale Gold

1. 2. 3. 4. 5.

Traditional

Trends may ebb and flow, but the colors in the Traditional palette withstand the test of time. These mid to deep tones call forth history, substance, connectedness, and stability. Even when they veer towards brightness, these traditional colors maintain a sense of restraint and propriety that give rooms a feeling of permanence and refinement.

COMBO 79-B

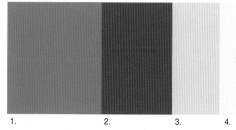

1. Coronet Blue
2. Eggplant
3. Silver Mink
4. Oyster Gray

1. 2. 3. 4.

COMBO 79-F

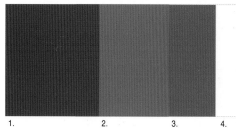

1. Grape Royal
2. Mallard Green
3. Stone Gray
4. Bone White

1. 2. 3. 4.

COMBO 79-C

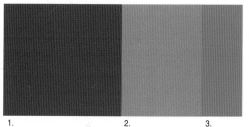

1. Blue Ribbon
2. Amber Green
3. Colonial Blue

1. 2. 3.

COMBO 79-G

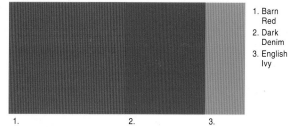

1. Barn Red
2. Dark Denim
3. English Ivy

1. 2. 3.

COMBO 79-D

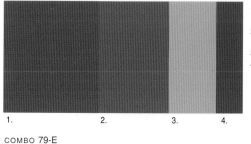

1. Deep Claret
2. Rose Brown
3. Bark
4. Loganberry

1. 2. 3. 4.

COMBO 79-H

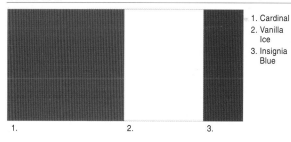

1. Cardinal
2. Vanilla Ice
3. Insignia Blue

1. 2. 3.

COMBO 79-E

1. True Navy
2. Burgundy
3. Four Leaf Clover
4. Misted Yellow

1. 2. 3. 4.

COMBO 79-I

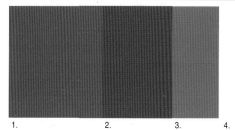

1. Partridge
2. Plum
3. Duck Green
4. Parchment

1. 2. 3. 4.

As a result, yellow-green in particular is very often the least popular of all colors unless there is a strong cultural or traditional tie to those shades. Because of their association to nausea, airlines, ships, and hospitals should never use yellow-greens like chartreuse and lime to decorate the surroundings of those who are already suffering a sickly complexion.

Sulfurous olive greens do not hold fond memories for most people. Especially for many men, the immediate association is one of government-issued socks, sheets, fatigues and shirts used day after dreary day—a whole world of drab military olives!

Pulsating neon chartreuse greens are trendy and youth-oriented and often intensely disliked in sophisticated markets where they are perceived as tacky. And this is precisely why young people like to use these electric greens. What better way to flaunt their disdain for the values of the older generation than wearing a color that their elders consider vulgar and obnoxious!

Nature's Green

But there are also some very positive associations to green. For most people a green path leads inevitably to thoughts of nature. Mother Nature painted more green on earth than any other color. It is the hue of foliage, grass, and growing plants; of graceful sheltering trees, dappled meadows and clinging vines; the shade of forest and jungle. It is the color of the country as opposed to the city; the romance of Robin Hood, wood urchins, elves, gnomes, and leprechauns; the product of the Irish patriot and St. Patrick's Day.

The sight of green is inexorably linked to the sense of smell—a freshly mown lawn, pine needles, and wet leaves after a sudden summer shower, a splash of lime and a crushed sprig of mint. Because our senses are intertwined, scents and colors are inevitably tied, one sense suggesting a specific color to another. We can look at a bottle of perfume and sense how it will smell before we sniff it. We can't help but associate a green fragrance with freshness and nature.

In Germany and Austria the loden coats and capes that many wear are part of a very old tradition that links people inevitably to lush summer greenery. Houses are bedecked with big sprigs of pine, humid greenhouses yield all kinds of plants, and giant cachepôts are filled with evergreen boughs. Hunting gear is always done in the camouflaging shades of the Black Forest greens. The privileged gentry who belong to the order of the "Green Tails" traditionally wear a brilliant emerald-green formal jacket to the evening of festivities after the hunt.

Green is so pervasive in nature that we never question it as a background for all other surrounding colors. Contrasting with purple pansies, pink azaleas, yellow daylilies, orange marigolds or red tulips (and any other color under the sun), leafy foliage greens are truly nature's perfect neutral.

This same natural versatility applies to the use of green in interiors. With the exception of the most attention-demanding neon yellow-greens, all other shades will fit comfortably into any color scheme because our eyes are so accustomed to the prolific world of greens around us.

Fruitful Green

The word "green" comes from the same root as "grow," so green symbolizes that which grows as well as the regeneration and the renewal of life. In several languages the words "grass," "grow" and "green" all spring from the same source. The Teutonic word *gro* and the Anglo-Saxon word *grene* both mean "to grow." In the ancient Egyptian language, the word for green, *akh*, meant "to blossom."

The first sign of spring, as the color of new vegetation that breaks through the hard wintry ground, green signifies rebirth, regrowth, regeneration, and renewal. As a hopeful symbol of new life and fertility, green gowns were worn by English brides until Elizabethan times.

For the Greeks, green was revered for still another form of fruitfulness—that of a beautiful garden. In the *Odyssey*, Homer describes the royal garden of Alcinous as "a smiling patch of never-failing green." Virgil and Cato expounded on the abundant greenery of the Roman kitchen garden filled with medicinal herbs and vegetables. In the first century B.C. the writer Columella loved green so much that he grew fifteen different varieties of cabbage! Aphrodite, the Greek goddess of love, was associated with the color green for much the same reason that the Romans revered Venus, the goddess of spring, beauty, and blossoms.

The ancient Egyptians symbolized the nature of green better than any other—the great Osiris was the god of both vegetation and death. They understood that green ultimately brings us full cycle: from the promise of the first buds of spring to inevitable and final mold and decay.

The Great Harmonizer—Restful Green

In the center of the spectrum, between the passivity of blue and the activity of yellow, green is known as the "great harmonizer" by Indian mystics who see green as the color of balance and harmony—the ray that bridges cause and effect. Used lavishly in verdant surroundings, the serenity of nature's green can indeed bring a sense of balance and harmony. As any nature lover knows, a walk in the woods, a mountain hike, or lying on your back in a grassy knoll gazing up through the leafy trees can be truly the best tranquilizer.

The ancient Romans knew that green is the most restful color to the eye. Pliny, the philosopher, once said that emerald delights the eye without fatiguing it. Nero watched his gory entertainments while peering through an emerald. Engravers kept a green beryl close at hand for a few moments after doing close work. This was a precursor to the green eyeshade worn by office clerks in later years, as well as the light green steno pads still in use.

In 1914, a surgeon at St. Luke's Hospital in San Francisco was disturbed by the glare of the white walls, drapes, towels, sheets, and so forth. He chose a lettuce-leaf green to have his operating room painted because it is the complementary (or opposite) color to red and pink—the colors of blood and tissue.

The color rapidly gained popularity. Thousands of surgical suites, uniforms, and drapes were eventually colored green—from lettuce to spinach green depending on the location. This "eye-ease green" has been scientifically proven to keep the surgeon's eyes acute to red and pink, to relieve glare, and to be psychologically cool. Green is also the color of the visual after-image that persists in the mind's eye after red is viewed.

In many hospitals green has given way to blue, but green is still considered the most preferred color for the operating room in many medical facilities. The use of "institutional" green spread to many other kinds of facilities, including educational and industrial.

At St. James Church in London there is a green room where those in need of solace can come for help. Theaters and television stations still have "green rooms" where performers may relax their eyes before facing the glare of the stagelights. Infamous for the many suicide leaps, the Blackfriar's Bridge, originally painted black, was repainted green by the city fathers of London and the suicide rate decreased by one-third!

Continues on page 84

COMBO 83-A

1. Green Haze
2. Winter White
3. Alabaster
4. Blue Ribbon
5. Pale Gold
6. Jasper

1.   2.   3.   4.   5.   6.

Contemplative

In a quiet sanctuary as designed by Michael Love, simplicity and understatement prevail in this Color Mood, and attention is drawn to important focal points—the colors of the art on the wall, a special glass piece in a niche, or the amazing view from a picture window. The surrounding colors in the interior designed by may be either monotone or monochromatic: there is minimal color to distract from the starring hues.

COMBO 83-B

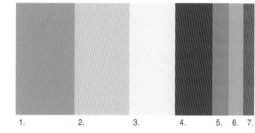

1. Deep Taupe
2. Light Taupe
3. Angora
4. Ethereal Green
5. Cinnabar
6. Deep Blue

1.   2.   3.   4.   5.   6.

COMBO 83-F

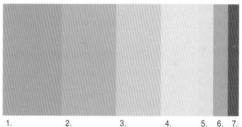

1. Charcoal Gray
2. Neutral Gray
3. Limestone
4. Blue Gray
5. Royal Purple
6. Directoire Blue
7. Deep Peacock Blue

1.   2.   3.   4.   5.   6.   7.

COMBO 83-C

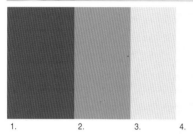

1. Natural
2. Shifting Sand
3. Pastel Parchment
4. Byzantium
5. Biscuit
6. Cadmium Orange
7. Rose Of Sharon

1.   2.   3.   4.   5.   6.   7.

COMBO 83-G

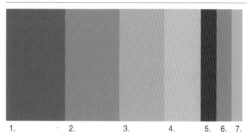

1. Elm
2. Eucalyptus
3. Pale Gray Green
4. Celadon
5. Sky Blue
6. Coral Haze
7. Twilight Purple

1.   2.   3.   4.   5.   6.   7.

COMBO 83-D

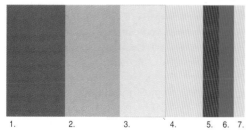

1. Pewter
2. Storm Gray
3. Vapor
4. Golden Mist
5. Bright Red Violet
6. Imperial Blue
7. Gray Violet

1.   2.   3.   4.   5.   6.   7.

COMBO 83-E

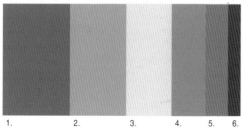

1. Walnut
2. Bark
3. Bleached Sand
4. Deep Periwinkle
5. Porcelain Rose
6. Purple Wine

1.   2.   3.   4.   5.   6.

DESIGN: OLSON SUNDBERG ARCHITECTS WITH ED CARPENTER   PHOTO: EDUARDO CALDERON

Goethe was so impressed by the refreshing and restful qualities of the hue that he wrote: "The eye experiences a distinctly grateful impression from this color."

Eternally Green

Numerous people over the centuries have claimed the ability to read auras, what they see as the luminous radiation of colors that emanate from the body. Religious idols have often been depicted as possessing the divine light of energy. There are many interpretations of what these emanations mean, but the following messages are linked to the auras surrounding the body in various shades of green: gray-green means deceit, pale green means sympathy, and bright green stands for ingenuity, abundance, and the ability to heal.

In many religions green carries implications of immortality, faith, and contemplation. During Easter, it symbolizes the resurrection. Pale green is the color of baptism. The olive branch is the symbol of peace and the laurel wreath, immortality. The legend of the Holy Grail tells us that the cup was green, signifying an eternal life.

For the Muslim, green is associated with World Mother; and only the holiest—those who are descendants of the Prophet Mohammed and have made a pilgrimage to Mecca—are allowed to wear a green turban. This relates to the dark green gardens of the eternal abode filled with fruit trees and fountains that the Koran promises the devout. Life eternal is predicted as harmonious, and everywhere is the color green.

In the desert, green clearly marks the space between life and death. For that reason, it became Mohammed's special hue. It is one of the sacred colors of Islam, present in the flags of nearly every Muslim country, including Iran, Iraq, Pakistan, the Sudan, and Jordan.

When Lord Louis Mountbatten was viceroy of India, he made the lucky choice (quite by accident) of wearing his green uniform to meet the formidable Mohammedan tribesmen. They took this as a compliment and a good omen, and they embraced their new envoy.

In the classic book, *The Enjoyment and Use of Color* (Dover Publications, 1964) Walter Sargeant quotes William Beebe, the explorer, as he describes greens:

> When I have left behind the world of inharmonious colors, of polluted waters, of soot-stained walls and smoke-tinged air, the green of the jungle comes like a cooling bath of delicate tints and shades. I think of all the green things I have loved—of malachite in matrix and table-top; of jade, not factory-hewn baubles, but age-mellowed signets, fashioned by lovers of their craft, and seasoned by the toying fingers of generations of forgotten Chinese emperors . . . jade . . .of the exact shade of the right color . . . I think, too, of dainty emerald scarves that are seen and lost in a flash at a dance; the air-cooled, living green of the curling breakers; of a lonely light that gleams to starboard of an unknown passing vessel, and of the transparent green of the northern lights that flicker and play on winter nights high over the garish glare of Broadway. Now in the late afternoon, when I opened my eyes in their little gorge, the soft green vibrations merged insensibly with the longer waves of the dove's voices . . .Soon the green alone was dominant.

To the Japanese the word for green, *midori*, is seen as the color of eternal life—as in the evergreens that never change color. *Midori* also implies vegetation: the greens of the Japanese people's highly treasured gardens and of their daily sustenance based primarily on a vegetable diet.

Fashionable Green

In the Middle Ages, emerald green gemstones were believed to protect a woman's chastity. This tradition persisted through the years and overanxious men of wealth presented their marriageable daughters with emerald rings or brooches. In the previously mentioned classic *Wedding Portrait* by Jan Van Eyck, the very pregnant bride wears green—she evidently neglected to wear her emerald green jewelry!

In the Orient of the Middle Ages, jade was believed to have mysterious occult and restorative powers, especially when ground into a powder, combined with liquid, and used as a potion by jealous lovers (the green-eyed monster who turned green with envy) so that they could regain the attention of the beloved.

In the 17th century, ladies of the French court carried limes around with them because they had discovered that when they bit into the pungent citrus fruit regularly, their lips would redden. A bit messy and not a very practical substitute for modern lipstick, but it might have been the first form of time-released Vitamin C!

Many years later, Empress Eugenie started the rage for green when she appeared at the opera one night in 1864 in a spectacular deep green gown that actually kept its color under the gas lighting—not an easy task in those days before the advent of electricity. The chemically produced dye was more impervious to gaslight than were natural dyes.

Oddly enough, in spite of the plenitude of green in nature, natural resources for green dyes are not bountiful. In the 19th century, the world of fashion and design was delighted with the increased range of color made available by chemical processes. "Paris Green" became a very fashionable emerald shade, used extensively in decorating. When it was discovered that the deadly arsenic-based pigments used in wall coverings of this color had caused many mysterious deaths, it was aptly re-named POISON GREEN!

And across the channel, the English were responsible for the invention of khaki. It doesn't sound very British because it isn't. The name is derived from the Hindustani word for dust. Not a very fashionable name for a color, but khaki was never intended to be fashionable. That happened entirely by accident when a clever chap in the British East India Company tore off his stifling (not to mention attention-getting) scarlet uniform to do battle in the comfy pajamas that he had dyed the color of mud. Not an illustrious beginning, but armies all over the world soon followed suit and a new color classic was created.

We often think of olive-greens as a 20th-century phenomenon—the olive drabs of World War II, the avocado shag carpets of the 1970s, the designer citron greens of the 1990s. But it was during the turn of the century that the Victorians used these yellow-greens in complex combinations of OLIVE GREEN with PEACOCK BLUE, OLIVE GREEN with MAROON, or most dramatically, OLIVE GREEN with MAGENTA.

So important were the yellow-greens that Gilbert and Sullivan paid homage to the color, calling it "greenery-yallery" in their popular operettas. The artist Kandinsky emphatically believed in the connection between music and color. He wrote: "In music, absolute green is represented by the placid middle notes of the violin."

Blue-Green

While most greens emanate from the earth, blue-greens are associated with the sea—calm, spacious, and cool. Some languages have a single word for the entire range of blue-green, and that word is also the word for the sea. Aqua in the romance languages as well as in English, actually means water, so that blue-greens, light and dark, are always thought of as "wet" colors. In many of the world's languages, including certain American Indian dialects, there is a term for the combination of green and blue called, simply and logically, *grue*.

Continues on page 88

COMBO 87-A

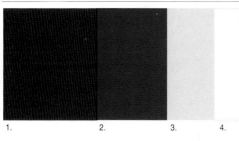

1. Mars Red
2. Gunmetal
3. Neutral Gray
4. Star White

1.　2.　3.　4.

Dynamic

A Dynamic mood is just that: high energy, exciting, and very dramatic. It can be created in two ways: bold colors in combination with black, neutrals, and whites, or unusual combinations of glamorous show-stopping jewel tones that the less adventurous would never dare put together.

COMBO 87-B

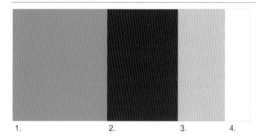

1. Byzantium
2. Foggy Dew
3. Smoked Pearl

1.　2.　3.

COMBO 87-F

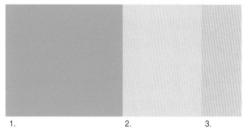

1. Lapis
2. Opaline Green
3. Silver

1.　2.　3.

COMBO 87-C

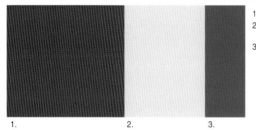

1. Brilliant Blue
2. Raven
3. Storm Gray
4. Pristine

1.　2.　3.　4.

COMBO 87-G

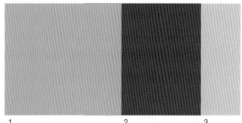

1. Peridot
2. Amethyst
3. Antique Gold

1.　2.　3.

COMBO 87-D

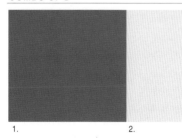

1. Violet Storm
2. Light Gray
3. Black Ink

1.　2.　3.

COMBO 87-H

1. Garnet
2. Dusty Turquoise
3. Sauterne

1.　2.　3.

COMBO 87-E

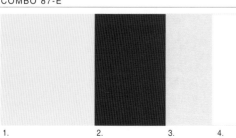

1. Lemon Chrome
2. Black Olive
3. Silver Lining
4. White Asparagus

1.　2.　3.　4.

COMBO 87-I

1. Jade Green
2. Carmine
3. Bright Gold

1.　2.　3.

The origin of the word "turquoise" comes from the French meaning "Turkish" because the stone was first brought from Turkey to France. The ancient Persians protected themselves with turquoise gemstones called piruseh, which meant joy and carried them as talismans against the "evil eye." They also loved turquoise glazes on bricks and tiles, so that many of their buildings glistened with the lively shade that they considered to be a lucky color. That same reverence for turquoise has carried through to modern times.

Teal green, a variation of blue-green, is seen as sophisticated and upscale, as are the bluer versions of teal and teal blue. When deep blue is added to green, the shade becomes more serious and pensive. Dr. Max Luscher, the Swiss psychologist known for his color work, stated:

> The more a darkening blue is added to green the more solid, the colder, tenser, harder and more resilient the psychological effect of the color . . . fir-green corresponds to stability, solidity, constancy, persistence, resilience of will.

Word association studies show many positive responses to blue-greens. The words used most often to describe the blue-greens are these: cool, fresh, refreshing, liquid, soothing, ocean and water.

The Perception of Green

In color effect experiments in the 1930s, Dr. Kurt Goldstein found that ". . . green induces a state of tranquillity and a withdrawal from external pressures which occurs on both a motor and emotional level." He felt that green induces a relaxation of the muscle. The motor he was referring to were the designating nerves that carry impulses from the nerve centers to the muscles.

Goldstein compared the effects of red to green. He found that while red is more effective than green in stimulating ideas and energy for mental activity, green aids in the actual development of those ideas. He said in his book, *The Organism* (D.C. Heath and Co.,1939):

> One could say red is inciting to activity and favorable for emotionally determined actions; green creates the condition of meditation and exact fulfillment of the task. Red may be suited to produce the emotional background out of which ideas and actions will emerge; in green these ideas will be developed and action executed.

Later tests by other researchers also indicate that although red may be more arousing than green, and the strength of hand grip is greater in the presence of red visual stimulation than green, there is greater hand tremor under red than green. Again, red may stimulate the activity, but green helps the respondents to keep cool. Because of this calming effect, blue-green lighting is being tested for the treatment of depression.

Our perception of time, weight, and length can be affected by color. Time is perceived as moving more quickly in a green room; length is judged to be shorter and weight heavier when viewed under a green light.

Green has also been shown to "lighten" moods. If you're inviting friends in for a friendly came of cards, use a green tablecloth. Studies show that while a red tablecloth causes disagreements and interruptions 31 percent of the time and a black tablecloth disrupts the game 27 percent of the time, green hardly causes a riffle in the players' irritation level.

Decorating with Green

Because of our eyes being accustomed to the ubiquitous green found in nature, this hue is equally at home in every room in the house. There are some shades that work better than others, however.

The Den: If this is your "retreat and restoration" room, the deepest greens will work best here. It is a perennial favorite when paired with navy and red in plaids and checks, but deep solid greens are equally effective on major areas such as walls and floors, imparting a hushed and stable atmosphere.

Entry Areas and Living Rooms: Green is not only the color of nature, but it is also the color often identified with money. So if your goal is to impart a prosperous air to the entry or living room areas, medium to dark greens (especially the color of legal tender!) will impart that message. It is an excellent color for waiting rooms in offices where the responsible handling of money is an issue—accountants, stock brokers, investment counselors, and so on.

Bedrooms: Like blue, green imparts a calm, cool, and collected feel to the environment. The blue-greens are an especially good choice for the bedroom as they embody the most tranquil aspects of both color families, doubly reinforcing the serene mood. If your bedroom is your sanctuary, then the blue-greens will help you achieve the nirvana you are seeking.

Bathrooms: If you want your bathroom to feel like a spa, the softer sage greens and blue-greens are your best choice. Cool, soothing and refreshing, submerging yourself in this color is the antidote to a particularly stressful day.

Exteriors: Because of its ability to blend so well into the outdoor environment, green is an especially handsome color on the exterior, especially when a more subtle look is preferred. In every shade other than neon or bright green, it is unobtrusive as an outdoor color.

Green and Personality

If Green Is Your Favorite Color: Nature's most plentiful color promises a balance between warmth and coolness, so green people are usually stable and balanced types. This is the good citizen, concerned parent, involved neighbor, and PTA member—the joiner of clubs and organizations. You are fastidious, kind, and generous.

It's important for you to win the admiration of peers, so you are often a "do-gooder." You are a caring companion, loyal friend, partner, or lover, with a high moral sense, and are super-sensitive to doing the right things.

You are intelligent and understand new concepts. You are less inclined to risk something new than to do what is popular and conventional. The bad news for green people is that they often have big appetites for food. If you are dieting, it is difficult for you to lose your lumpies. The worst vice for green lovers is the tendency to gossip. Are you that way because you're a little green with envy?!

If Green Is Your Least Favorite Color: Since lovers of green are usually very social, and keeping up-with-the-neighbors types, dislikers of green will often put those qualities down. You may have an unfulfilled need to be recognized that causes you to pull away from people rather than join them. You don't like thinking, looking, and doing things the way you see the majority of people thinking, looking, and doing them. Picnics, cocktail parties, and Saturday night at the Elks Club do not interest you in the least.

Remembering that snakes, lizards, dragons, and various other creepy-crawlies are green, the most important thing to look at is the question: Did something green and slithery frighten you as a child?

90   COLORS FOR YOUR EVERY MOOD

COMBO 91-A

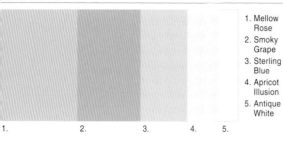

1. Mellow Rose
2. Smoky Grape
3. Sterling Blue
4. Apricot Illusion
5. Antique White

Romantic

A tasteful take on nostalgic colors, a Romantic mood is created when midtones, in variety of hues, are combined in low-contrast or closely related combinations. There is nothing to jar the eye here as we follow the easy visual pathway around the room--the result is a mellow, inviting, intimate, comfortable and comforting mood.

COMBO 91-B

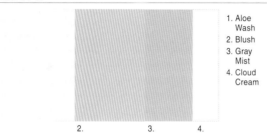

1. Aloe Wash
2. Blush
3. Gray Mist
4. Cloud Cream

COMBO 91-F

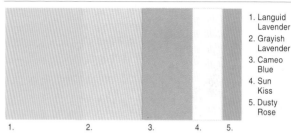

1. Languid Lavender
2. Grayish Lavender
3. Cameo Blue
4. Sun Kiss
5. Dusty Rose

COMBO 91-C

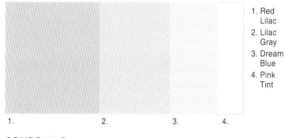

1. Red Lilac
2. Lilac Gray
3. Dream Blue
4. Pink Tint

COMBO 91-D

1. Forget-Me-Not
2. Rose Dust
3. Cameo Green
4. Cocoon

COMBO 91-E

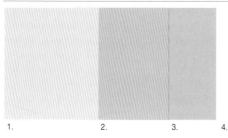

1. Evening Sand
2. Deauville Mauve
3. Elm
4. Pastel Parchment

PHOTO: DON PAULSON

CHAPTER 9

Purple
Passion and Magic

The purple family—the most enigmatic of all colors—is a combination of the excitement of red and the tranquillity of blue, the marriage of two diametrically opposed emotions. A critical balancing act always exists: which emotion takes the lead?

The Rainbow's Most Complex Color

From passionate red-violets to strong, silent indigo purples, this is the rainbow's most complex color and so are the people who prefer it: artists, mystics, performers, designers, widely (and often wildly) divergent types who have one thing in common—they are nonconformists (or longing to be!).

It is no wonder that highly creative artistic types (as well as eccentrics) have a predilection for purple. They enjoy the uniqueness inherent in this extraordinary hue. Wagner composed his magnificent operas in a room surrounded by purple curtains. Leonardo DaVinci felt that the power of meditation was increased tenfold if done under rays of violet light. Chromotherapists claim that purple light has the power to heal hacking coughs, hoarseness, high blood pressure, and even lunacy! The oil of violets was used for medicinal purposes in medieval times, particularly as an aid for insomnia.

The Ancient Passion for Purple

The most precious dye color in all the ancient world was purple. Phoenicia was the original home of purple dye. As a matter of fact, the word "Phoenician" is derived from the Greek common noun *Phoinix* which meant "purple-red." The Phoenicians discovered the hue in a shellfish, purpuridae (*murex*). Only a single drop of glandular mucous could be extracted from the tiny mollusks, which made the color rare and extremely expensive. Enormous amounts of shells had to be crushed to obtain the smallest quantity of the purple dye: 336,000 snails to produce one ounce of dye! Huge mounds of murex shells—12 miles long and eight feet high—were excavated in the city of Tyre. Little stone hammers used to break the tiny glands, were also unearthed.

The Phoenicians traveled through Morocco, Italy, and Syria seeking the shellfish to yield the famous "Tyrian Purple" that was used to dye woolens and linens. Legend has it that wherever they found people with purple lips (from eating the snails), they established dye works and centers of trade. After the snails were extracted from their shells, they were placed into vats where their putrefying bodies excreted a yellowish liquid. This liquid yielded various shades ranging from rose to violet, depending upon the amount of water added. Because of the awful odors, the dyeing sites were placed well away from town centers.

There is a certain mystical or spiritual quality attached to purple. In the language of metaphysics the term "purple power" means psychic ability. Because violet has the highest frequency in the visible spectrum, many mystics and New Age believers see violet as the highest spiritual intuition—the connecting link in the color spectrum between the life-sustaining red and heavenly blue.

To the ancients, this transitional, transcendental color was a spiritual rather than physical phenomenon. A violet flame was believed to issue forth from the heavens above the highest white lights, and this indiscernible light was called the "seventh ray." It was believed that in this heavenly ray was the energy of mercy and forgiveness.

Those who claim to read auras, the luminous radiation of colors that emanate from the body, say that a violet aura means a free-spiritual soul. In the Kaballah, a mystical interpretation of the scriptures developed by Jewish rabbis during the sixth century and ultimately adopted by many Christian mystics in the Middle Ages, purple held the quality of leadership—full of "pomp and splendor." They saw amethyst as spiritual and magical. The learned rabbis were so sophisticated about color that they saw the merging of gray with purple as producing violet— "a higher octave of purple than purple itself . . . the influences flowing through . . . are humility, reverence, and spiritual dedication."

Purple in Religion

There are many mentions of purple in the *Old Testament*, where it is associated with splendor and dignity. Moses decreed that a curtain of purple separate the "Holy of Holies" from the rest of the temple. The high priests of the Israelites wore majestic purple robes.

Jesus wore a purple robe when Pontius Pilate's soldiers placed a crown of thorns on his head. Purple became symbolic of suffering, sacrifice, and penance and was designated for liturgical vestments during the time of purgation, Advent and Lent. Catholic priests were "raised to the purple" when they became bishops or cardinals. In the 17th century an Italian cardinal living in Paris chose a brilliant cyclamen for his robes. Some writers and historians feel that the original purple was possibly magenta or crimson.

Dr. H. Zollinger of Tehnisch-Chemisches Laboratorium, in Zurich, Switzerland, an expert on ancient color use, wrote: "Most astonishing was the shade of ancient purple. The fabrics used today by Vatican tailors for the gowns of cardinals correspond to a brilliant bittersweet red, a red which is even more on the yellowing side than magenta." Dyed on wool (as it was in Roman times) it was a deep plum, not a red.

So it seems there were several variations of purple-crimson-magenta-plum and eventually cardinal red in ecclesiastical dress. This was probably caused by variations in the dye lots or a color-blind tailor!

Purple's Healing Powers

In Egypt, amethyst was cherished as a healing amulet, a divine protection from evil. The Egyptian warrior wore an amethyst to protect himself in battle, as did soldiers in the Middle Ages. It was believed that wearing an amethyst brought peace of mind, cured insomnia, and enabled the wearer to dream many dreams.

In Greek, amethyst means "not drunk." Legend has it that the color of ecclesiastical rings were amethyst, not only because of religious symbolism, but also to protect the wearer from imbibing too much of the fermented grape! The Vikings drank their wine from cups made of amethyst, calling it the "sobering stone." It was also thought to guard against evil thoughts and contagious diseases.

Lucian, the Greek historian, described a fabled city of gems whose alters were huge blocks of amethyst. The frescoes preserved on the island of Crete show that

Continues on page 96

COMBO 95-A

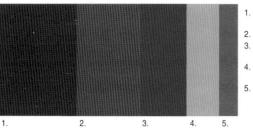

1. Aurora Red
2. Tabasco
3. Purple Mountain
4. Golden Apricot
5. Kashmir

Sensuous

When rich, predominately warm, luxurious hues are combined in complementary schemes, they infuse a room with an aura of sensuality and opulence. The heightened intensity of the hues creates an atmosphere that is sultry, exotic, and daringly inviting.

COMBO 95-B

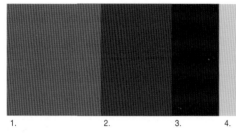

1. Aragon
2. Purple Passion
3. Pompeian Red
4. Desert Dust

COMBO 95-F

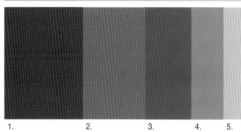

1. Burnt Henna
2. Raw Umber
3. Velvet Morning
4. Topaz
5. Amber

COMBO 95-C

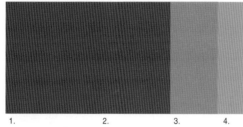

1. Tulipwood
2. Cinnabar
3. Carnelian
4. Green Eyes

COMBO 95-G

1. Mandarin Orange
2. Flame Orange
3. Cadmium Yellow
4. Turkish Sea
5. Blue Nights

COMBO 95-D

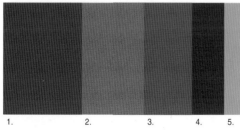

1. Greyish Purple
2. Arabesque
3. Corsican Blue
4. Persian Red
5. Chinchilla

COMBO 95-E

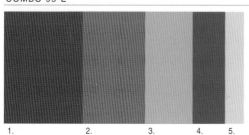

1. Marsala
2. Ginger
3. Silver Mink
4. Blue Iris
5. Buff Orange

DESIGN: JAMIE DRAKE ASID   PHOTO: EDWARD J. NORTH

the inhabitants had a passion for bright colors, including purple. The tombs of the rich were filled with rings, bracelets, collars, and hairpins, often fashioned of amethyst. Purple dye was so expensive that commoners could not afford to buy the precious purple coloring for their clothing or their homes. In spite of this limited number of potential customers, the glorious color was held in such high esteem that 2,000 people were employed in the sewing of purple garments in 12th-century Greece.

Regal Purple

For thousands of years the wearing of purple was the prerogative of kings—those "born to the purple" and ultimately to the very wealthy. The rulers of Assyria and Babylonia wore purple, as well as Alexander the Great. Caesar and Nero proclaimed purple exclusively for the emperor, and the Roman senators were limited to purple trim only. Many pharaohs were placed in sarcophagi made of porphyry, a reddish-purple rock mined in Egypt.

The bards of Homer's *Odyssey* were wrapped in purple robes and Agamemnon's wife rolled out a purple-crimson carpet—a color reserved only for the gods when he returned from Troy. Cleopatra regally displayed purple sails on her flagship (a preference she may have picked up from her good friend, Julius Caesar).

In England, the huge wardrobe inventories of Henry VIII disclosed a purple velvet doublet embroidered in gold, a gift from Thomas Cromwell. However, it was often difficult to see the color of Henry's clothes because they were so heavily encrusted with the English royal diamonds, rubies, and pearls. Henry, as history has told us, was not prone to understatement.

The regal connotations have held on through the years for many socioeconomic levels. In Alice Walker's *The Color Purple* (Harcourt, Brace, Janovich, 1982) the main character, Celia, chooses a dress for her friend and mentor, Shug. She says, "I think what color I should wear. She like a queen to me, so I say . . . Somethin purple . . ."

In ancient China, the well-read, scholarly intellectuals affected purple garments. But the great philosopher Confucius warned his followers that the expense of the desirable dye would cause social disorder. He admonished his followers never to use anything so base as a dark purple or puce in their ornaments or their dress.

In Indian folklore purple means decadence. The book *A Second Paradise* by Naveen Patnaik tells of the "Orchid House," a 19th-century court of the kingdom of Oudh where the king had absolute power of life and death over his subjects. He had a particularly large harem made up not only of the royal ladies, ladies-in-waiting, and maid-servants, but also the concubines. The women were condemned to a life of idle leisure and enforced companionship. Most of them came to the harem as children and never left. His harem eventually became so unwieldy and oversized that it had to be guarded by still more women—a whole regiment of them armed with muskets and bayonets!

During the 19th-century Regency and French Empire periods, hyacinth purple was favored by the European elite. When chemical dyes became more readily available in the latter part of the 1800s, women luxuriated in wearing purple. Because it faded so quickly when exposed to light, however, many women were forced to "turning" their purple garments, literally picking the stitches out, turning the clothes inside out and resewing them so that they could get more wear out of them. Imagine having to do the same with draperies and upholstery fabrics.

Nostalgic Purple

As a reaction to the garish purples brought on by experimentation with the new chemical dyes, purples were softened by the end of the century. These subtle tints of lavender, lilac, heathered tones, and "swooning mauves," as they were called at that time, hint of nostalgia, delicacy, and refinement, especially as Lalique's amazing Art Nouveau dragonfly designs, typically executed in orchids and opals, were ushered in.

In 1845 August Wilhelm Hofman, a German professor at the Royal College of Chemistry in London, experimented with coal-tar derivatives—a waste material left over in the manufacture of gas. One of Hofman's students, William Henry Perkin, in an effort to synthesize quinine, mixed one of the coal-tar chemicals called aniline with a form of potassium. He was about to discard the mess when a glint of purple caught his eye. He diluted this with alcohol, and the solution turned to a beautiful purple. Not only did it dye silk, but more importantly, it resisted fading in both water and light. The solution was called *mauve* after the French word for the delicate purple wood mallow flower that provided the natural dye.

Perkin gambled on the entrepreneurial possibilities of the first commercial production of organic dyes, and he won handsomely. Upper-class ladies followed the fashion of Queen Victoria who favored the shade and wore a mauve gown to the Great Exhibition of 1862. The color remained popular for ten years and was dubbed the "mauve decade." At the age of 23, Perkin was the acknowledged world authority on dyes. Not to be outdone by his now-wealthy former student, Hofman developed a rosaniline dye called Hofman's violet.

There has also been the association of aging older ladies with those softened tints, a sort of "lavender and old lace" stigma. That attitude is rapidly changing, particularly in the Western world where Grandma is more apt to jog in lavender sneakers or color her formerly purpled-gray hair with an exciting red or blonde tint!

Decadent Purple

But purple also has its mournful side. As the deepest tones of purple are closely akin to black, some of black's connotations rub off on purple. In Victorian England, purple was the accepted shade of half-mourning, the color worn after the first few months of obligatory black. In some cultures, dark purples are viewed as melancholy and funereal, while in others the deep shades such as WOOD VIOLET or PLUM are seen as very sophisticated.

In other cultures, vivid red-purples and bright orchids bear the taint of prostitution and poor taste. In 1926 Oswald Spengler showed little tolerance for violet in his book, *Decline of the West* (Knopf, 1938). He said, "Violet, a red succumbing to blue, is the color of women no longer fruitful and of priests living in celibacy!"

In spite of that very haughty pronouncement, shades of orchid were considered very chic in the 1920s, a time of flappers flagrantly defying established conventional rules. In more recent times, purple has had its highs and lows in public awareness and acceptance. In the 1960s it was very much a part of the psychedelic scene as well as the color adopted by many non-conforming "hippie" types. In the 1970s, it all but disappeared from view entirely as earth tones took over. In the 1980s, the pendulum swung in the opposite direction as the "mauving of America" (as *Time* magazine labeled it) took over and mauve was a ubiquitous presence in every living room, hotel, motel, and doctor's office in America.

Continues on page 100

COMBO 99-A

1. Mosstone
2. Tarragon
3. Seedling
4. Mineral Red
5. Oak Bluff
6. Rose Violet

1.   2.   3.   4.   5.   6.

Foraging the Forest

Of all the colors in the spectrum, there are more shades of green than any other, and there is no lack of greenery in any forest scene. Look at all the nuances of Nature's greens and draw your inspiration from them. There is green, yes, but add to this leafy color all those on the forest floor: the mineral reds, purples, golds, grays, taupes and browns of rocks, stones, and moist mosses near the liquid greens of the nearby stream.

COMBO 99-B

1. Elm Green
2. Aspen Green
3. Spruce
4. Burnt Russet
5. Wineberry

1.   2.   3.   4.   5.

COMBO 99-C

1. Butternut
2. Antelope
3. Misted Yellow
4. Chrysanthemum
5. Acorn

1.   2.   3.   4.   5.

COMBO 99-D

1. Jade Gray
2. Feldspar
3. Fir
4. Rose Taupe
5. Faun
6. Moonlight Mauve

1.   2.   3.   4.   5.   6.

COMBO 99-E

1. Verdant Green
2. Loden Frost
3. Shadow Green
4. Bison
5. Heather Rose

1.   2.   3.   4.   5.

COMBO 99-F

1. Cypress
2. Tendril
3. Boysenberry
4. Cranberry
5. Golden Yellow

1.   2.   3.   4.   5.

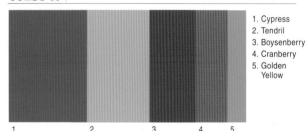

PHOTO: DON PAULSON

The mid-1980s saw grape take shape as the leading purple, on the heels of the Miami Art Deco-inspired *Miami Vice* television series. At that point, it gained a new acceptance from men in clothing choices; what had once been a nonentity in men's color preferences became a featured color player as a result of the series.

Purple's Messages

Although it is classified as a cool color, purple does contain red. Testing of galvanic skin response has shown that violet, like red, is more emotionally arousing than cooler greens. The redder the purple, the hotter and more passionate it gets and the more it is imbued with red's persona of dynamism and excitement. It advances to the eye—defying the viewer to ignore its presence.

The bluer purples are the more subdued side of purple and take on many of the serene qualities of deepened blue. They do not move forward in the field of vision as do the redder purples. There is more dignity in a blue-purple than in a red-purple, and, like blue, ir has a more contemplative demeanor. The subdued grayed purples such as GRAPE and MULBERRY are very quiet and low-key.

There are many components of this very complex color, as well as many meanings. Because of its mystical associations, it is also seen as the color of enchantment. Used in colored lighting on-stage, purple lights add an ethereal, even eerie quality.

As the psychological message is not quite clear, the most difficult purples for many people to deal with are the shades that seem to contain equal amounts of blue and red undertones. This "split" personality of two very different moods can cause an ambivalence in purple's meaning and our reactions to it. Most people feel more comfortable when purple has a definite red or blue undertone and the message becomes clearer.

The Language of Purple

The origin of the word "purple" is derived from the Latin *purpura* and the Greek *porphyra*, a kind of shellfish that yielded the purple dye. Most all other variations for this color family come from floral names, as purple is most abundant in flowers, such as lilac, orchid, cyclamen, pansy, mauve, lavender, viola and violet. Violet is derived from the French *violette*, the old French *viole* and the Latin *viola*. Lavender comes from the Latin *lavendula*, the pale purple spiky plant of the mint family, used in sachets, toilet waters, and as a preservative.

Although purple is a commonly known color word in many cultures, a study done in Sweden showed that for many people purple was the least known color word of seventeen colors presented; many of the subjects had no comment on the color, and some guessed it was among the yellow-reds!

Nature's Purples

Purple rarely appears in wildlife (most frequently in butterflies), and when the hue does make its splashy appearance in the sea, it is often iridescent and blatantly beautiful.

Some purple flowers are very short-lived. The giant water lily changes from white to purple in the single day in which it matures. When purple make its appearance in flowers, it can upstage every other color surrounding it.

The range of purple flowers is diverse and reflects every purple mood: from delicately scented lilac to wistful wisteria, exotic orchid to almost black pansies,

COLORS
FOR
YOUR
EVERY
MOOD

100

purple intrigues the eye in every landscape. Purple is breathtaking when it is splashed across a desert sky or reflected into a tropic sea.

Somehow, it is the least expected color in vegetation. Our eyes are accustomed to orange leaves in autumn, but an orange leaf turning to purple fascinates us. A white potato is to be expected, but a purple potato in a gourmet grocery never ceases to amaze!

From the dazzling beauty of a hot purple Santa Fe sunset to the cool retreating magnificence of a distant mountain range at dusk, purple paints an imposing picture. It is a distinctive color demanding special attention—definitely not the shade for shrinking violets!

Decorating with Purple

A unique color demands a unique person—this is a color that is not for everyone. But before you turn away from all things purple in the home, think of all the nuances. A vivid purple may not work for you, but think of purple in terms of undertones, lightness and brightness. There are so many shades of purple—they are extremely varied, and some shades will work better than others for specific areas.

The Kitchen: Absolutely the most fun place to use brighter shades of purple. Think of Italian ceramics and interesting glassware and endless possibilities on the tabletop.

Bedroom: The bluer purples such as violet work best in the bedroom—those that are quieter and more serene than the red purples.

Powder Room: This is where the deep sumptuous aubergine purples are really spectacular, the darker the better. A wonderful surprise when the door is opened by your guests and quite unexpected.

Dining Room: This is best place for grape tones. It's sophisticated and subtle and suggestive of delicious fruits. The cool grape tones are also excellent in a dining area that faces south, especially in hot climates.

Living Room: Grape or aubergine will work here as well. It's just a question of what suits your psyche best: the depth and elegance of the plum shades or the subtlety of grape. If you like to keep your living areas light, lavender might work, but don't use too much of it as the effect can get sugary sweet. It's best to combine your lavenders with darker shades of plum to give a more sophisticated feel.

Children's Rooms: Typically, young girls go for lavender, especially if it's skewed to pink. This is Barbie doll lavender, so the boys won't go for it at all!

The Den: This is another good spot for aubergine, but any purple skewed to wine would be excellent. These shades are in the warmer purple category and create a cozy, comfortable feeling.

Bathrooms: Any color mindful of flowers, such as lilac or lavender, can impart a pleasantly scented ambiance. As lavender has many of the same calming qualities of blue, it is an excellent color to use in an area where a quiet restful "spa" can be created.

Purple and Personality

If You Like Purple: This hue has an aura of mystery and intrigue. The purple person is enigmatic and highly creative, with a quick perception of spiritual ideas. Purple is often preferred by artists. People who like to consider themselves different from the common herd or unconventional often prefer purple.

Continues on page 104

COMBO 103-A

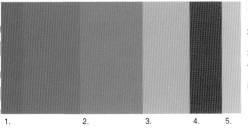

1. Dusky Green-Blue
2. Bleached Denim
3. Roebuck
4. Aurora Red
5. Eucalyptus

1.   2.   3.   4.   5.

COMBO 103-B

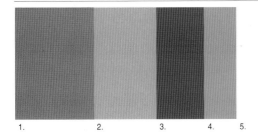

1. Rose Canyon
2. Buckskin
3. Cowhide
4. Otter
5. Dusky Green

1.   2.   3.   4.   5.

COMBO 103-C

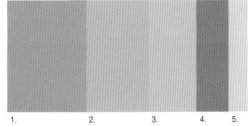

1. Burro
2. Faded Denim
3. Sage Green
4. Raw Sienna
5. Winter Wheat

1.   2.   3.   4.   5.

COMBO 103-D

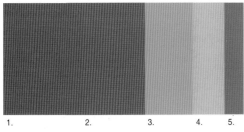

1. Mineral Red
2. Magenta Haze
3. Khaki
4. Golden Nugget
5. Purple Sage

1.   2.   3.   4.   5.

COMBO 103-E

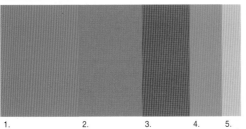

1. Sage Brush Green
2. Beaver Fur
3. Cactus Flower
4. Dusk
5. Tan

1.   2.   3.   4.   5.

Rustic Remembrances

Weathered wooden surfaces, exposed timbers, Navajo rugs, honeyed chamois and tanned buckskin, an old faded blue tin canteen—all of these elements are earthy, well-worn, and comfortably lived-in. These are the closely related earthtones, khaki greens, and denim blues that sometimes surprise us with the sudden infusion of complementary desert and wildflower pinks.

COMBO 103-F

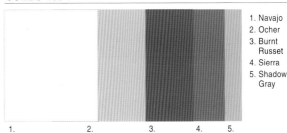

1. Navajo
2. Ocher
3. Burnt Russet
4. Sierra
5. Shadow Gray

1.   2.   3.   4.   5.

PHOTO: DON PAULSON

They are generous and, at times, charming. Purple is also associated with wit, keen observation, supersensitivity, vanity, and moodiness. Because purple is a combination of red and blue, which are opposites in many ways, you often have conflicting traits. You are constantly trying to balance those opposites—the excitement of red with the tranquillity of blue.

It has been said that purple people are easy to live with but hard to know. You can be secretive, so that even when you seem to confide freely, your closest friends might never know your innermost feelings.

If You Dislike Purple: When people are anti-purple, they need sincerity, honesty, and a lack of pretense in their lives. You do not like to get involved in any activity unless you know exactly what you are getting yourself into. You usually exercise good judgment, and frankness is a quality you look for in friends and colleagues. They may not have any particular artistic talents, but you make good a critic!

Purple may seem a bit "puffed-up" to you because of its association to royalty, or perhaps you come from a culture where its association to mourning is deeply ingrained. In certain areas, it was equated with immorality. So it could be that you are still hearing that little inner voice saying that "nice" people don't use purple!

Loving Lavender

If You Like Lavender: People who like this tint use it sometimes to the exclusion of all other colors. Just as with purple, they like to be considered "different." They are quick-witted, though not usually intellectual.

The lavender person seeks refinement in life. Yours is a fantasy land where ugliness and the baser aspects of life are ignored. Outward appearances are very important. Gentility and sentimental leanings go along with this color, as do romance, nostalgia, and delicacy. Since lavender is first cousin to purple, lavender lovers may aspire to creativity, but if not capable of it, you tend to encourage those who do have talent.

If you dislike lavender, it shows a no-nonsense approach to life. These people don't like others to be coy with them; they appreciate directness. Nostalgia is not your thing, you live in the present. You don't like superficiality in manners or appearance and usually let people know about it (or wish you had)!

COLORS
FOR
YOUR
EVERY
MOOD

104

CHAPTER 10

Brown
Earthy and Real

Brown is the color of hearth and home—of dried herbs and stone-ground bread and freshly baked cookies. It represents all of the nurturing, life-sustaining, down-to-earth qualities of terra firma, the very shade of earth itself. Just as in the sturdy oak, brown represents roots, a steady, stable source of security, comfort, and normalcy.

It is the fertile soil that sustains growth and nourishment; the color of plowed earth, buckskin and rawhide, weathered redwood, bison and mustang, frontier land—rugged and outdoorsy. It is pine cone and bracken, chipmunk and acorn, beaver and doe, and all other manner of woodland inhabitants. Even in its more sumptuous state of fine suede and supple kid leather, brown is considered a classic shade of solid substance.

Brown as Coloring

Brown has always been easily obtainable with little or no cost as a dye from natural sources. Cloth dyed brown shows no dirt—a very important consideration in predetergent days. When the Puritans and other religious sects banned brightly colored garments (said to produce lust and pride), brown was looked upon with great favor as humble, hard-working, and unpretentious. Sackcloth was worn by the poor or pious. So it came to be associated with economy, simplicity, and modest ambitions.

Like the soil that sustains growth and nourishment, brown broadcasts earthiness and fertility. Auburn brown tinged with orange is exuberant as autumn leaves, but dark brown turning to black becomes more wistful, as in autumn turning to winter.

Brown came from the soil, tree bark of hemlock, maple, and alders, the husks of walnuts and kola nuts, the stalks of hops, water lily, and other plant roots. The inkbag of the cuttlefish provided sepia. It was eventually discovered that cooking brown dye in an iron pot produced black dye.

Sheltering Brown

From the beginning of time, nature has been abundant with a wide variety of brown materials to build human habitats: from the hardened mud color of the dark earth itself to sandstone, clay, and adobe. Word association studies show that some people respond to brown as "dirty" or "dirt." But dirt isn't always grime and grunge. It is also the color of the soil, and as any passionate gardener knows, where would we be without lots of that rich, nurturing, fragrant (yes, fragrant) stuff?

Although brown in wood tones is not often thought of as a color, it is still a psychological presence carving an impression on the human mind. Even those people who express a dislike for brown as a color will often surround themselves with brown wood furnishings and floors and feel quite comfortable and content. Because it is ever-present in the earth, the color of tree bark, twigs, and every other source of wood that has always provided human shelter, in reality, brown is very easy to live with; and because of its earthy and grounded associations it is viewed as protective.

BROWN

Continues on page 108

COMBO 107-A

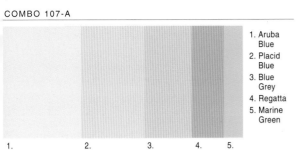

1. Aruba Blue
2. Placid Blue
3. Blue Grey
4. Regatta
5. Marine Green

1.   2.   3.   4.   5.

Beach Scenes

Sand dunes, beach grass, the whitecaps of waves, the sea, and the sky, iridescent pastel shells, coral reefs, and secluded blue-green lagoons—whatever your dreams are made of, sandy warm or watery cool, these contrasting elements make for beautiful inspiration.

COMBO 107-B

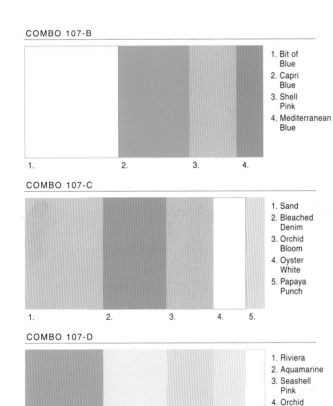

1. Bit of Blue
2. Capri Blue
3. Shell Pink
4. Mediterranean Blue

1.   2.   3.   4.

COMBO 107-C

1. Sand
2. Bleached Denim
3. Orchid Bloom
4. Oyster White
5. Papaya Punch

1.   2.   3.   4.   5.

COMBO 107-D

1. Riviera
2. Aquamarine
3. Seashell Pink
4. Orchid Pink
5. Whitecap Gray

1.   2.   3.   4.   5.

COMBO 107-E

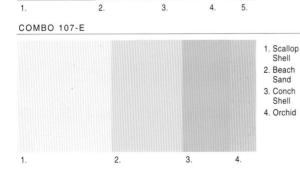

1. Scallop Shell
2. Beach Sand
3. Conch Shell
4. Orchid

1.   2.   3.   4.

COMBO 107-F

1. Billowing Sail
2. Evening Sand
3. Sea Pink
4. Zephyr
5. Marine Blue

1.   2.   3.   4.   5.

PHOTO: DON PAULSON

Delicious Brown

There are many delicious variations of the hue, from PECAN BROWN and BROWN SUGAR to the deepened delectable shades of BITTER CHOCOLATE, COCOA BROWN, COFFEE and COGNAC. In the 1990s brown became very chic and stylish because of the trendy "coffee craze" with tones ranging from CAFE CREME to CAPPUCCINO. It is a curious and delicious dichotomy that brown as a food color can be the most calorie-laden, sugary sweet, and seductive or the most organic and nutritious; from chocolate mousse, double-double chocolate ice cream, luscious caramel, and brownies to whole-grain bread, bran muffins, brown rice, toasted almonds, and sesame seeds. Whether wholesome or enticingly decadent, brown is always a staple presence and persistent persuader on the kitchen shelf.

Word associations show that many people react to the word "brown" with the instant response of "chocolate." It's a given that decadent goodies are usually a delicious chocolate brown. What would a double scoop of fudge ripple be without the fudge? Would a greenie be as enticing as a brownie? Would chartreuse mousse be as appealing as chocolate mousse? Possibly. But only if you had your eyes closed.

Brown and Culture

The artful interiors of stately homes often favor the patina of elegant antiques and polished wood floors or paneling in dark brown tones such as satin smooth mahogany or cherry woods. Sir George Howland Beaumont, the 19th-century British art connoisseur, always said that a good picture, like a good fiddle, should be brown. Brown does have its more luxurious side—but always subtle and understated, never noisy or vulgar.

Every artist knows the pigment called burnt sienna, which results when raw sienna is put through a burning process and mixed with oils. This typical color of Renaissance painting is used today, as are burnished umbers, to "gray" a wall color to which it has been added.

Rarely is brown thought of as a shade favored in Japan, but in the Hiean era (794 to 1192) a precise prescription for the color of clothing according to social rank or office was decreed. The emperor wore yellowish-brown outer silk garments in winter and brown over strong purple-red in summer. The crown prince was much more colorful. His inner garments were the same as the emperor, but his outer garment was a bright orange.

The Japanese do not have a word for generic brown; they prefer instead to be much more color specific in their descriptions of the shades with words such as "tea color" or "fox color." The colors worn while hunting were also decreed. Among the acceptable shades were "fallen leaves" (a gray brown) or "green maple leaf," which wasn't green at all, but in fact a brilliant blue worn with grayish-brown.

Brown is treated with a healthy respect in European countries where it is considered the most realistic of all colors, utilitarian but not vulgar, embodying a hearty life and the work ethic. As it is so rooted and steady, historically there has always been a resurgence of brown when economies have been depressed and people need the reassurance of down-to-earth brown in their surroundings.

In Scottish folklore, a merry (and energetic) elf called a brownie came out secretly at night after everyone was asleep to do the household chores. In Nazi Germany, the shade took on a more ominous meaning because the brutish storm troopers were called Brown Shirts.

COLORS
FOR
YOUR
EVERY
MOOD

108

Carefully Neutral

First cousin to brown is the lighter beige family, generally warm neutrals that include the light to medium browns of BUFF, BEIGE, NUDE, BISQUE, ECRU, and CARAMEL CREAM. Often referred to as naturals, these are the subtle, comfortable, and unpretentious classics that withstand the ebb and flow of color trends. The very word "neutral" evokes "natural," and many more neutrals are named accordingly: GOLDEN STRAW, DESERT DUST, LAMB'S WOOL, and CORNHUSK.

But beiges are not as nondescript as gray. Because beige is inherently warm and the lightest of earth tones, it brings to mind the glowing warmth of wheat fields and sandy beaches, of wicker on a sun porch, and country pine in the kitchen.

Neutral colors in interior design gained a foothold in the 1920s when the Bauhaus School of Architecture and Art with its very simple and basic approach to interiors brought a flood of neutral beiges and cream into the marketplace. Prior to this period, Elsie DeWolfe, a socialite and former actress, became the first American "interior decorator." She had lived through Victorian times and detested what she called "the uncomfortable chairs and sofas on which one could do nothing but sit upright, and its red, green, or saffron upholstery—all invariably arranged against a background of wallpaper on which colors that should never be allowed out together made faces at one another."

Her work took on a decidedly "modern look" in the 1920s as she embraced comfortable informality done in neutral colors. She so loved beige that it is reported when she visited the Parthenon for the first time she cried: "It's my color—it's beige," as if she had invented the color before the ancient Greeks!

Coco Chanel designed her very modern new fashions using a great deal of head-to-toe beige (reportedly because she got a great deal on army surplus). Her sleek understated salon was also done in beige and provided inspiration to the rich and famous.

Beige remained a favorite through the 1930s, and there has rarely been a decade when it has not surfaced since that time.

Taupe

Taupe also has an inherent warmth because it is brownish gray or grayish brown. The chameleon shade among the neutrals, it often contains a bit of rose, or a dollop of mauve, a hint of green.

In the 1930s, variations of taupe were very popular. So popular in fact that the monotony of taupe interiors, exteriors and clothing caused Matthew Luckiesh in his book *Color and Colors* (D. Van Nostrand Co., 1938) to state: "For the most part ignorance of color, due to lack of conscious experience is largely responsible for the Taupe Age, particularly in homes . . . the householder who wishes to escape the Taupe Age may begin by observation and gradual adoption [of color]." Other critics disparaged decorators who worked extensively with neutrals, calling them "the bland leading the bland."

In spite of their admonitions, taupe and beige have remained a practical and popular choice for home and office decor, especially in carpeting. The many variations of undertone make them favorite neutrals to combine with many other colors; to quiet noisy prints or to serve as subtle background. They are associated with the sands of time and antiquity; of ancient monuments, buildings, temples, pillars, and pyramids that seem to last forever. These are the eternal "upscale" patrician shades, understated and never ostentatious. These shadings give a timeless dependable appearance of quality in any product line—from cars and carpets to kitchen cabinets.

Continues on page 112

COMBO 111-A

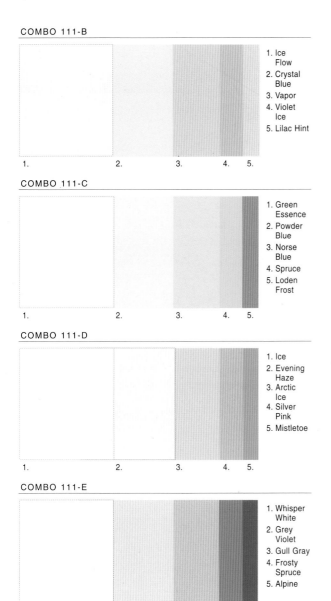

1. Snow White
2. Air Blue
3. Swedish Blue
4. Frosty Spruce
5. Winter Pear

1.   2.   3.   4. 5.

COMBO 111-B

1. Ice Flow
2. Crystal Blue
3. Vapor
4. Violet Ice
5. Lilac Hint

1.   2.   3.   4. 5.

COMBO 111-C

1. Green Essence
2. Powder Blue
3. Norse Blue
4. Spruce
5. Loden Frost

1.   2.   3.   4. 5.

COMBO 111-D

1. Ice
2. Evening Haze
3. Arctic Ice
4. Silver Pink
5. Mistletoe

1.   2.   3.   4. 5.

COMBO 111-E

1. Whisper White
2. Grey Violet
3. Gull Gray
4. Frosty Spruce
5. Alpine

1.   2.   3.   4. 5.

Winter Frost

Although white is often an essential color element in this clean environment that evokes the absolute silence of snow falling on cedars, it is not always the purest white—there may be faint undertones of cool blue or icy green. The colors are closely related cool tones; but for a bit of balancing warmth, look to the glimmering rose, violet or yellow-green tinges of winter foliage that sparkle under a sprinkling of frost.

COMBO 111-F

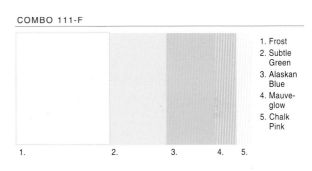

1. Frost
2. Subtle Green
3. Alaskan Blue
4. Mauve-glow
5. Chalk Pink

1.   2.   3.   4. 5.

PHOTO: DON PAULSON

Beiges and taupes, as well as gray, are considered the most classic of colors. Regardless of fads, they linger on. Rarely named as the most favorite colors, they fit well into most people's "comfort zones" because, though not exciting, they seem safe and noncommittal. And this is precisely why so many people are drawn to using neutrals in the "big ticket" purchases like upholstered pieces and carpeting.

The downside of using too much beige and other neutrals is that they can lead to boredom and a lack of visual stimulation. But they can be the perfect background for lively touches in accessories or patterns.

Rooted in Language

Interestingly, even though the brown of earth is present in every society, it was not one of the first colors to be named in the evolution of color words. Black, white, red, yellow, green, and blue were all named before brown. Many languages share the root word frequently related to the word for burn—Aryan *bhru*, Italian *bruno*, French *brunir*, Danish *bruun*, Swedish *brun*, Dutch *bruin*, German *brawn*, and Old English *brun*.

There are many English words that imply brown, such as burnish, bronze, brunette, but some other languages lack any generic term for brown. In modern Greek, all brown hair is chestnut, a suntan is black, and most other browns are called coffee. In old High German, "brown" meant gleaming or dark.

It is not surprising that there are many Arabic words for various shades of sand or that Eskimos have no word for brown in their vocabulary, but instead, a multitude of words for different shades of white!

Brown's Messages

Brown is a color that must be thought of in terms of its context. An ice cream sundae dripping with a delicious hot fudge sauce is decidedly more appealing than a brown worm wriggling out of a half-eaten apple! Although brown does not evoke an emotion as strong as yellow-green, for example, the psychological connotations for brown range from delectable to dull.

As Dr. Benjamin J. Kouwer says in his book, *Color Their Characters* (Martinus Nyhoff, 1949):

> It possesses a sturdiness, a strong powerfulness which is not immediately evident. It is an inner force, a never-actualized energy. . . . It exists as a necessary support, as an unquestionable but not very conspicuous factor.

So the brown family ultimately does represent the most honest, stable, and secure qualities. There is, after all, safety in umbers.

Decorating in Browns and Neutrals

As brown tints and tones are ever-present in wood tones, they can be used in any room. But some shades will work better than others.

Living Room: From dark, traditional mahogany to the lightest casual country pine, wood floors, cabinetry, and furnishings instantly impart warmth to this room which is primarily a gathering place for friends and family.

Studies, Dens, Libraries: These are the areas where darkened brown tones in wall paneling, cabinetry, and flooring seem most at home. They are cozy, often cloistered areas conducive to curling up with a good book. If too much dark brown seems oppressive to you, these are the rooms where accents, patterns, and paints in sumptuous jewel tones like AMETHYST, GARNET, or EMERALD will show off beautifully against a brown background.

COLORS
FOR
YOUR
EVERY
MOOD

112

Kitchens and Dining Rooms: Often described as delicious, the very best neutral to use in these food areas is cream, as many people respond to it as warm and delectable. This classic appetite-appealing hue with a hint of custard color is the closest a neutral can get to being an actual color and still provide a background suitable for accessories ranging from fine china to fun collectibles.

Hallways and Entries: Cream really is a good choice for these are often cramped and smallish spaces. It provides a welcoming warmth with just a suggestion of sunshine.

Powder Rooms: Interestingly, taupe can be the most dramatic of the neutrals, depending upon its undertones. A touch of wine against taupe, a glimmer of gold (especially in faux layering techniques) can provide an unexpected surprise to your guests, the primary users of this room.

Brown and Personality

If You Like Brown: The color of Mother Earth, brown is the hue that is associated with substance and stability. A preference for brown means that you have a steady, reliable character with a keen sense of duty and responsibility. You are the down-to-earth person with a subtle, earthy sense of humor. Browns love simplicity, comfort, quality, harmony, hearth, and home.

You are a loyal friend, receptive, understanding, but firm, have strong views and may be intolerant of others who think, talk, or act too quickly. You strive to be good money managers (we won't say cheap) and drive a good bargain.

You are the person who might find it difficult to be carefree and spontaneous, but will often rebel internally against accepting things the way they are. You feel very uncomfortable about losing control, but will work hard to change a situation that seems unjust or unfair. With a strong need for security and a sense of belonging, family life is very important to you.

If You Dislike Brown: You have probably either fantasized about a lot of exciting things like bungee jumping or racing cars, or have already participated in some risk-taking sports activity. Novelty excites you, and routine drives you crazy. You are witty, impetuous, and generous. Living on a farm is not for you. Homespun people bore you. You do like people, but they must be bright and engaging. A meaningful relationship with you could be risky business—it's hard to get you to sit still.

If You Like Beige: You have many of the same qualities as people who prefer brown, though probably less intense. Creamy beiges and honeyed tones take on a lot of yellow qualities, while rosy beiges take on pink characteristics. You are warm, appreciate quality, and are carefully neutral in most situations. You are usually well-adjusted and practical.

If You Dislike Beige: You are less frenetic and impetuous than a disliker of brown, but possess many of the same characteristics. Beige represents to you a beige existence—boring and tiresome. You hate routine.

If You Like Taupe: This color also speaks of neutrality, but combines the character and dependability of gray with the warmth of beige. You like classic looks and are careful about allowing too much excitement into your life. You are practical, fair, well balanced and would make a good arbitrator.

If You Dislike Taupe: If taupe doesn't appeal to you, it may be because it is so balanced and classic. You'd rather make a more definite statement, whether with color or otherwise. You are probably not known for your subtlety.

PHOTO: DON PAULSON

COLORS FOR YOUR EVERY MOOD

COMBO 115-A

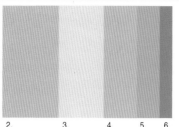

1. Vapor
2. Ash
3. Almost Aqua
4. Burnished Lilac
5. Granite Green
6. Quail

1.   2.   3.   4.   5.   6.

Dawn and Dew

Think of the early morning hours before dawn as the curtain of night is lifting— the cool, shaded grays, the shrouded blues, hazy greens, misted mauves, and veiled violets. There is very little contrast here, just one deepened shade dissolving into the shadowed midtones of the beginnings of another day.

COMBO 115-B

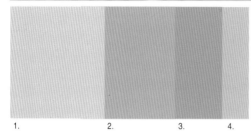

1. Moonbeam
2. Shadow Gray
3. Slate Gray
4. Dawn Pink

1.   2.   3.   4.

COMBO 115-F

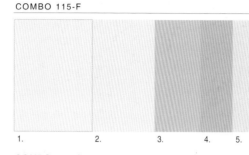

1. White Swan
2. Almost Mauve
3. Smoke Gray
4. Burnished Lilac
5. Dawn Blue

1.   2.   3.   4.   5.

COMBO 115-C

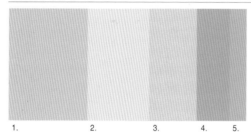

1. Gray Morn
2. Pinkish Gray
3. Hushed Violet
4. Abyss
5. Eucalyptus

1.   2.   3.   4.   5.

COMBO 115-G

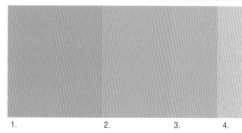

1. Silver Blue
2. Malachite Green
3. Tourmaline
4. Maple Sugar

1.   2.   3.   4.

COMBO 115-D

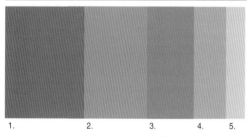

1. Rose Gray
2. Smoke Blue
3. Cinder
4. Atmosphere
5. Silver Fern

1.   2.   3.   4.   5.

COMBO 115-H

1. Gray Violet
2. Gray Dawn
3. Lavender Gray
4. Ether
5. Pink Tint

1.   2.   3.   4.   5.

COMBO 115-E

1. Misty Lilac
2. Green Haze
3. Arona
4. Sparrow
5. Silver Pine

1.   2.   3.   4.   5.

COMBO 115-I

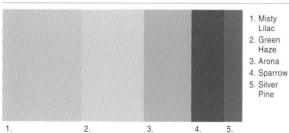

1. Rose Smoke
2. Deauville Mauve
3. Antler
4. Rose Taupe
5. Duck Green

1.   2.   3.   4.   5.

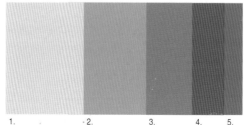

CHAPTER 11

Black
Sleek and Sophisticated

To some, it is sinister and eerie; to others, the height of sophistication. In fact, no other color evokes such a variety of feelings. At various times it is described as foreboding and funereal; magical or mysterious; suave, sexy, or sober; powerful or pretentious; practical yet glamorous. But always it is a presence not to be ignored.

From the beginning of time and the earliest associative response to color, black has raised ambivalent feelings. To primitive peoples the black of night represented a needed respite from the struggle for existence and their vulnerability in the full light of day. Under cover of darkness they could rest and regain their strength and power.

But the color of darkness could also mask the possibility of danger. Fear of the dark is a spontaneous reaction. It is unknown, an association with death. It is the black hole, the bottomless pit, the unexplainable, the mysterious. Ultimately, because of this dichotomy of emotions, black symbolically combines mystery with powerful forces and mysterious good or evil purposes. There is also power in abstinence and strict self-control. Throughout the ages the wearing of black demonstrated a denial of the sensual life—monks, mourners and misers, priests, penitents and Puritans, widows' weeds. As Alison Lurie points out in her book *The Language of Clothes* (Random House, 1981): "Just as white suggests innocence, black suggests sophistication—which, after all, often consists in the knowledge or experience of the darker side of life: of evil, unhappiness and death." Today, however, the most accepted meaning of black as sophistication is far less gloomy.

Black has come to denote great chic as well as the ultimate in elegance and drama—on the body as well as in the home. It also signifies solid, basic strength—a deep abiding powerful presence.

Artsy Black

Authors and artists have always recognized the dramatic impact of black. In Anton Chekhov's *The Seagull,* Masha's friend asks her why she always wears black. "I am in mourning for my life," she declares. Shakespeare put the long suffering Hamlet in a "customary suit of solemn black."

The Mafioso thugs always wore black suits and shirts in the classic gangster movies and to add to the mood, the films were always shot in black and white. George Raft was typical of this look, complete with black hair slicked back and a white tie to further accent the black pin-striped suit. A black comedy is a play or film with a sardonic and perverse sense of humor especially on such deadly serious subjects as death, war, or illness. "Film noire" describes a dark, brutal and violent world of corruption inhabited by sordid and neurotic figures. Classic film noire are the *Maltese Falcon* with Humphrey Bogart and *Double Indemnity* with Fred MacMurray and Barbara Stanwyck. More contemporary examples of film noire are *Chinatown* with Jack Nicholson and Faye Dunaway or *L.A. Confidential* with Kim Basinger. The sets are full of heavy shadows and sharp contrasts of light and dark.

COLORS
FOR
YOUR
EVERY
MOOD

116

Edgar Allen Poe used the symbolism of malevolent black brilliantly. Is there any mystery more sinister than his classic *The Raven?* Or think of the villain tying a pretty young thing to a railroad trestle, the spine-tingling effect of Dracula rising from the coffin, or the heavy breathing of the menacing Darth Vader. What are they all wearing? The heart-stopping black cloak, dramatic evidence of lurking evil.

Mourning Black

In the United States and Britain the custom of wearing black almost exclusively started at the turn of the century. Black became the basic mourning shade in Victorian times. Geoffrey Gorer writes of his memories of the death of King Edward VII of England in 1910 when everywhere he looked he saw people in black, from head to toe.

He goes on to tell about nagging his mother to "get out of those horrid clothes." She finally agreed to wear "half-mourning" (gray or purple) in the house, but convention decreed that she simply had to wear black when she was out in polite society.

In many countries around the world, the custom of wearing black for mourning has existed for centuries. As far back as 14th-century France, black was not only worn on the body, but it was also draped liberally over the walls and beds of the homes during mourning.

Mourning was more strictly enforced for women than for men. A 15th-century queen of France had to remain in her black-draped bedroom draped for an entire year. Princesses were expected to stay in the mourning room for six weeks, but the wives of knights got off with only nine days!

In New Guinea widows literally wallowed in their grief by throwing themselves into a bed of black mud; while in other countries, such as Greece, widows lose not only their husbands but tradition decrees that they abandon color as well. A very old custom in Jewish orthodoxy is the wearing of a black ribbon during the mourning period, and all the mirrors in the home are covered with black. In other religions, the black arm band signifies mourning.

For the ancient Egyptians, black symbolized two extremes of life and death. Because of the life-sustaining fertile black humus earth of the Nile delta, the hue stood for fertility. And, as they believed so fervently in life after death, black also symbolized renewal. Two black-skinned life-sized statues of Tutankhamen guarded the doorway to his burial chamber. Black is also the color of Anpu, the jackal-headed god of the dead who presided over the art of embalming.

Formal Black

The use of black for formal occasions goes back to the Spanish court of the late 16th-century and soon spread to most other European countries. Until recent times, black was the color worn by Spanish brides. In Italy, Baldassare Castiglione wrote a book of etiquette in 1528. He advised, "Black is more suitable than any other color . . . I would have our courtier's dress display that sobriety which the Spanish nation greatly affect—for things external often bear witness to the things within." (Baldassare was not a fun kind of guy!)

The black tuxedo was born in the United States in 1886 when the youthful tobacco heir Griswold Lorillard shocked his society neighbors in Tuxedo Park, New York, by cutting off his dress coat and wearing this brazen nonconforming outfit to

Continues on page 120

COMBO 119-A

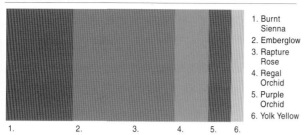

1. Burnt Sienna
2. Emberglow
3. Rapture Rose
4. Regal Orchid
5. Purple Orchid
6. Yolk Yellow

Sunset and Fire

These are the shades that radiate resplendently across the evening sky. There is no mistake about the temperature here: this is the palette that speaks of heat and intensity. Emulating sunset, the colors are dramatically darkened or brilliantly heightened warm shades, often splashed with a contrasting blue to keep the fire from burning too brightly.

COMBO 119-B

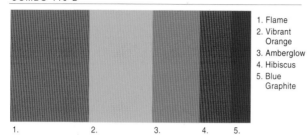

1. Flame
2. Vibrant Orange
3. Amberglow
4. Hibiscus
5. Blue Graphite

COMBO 119-F

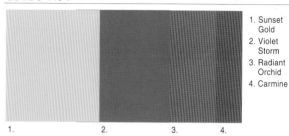

1. Sunset Gold
2. Violet Storm
3. Radiant Orchid
4. Carmine

COMBO 119-C

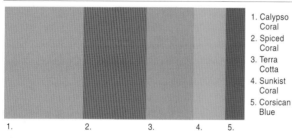

1. Calypso Coral
2. Spiced Coral
3. Terra Cotta
4. Sunkist Coral
5. Corsican Blue

COMBO 119-G

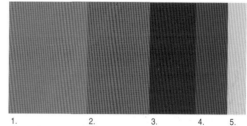

1. Hot Pink
2. Pink Flambe
3. Lipstick Red
4. Sunset Purple
5. Orchid Bloom

COMBO 119-D

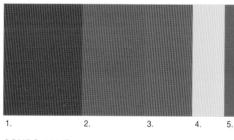

1. Rococo Red
2. Paradise Pink
3. Rose Violet
4. Vibrant Yellow
5. Amparo Blue

COMBO 119-E

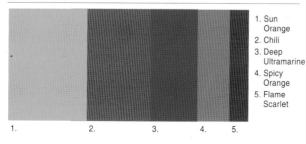

1. Sun Orange
2. Chili
3. Deep Ultramarine
4. Spicy Orange
5. Flame Scarlet

the very social Autumn Ball. This started a trend among the elite, and by the 1920s the first ready-to-wear tux was born.

Elegant occasions often calls for "black tie" for men, and, although it's not required for formal wear, many women opt to wear black because of its elegance and sophistication (and ability to make them look slimmer!). In interiors, polished black surfaces speak of formality: sleek black marble and granite, black lacquer furniture, handsome grand pianos, ebony accents.

Culture and Black

For the Romans black was a symbol of immortality. The Japanese see black as the color of solemnity and mystery, expressing the depth of the unknown. Their view is that black stimulates the imagination because it springs from the darkness of night—a world very different from the light of daytime realities. From Africa came some of the best sources of black dye: fermented mud, various leaves, soot, oil smoke, charcoal, seeds, roasted animal teeth, burnt ivory, and bones. One of the main dyestuffs of the ancient world was made from the crushed and fermented leaves of woad, a plant of the mustard family. The fresh solution yielded a black dye that when diluted became blue or green. And just as some manufacturing processes do today, the processing of woad caused contamination of water, noxious fumes fouled the air, farming land was ravished; all of this necessitating the passage of laws separating commercial sites from residential! Many Hindus and Buddhists regard black as "Tamas"—people who have become demons or have low moral or intellectual capacity.

In various African societies, black was imbued with both positive and negative qualities. As in many other cultures, it is associated with death, illness, uncertainty, corruption, and antisocial behavior such as witchcraft. But it is also the normal skin color as well as fertile African earth, so it represents completeness and plenty.

For the female leaders of an African women's association, it is the color of their ceremonial masks representing the guardian spirit and expresses their ideal feminine beauty of gleaming black skin, triangular faces, elaborate hairstyles, and excessive weight!

For the Bangwa people of Cameroon their night society masks of dull black are terrifying symbols of the all-knowing, supernatural powers of a chief and his servants who are members of a secret regulatory society. The frightening dark masks look like human faces with grossly rearranged features.

In still other African societies, black masks were symbols of transformation. Chiefs and their servants are thought to be capable of changing into leopards, elephants, and other nonhuman forms. Blackened face masks in Nigeria are believed to be the dangerous spirits of persons who died in a strange way and wandered aimlessly through the night.

The black cat is an ambivalent symbol universally. Legend claims them to be sacred (to the Egyptians) or sinister; a friend to witches and Satan. In Europe, a black cat crossing your path means that money will come your way, but in the United States it is considered a bad omen. With his back arched ominously, he invariably accompanies the Halloween witch on her yearly sojourn across the sky.

Black has been used extensively as a cure. Faber Birren, in his book *Color, A Survey in Words and Pictures* (University Books, 1963), tells us:

Among ancient Greeks, it was thought that a raven's eggs would restore blackness to the hair. So effective was the remedy believed to be that the

COLORS
FOR
YOUR
EVERY
MOOD

120

Greek kept oil in his mouth while the egg was rubbed into his hair in order to keep his teeth from turning black. Black threads from the wool of black sheep cured earache in Ireland, England and parts of Vermont. Black snails were rubbed on warts. In France the skins of black animals, applied warm to the limbs of the body, relieved rheumatism . . . the blood of a black cat has been prescribed for pneumonia in places as remote from each other as England and South Africa.

The Language of Black

Black is seen as the opposite of white. *Webster's Dictionary* contains many definitions for black among them: "the darkest possible color or hue, like soot or coal; absorbing all light, or incapable of reflecting it . . . the opposite of white . . . "

The old English word for black, swart, is related to the Latin *sordes* (dirty or sordid), the old Norse word *svatr*, the old German *swarz*, the contemporary German *schwarz*, the Danish *sort*, the Swedish *svart*, the Dutch *zwart*. The modern English word, however, comes from the same family as the old Norse word for dark or black, *blakkr*, and to the Danish *blaek* and Swedish black meaning ink, as well as the old German *blah*—the probable origin of describing something which is nondescript or colorless.

In the romance languages, the hue is related to skin color: *negro* in Spanish; in Italian *nero* and French *noire*.

Black Power

Black has also been the symbol of countercultures. Black-leather-clad motorcycle gangs are invariably vroom-vrooming on big black bikes; Bohemians, artists, and poets of bygone days also wore black. Young people from beatniks to punk rockers, grungers, and street toughs have adopted black as a symbol of the negation of society's values and mores.

All colors ebb and flow according to the public whims and wishes. Up until the middle of the 20th century, products for more serious, practical use were usually black: telephones, cameras, cars, office equipment, whereas products used in the bathroom, laundry, or kitchen had to be white for cleanliness.

In the 1920s, Henry Ford advertised that consumers could have a Model T in any color "as long as it was black." White and beige were the colors of the 1930s, wartime khakis and tans abounded in the 1940s, while pink became the darling of the 1950s.

In the 1960s and part of the 1970s, polychrome and psychedelic burst onto the scene and black was practically banned, except for ritual or formal intent—clerics and hearses, limos and tuxes. Anyone with a black telephone was considered hopelessly outdated. After a hiatus of nearly 30 years, the late 1970s brought a reawakening to black.

As color often reflects social change or causes, the struggle for equality of black Americans, the Black Power movement, gained momentum during this period. The group's slogan "black is beautiful" also had its impact on the world of design and color.

In the 1980s, the enormously ominous appeal of Darth Vader in *Star Wars*, as well as other media heroes driving macho black sports cars across the screen in the inevitable chase scenes, contributed to the color pendulum swinging back to

Continues on page 124

COMBO 123-A

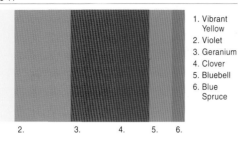

1. Vibrant Yellow
2. Violet
3. Geranium
4. Clover
5. Bluebell
6. Blue Spruce

1.   2.   3.   4.   5.   6.

Vivid Wildflowers

How can anyone resist the pure splendor of a meadow filled with wildflowers? They are Mother Nature's enticing invitation to fill our homes with their unbridled exuberance. The colors they inspire are bright, high contrasting hues that usually include some shade of green as a background—nature's ever-present neutral.

COMBO 123-B

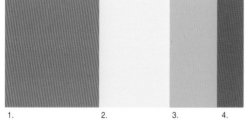

1. Raspberry Rose
2. Vanilla
3. Primrose Yellow
4. Blue Bonnet
5. Tender Shoots

1.   2.   3.   4.   5.

COMBO 123-F

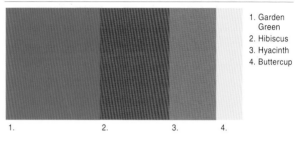

1. Garden Green
2. Hibiscus
3. Hyacinth
4. Buttercup

1.   2.   3.   4.

COMBO 123-C

1. Nasturtium
2. Saffron
3. Foliage
4. Reddish Blue

1.   2.   3.   4.

COMBO 123-G

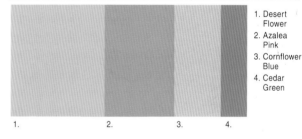

1. Desert Flower
2. Azalea Pink
3. Cornflower Blue
4. Cedar Green

1.   2.   3.   4.

COMBO 123-D

1. Lily White
2. Freesia
3. Amparo Blue
4. Phlox Pink
5. Mint Green

1.   2.   3.   4.   5.

COMBO 123-H

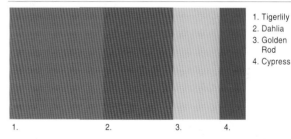

1. Tigerlily
2. Dahlia
3. Golden Rod
4. Cypress

1.   2.   3.   4.

COMBO 123-E

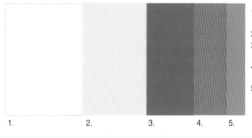

1. Georgia Peach
2. Rose Violet
3. Meadow Green
4. Dahlia Purple

1.   2.   3.   4.

COMBO 123-I

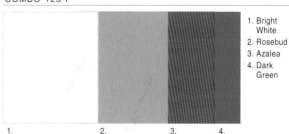

1. Bright White
2. Rosebud
3. Azalea
4. Dark Green

1.   2.   3.   4.

black—especially for the masses. Sears surprised customers by offering black refrigerators and dishwashers. Toilets and sinks became readily available in black. Eurostyle, the sleek and stylized European-inspired contemporary design became very popular, and all manner of high-tech gadgetry, household appliances, as well as the emergence of big-screen TV and microwave ovens, were featured in black.

For the upscale market, black has been a presence associated with prestige and worldly knowledge—a "discreet ostentation." Black-tie formality is "in" again. Both the sleek futuristic design of high-tech and the glossy lacquers of art deco or Asian artifacts are expressed importantly in black.

Whether the ultimate in chic, or in the expression of adolescent arrogance, black wields a powerful psychological force in the world of design and color.

Messages and Meanings

As a result of lifestyle changes and trends, feelings about black have changed considerably in recent years. Until the 1980s more people responded negatively to black with descriptions like "gloomy," "funerals," "death," "despair."

Attitudes have done an 180-degree turn, and many people (especially the younger generations) do not think of black as funereal; black is no longer required funeral wear. The positive responses to black outweigh the negative, with words like these: sophisticated, elegant, powerful.

Until recently, black was virtually verboten for kids—it was limited to tights and toe shoes, shiny Mary Janes, black velvet party dresses trimmed with proper lace, but now even the littlest tikes are sporting black jeans, sneakers, and baseball caps. It's doubtful that Mom, however, would do a black room for a three-year-old—there are still limitations, no matter how precocious the little ones are.

Black is highly preferred by people living in big cities like New York. They like to decorate with it as well as wear it. Aside from the practical elements of black "showing no soil" in a dirty metropolitan area, most people queried about black will say that black makes them feel less vulnerable, forming a protective shield and anonymity around them. Young people in particular say they feel "empowered" by black.

It also is very "in" to do whatever your peers are doing, and it takes a great deal of self-confidence to break away from that mold. However, psychologists say that people who use black to the exclusion of all other colors are depressed. Perhaps living in a big city is depressing—but it is true that too much black could lead to a major case of "color deprivation." We never outgrow that need for a box of shiny new crayons for coloring our world, so the best solution is to use black in appealing and satisfying combinations.

As to the argument that black is sexy—it depends on whether you are a man or a woman. Before you rush out to buy those expensive black satin sheets, you should know that women view black as sexy while most men do not.

Decorating in Black

Although attitudes about black have changed in general, most people would agree that too much in the home or office is literally "overkill"—too somber, too depressing, too dark. To live in too dark an environment would be like returning to the cave! Although dark colors can be used in some areas of the home where enclosure might be cozy and comforting (like HUNTER GREEN walls in the den), solid black is simply too oppressive and light-absorbing on major space like the walls.

COLORS
FOR
YOUR
EVERY
MOOD

124

It is less of a problem on the floors, except that solid black shows every microscopic piece of lint! Black can add an elegant presence to furnishings like leather sofas, lamps, chairs, table-top accessories, towels, or in printed patterns on upholstered pieces, bed linens, wall, window, and floor coverings. And black is very dramatic in marble, laminates, granite, tile, and slate, but it is generally limited to specific areas such as countertop or entries and/or contrasted with another color. Interestingly, most people prefer luminous or glossy black to dull (matte) finishes.

Black also makes an imposing trim color on the exterior. The black shutters on a white house and a front door in black lets you know that someone powerful lives within!

Black and White

The quintessential classic combination of black and white never goes out of style. It is the salt and pepper of decorating, the marriage of black's power and white's purity. They are, in fact, symbolic of the ancient Chinese dualistic philosophy of yang and yin: the balancing of opposite, yet necessary, forces such as night and day, masculine and feminine.

In the home, the starkness of the combination may start to take its psychological toll if another color is not introduced. Although we are not always overtly aware of it, we can be without color only so long and start to look for a color to alleviate the starkness.

Fortunately, black and white provide the perfect foil as a background for another color—even if it's just in limited amounts. In a black and white bath, we may want to add yellow towels; in a black and white kitchen, red dishes on the tabletop, and if you're a black and white purist, just a vase of colorful flowers.

Black and Personality

If Black Is Your Favorite Color: This is rarely chosen as a favorite color because it is actually the negation of color. The person who chooses black may have a number of conflicting attitudes. You may be conventional, conservative, and sophisticated, or you may like to think of yourself as rather wordly and serious, a cut above everyone else, or very dignified. You may also want to have an air of mystery or think of yourself as very sexy. Wit, cleverness, personal security, and prestige are very important to you.

If You Dislike Black: As black is the negation of color, it may be a complete negative to you. It is the eternal mystery, the bottomless pit, the black hole, the road to nowhere. It may represent death and mourning to you. Things that go bump in the night are black. Were you frightened by the dark in your childhood? That experience may still be buried in the recesses of your mind and may still haunt you when you look at anything black. Black may simply be too heavy for you to handle at this point in your life.

You are uncomfortable with the supersophisticated and feel insecure in their company. You like real people and are not dazzled by dignitaries.

COMBO 127-A

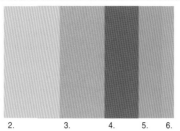

1. Bridal Blush
2. Peach Blossom
3. Lupine
4. Pansy
5. Jacaranda
6. Aspen Green

1.   2.   3.   4.   5.   6.

Summer's Gentle Petals

These are the hues that charm us with their intricate color details and nuances: a touch of peach that's not quite pink, a purple that glides from grape to petunia, a yellow with the slightest suggestion of orange. Subtly contrasting or closely related, the combinations are really more complex than they seem at first glance. Look to nature and imitate the combinations glimpsed in a garden: a purple pansy with a yellow center, a pink-tipped white rose.

COMBO 127-B

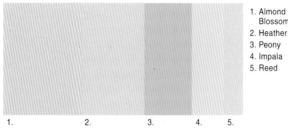

1. Almond Blossom
2. Heather
3. Peony
4. Impala
5. Reed

1.   2.   3.   4.   5.

COMBO 127-F

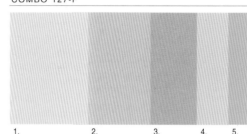

1. Rose Shadow
2. Orchid Bouquet
3. Rosebloom
4. Buff Orange
5. Leaf Green

1.   2.   3.   4.   5.

COMBO 127-C

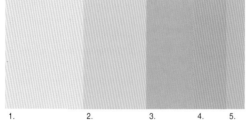

1. Golden Fleece
2. Peach Bud
3. Geranium Pink
4. Cornflower Blue
5. Sweet Pea

1.   2.   3.   4.   5.

COMBO 127-D

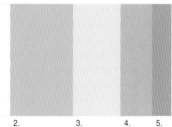

1. Bridal Blush
2. Morning Glory
3. Snapdragon
4. Sunkist Coral
5. English Ivy

1.   2.   3.   4.   5.

COMBO 127-E

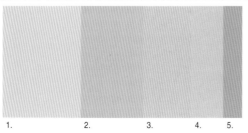

1. Impatiens
2. Candlelight Peach
3. Pastel Lavender
4. Forget-Me-Not
5. Basil

1.   2.   3.   4.   5.

PHOTO: DON PAULSON

CHAPTER 12

Gray
Quiet Gray

For many of us, gray inevitably reminds us of days when we were imprisoned indoors—standing with our noses pressed against wet window panes, looking out at leaden skies waiting for the gray day to disappear. We could hardly wait to hear the magic words: "You can go outside to play now!"

It's no wonder that gray suffers from a bad reputation. Those early gray childhood memories survive in our psyches to influence our attitudes forever. As a result, very few people choose gray as a favorite shade.

In the truest sense of the word, neutral gray is not actually a color, but is termed "achromatic"—devoid of hue. The direct descendent of black, gray slides down the value scale from deepest charcoal to the lightest pearly tints.

Many monastic orders wear gray as a symbol for quietude and introspection. The Emperor Charlemagne decreed gray as the color for the common people in keeping with his personal penchant for quiet clothing. *Grisaille* (from the French *gris* for gray), a method of decorative painting, has been used extensively in paintings, symbolizing tribulation and ecclesiastic themes. It is a long-suffering, no-nonsense, serious color.

In the book *Letters on Cezanne* (Fromm International Publishing, 1985), written by poet Rainer Maria Rilke, he spoke of Paul Cezanne's grays as a "particularly metallic white, aluminum or something similar. To Cezanne's immensely painterly eye, gray did not hold up as a color . . . he went to the core and found it was violet, or blue or reddish green."

He speaks of the grays in Cezanne's paintings as soft and mild, a "kind of atmosphere." He states: "The inner equilibrium of Cezanne's colors, which are never insistent or obtrusive produces this calm, almost velvety air."

Just as gold is related to yellow, silver is related to gray. In ancient Mesopotamia, the Chaldean society that was made up of Semitic peoples saw silver as a sign of calmness and serenity. They believed that the silvery moon sent wisdom and peace of mind. Silver projects that same reassuring message in packaging and advertising, along with the implied message of greater quality. Silver conveys a cool kind of elegance, catching the eye with its glossy sheen, glimmering, but not gaudy.

Eerie Gray

The darkest tones of gray share the same ambiguous feelings as black: powerful or sorrowful, sophisticated or sober, dominating or drab. Charcoal gray is less ominous than black. Demons like Dracula appear in black, but less frightening supernatural spirits appearing on stage or in film (in their civilian clothes) are often portrayed in the wispy grays of overcast days.

Gray can also be shrouded in a certain eerie quality reminiscent of twilight and moonbeams—day turning to the mystery of night, foggy, smoky, ashen, the cobwebs and ghostly shapes in the gray dust of a haunted house, a morning

COLORS
FOR
YOUR
EVERY
MOOD

128

mist. In England, gray as well as purple were considered the colors of half-mourning, the shades of clothing worn after the initial period of black bereavement.

If your dreams seem vaguely gray in color or you seem to be wandering around in a "gray fog," experts tell us that your outlook on life is very confining or confusing. It seems that when you start to dream in color, your mood starts to lighten up.

Solid Gray

Grays represent solid strength and longevity, an association stemming from the color of granite and gravel, stone, slate and rock; of ancient monuments, pillars, and temples that have withstood the ravages of time and technology. Tough modern cities are thought of as gray—cement and concrete, silvery-steel, metallic aluminum. Because of the consumer perception of gray, designers and architects use the neutrality of gray to depict products and buildings as sleek or high-tech; long-lasting or classic.

Gray is the color of intellect. It is thoughtful, contemplative, the gray matter of brain and mind; a striving for truth, knowledge, and wisdom. A certain venerable quality also comes with age and the association of the flowing gray beard and silver gray hair.

Medium grays are resolute, dignified, subtle, conservative: the understated authority of the man (or woman) in the gray flannel suit. Gray is the reasonable color of compromise, when extremes of black and white are tempered to "shades of gray."

It is easy to see why, for the most flamboyant personalities, gray is not a satisfying color. They see it as too modest, or mousy, controlled and inconspicuous.

Nature's Grays

Moving closer to white, gray becomes more innocent or fragile. Nature coats furry and fuzzy creatures and plants in various shades of gray: the delicate feathers of turtledoves and pigeons, seagulls, sparrows, pelicans, and quail; the plushy lushness of chinchilla, silver fox, the downy softness of rabbits, kittens, baby goats, and dappled ponies; cushy gray moss, silver birch, and pussy willow.

As gray nuzzles up to brown, it is perceived as warmer. Various shades of taupish grays are often given names associated with woodland animals, such as FAWN, ANTELOPE, and ANTLER. Other objects found in nature come in varying shades of gray—granite, stones, rocks, pebbles, shells—those weathered elements that add to gray's classic and timeless feeling.

Gray is nature's most perfect neutral, the color that designers and colorists use as background for color matching because it does not war with other colors. It's not a pushy color. It knows its place and slips quickly into the background to allow other colors to take center stage.

Just as the sky on a stormy, drizzly gray day inevitably opens to reveal a patch of bluish grays, these share the same assuring messages of blue: dependable, cool, and above all, constant.

Decorating with Gray

Gray has been called the "designer's workhorse" because there is always a tint, tone, or shade that will work with every color in the rainbow. On its own,

Continues on page 132

TRAVEL MOODS

Calypso Beat

If the words "fun vacation" instantly bring memories (or fantasies) of tropical islands, of sailboats and snorkeling, of dancing to the sound of steel drums, you can create this active and alive mood with vibrant sun-drenched yellows, corals, hot pinks and purples. And to keep the heat from getting too intense, freshen the combination with a splash of lime, or submerge yourself in scuba blues. This is the Color Mood of rich colors vibrating in high contrast with each other.

COMBO 130-A

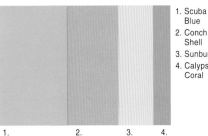

1. Nautical Blue
2. Parrot Green
3. Paradise Pink
4. Sundance

1.　　2.　　3.　　4.

COMBO 130-B

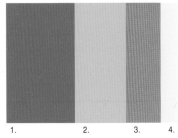

1. Scuba Blue
2. Conch Shell
3. Sunburst
4. Calypso Coral

1.　　2.　　3.　　4.

COMBO 130-C

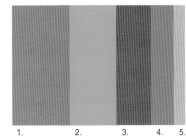

1. Super Pink
2. Capri Blue
3. Fandango Pink
4. Sugar Coral
5. Sand

1.　　2.　　3.　　4.　　5.

COMBO 130-D

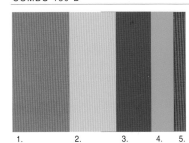

1. Orchid
2. Green Banana
3. Skipper Blue
4. Tropical Green
5. Fuchsia Purple

1.　　2.　　3.　　4.　　5.

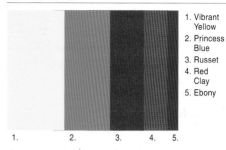

COMBO 131-A

1. Vibrant Yellow
2. Princess Blue
3. Russet
4. Red Clay
5. Ebony

1.   2.   3.   4.   5.

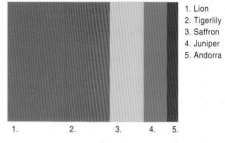

COMBO 131-B

1. Lion
2. Tigerlily
3. Saffron
4. Juniper
5. Andorra

1.   2.   3.   4.   5.

COMBO 131-C

1. Golden Glow
2. Black Olive
3. Bronze Green
4. Pristine

1.   2.   3.   4.

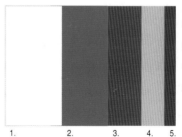

COMBO 131-D

1. Papyrus
2. Olympian Blue
3. Red Earth
4. Gold Earth
5. Peat

1.   2.   3.   4.   5.

COMBO 131-E

1. Ivory
2. Indigo
3. Sandstorm
4. Brown Patina
5. Ginger Spice

1.   2.   3.   4.   5.

TRAVEL MOODS

African Heritage

The colors of this Color Mood celebrate lush natural tones—the colors of earth, from red to gold reflected against the verdant green shades of vast African plains and endless blue skies. Africa is INDIGO and SAFFRON, EBONY, and IVORY, a land rich in the art of contrast, using dark robust shades with neutral tones, vivid hues or whites.

monochromatic gray can get very monotonous, so it is important to vary the textures, finishes, and shapes in a room that is primarily gray. Although they are both in the same color family, a silvery gray silk pillow against a charcoal chenille chair set in a bay window hung with pearl gray shantung drapes will alleviate visual boredom.

Gray can help prevent decorating mistakes. For example, if you bought a rather large and brightly patterned sofa in a moment of madness (or it was on sale) and the pattern happens to have some gray in it, you're in luck. Utilize the gray for accessories or other touches, and that will help to quiet the louder colors.

As to the most suitable rooms for gray—it does work best in a rather masculine den or in very "minimalist" surroundings like a very modern kitchen with smoky glass-doored cabinetry, and it can be very dramatic in marble and granite for the bath or entry areas. It's also excellent in "lodge" looks, especially when the inspiration for the other colors in the room comes from a handsome river rock fireplace, for instance.

Whatever gray might be, it is definitely not a fun color. It's just too serious. So the obvious places where gray does not function well as a dominant color are children's rooms and other recreational areas of the home.

Gray is dependable for a number of reasons: It ages gracefully because it is not a strongly recognizable "trend" color, it rarely shows the ravages of fading; it is quiet and peaceful and nonoffensive. And for some people, that's enough reason to do a gray room—it is simply safe. But if you're ready to make some changes in your life and living habits, if you want a little (or a lot of) excitement in your life, gray is not going to do it. Let it be dependably neutral and bounce some other colors off of it. Gray is perfectly happy to stay in the background.

Gray and Personality

If Gray Is Your Favorite Color: People who prefer this most neutral of all shades are carefully neutral about life. You like to protect yourself from the hectic world, wrapping yourself with the security blanket of a noncommittal color. You prefer a secure, safe, balanced existence, and unlike the lovers of red, you never crave real excitement, just contentment. It is important for you to maintain the status quo. You have often made compromises in your lifestyle. You are practical and calm and do not like to attract attention. You are willing to work hard (the gray flannel suit) and to be of service. You are the middle-of-the-road type: cool, conservative, composed, and reliable.

If Gray Is Your Least Favorite Color: To dislike gray is to dislike neutrality. You would rather be right or wrong, but never indifferent. Routine bores you. You are always seeking a richer, fuller life. This may lead you to get into one involvement, hobby, or interest after another in the pursuit of happiness. Gray may mean ghosts, ashes, cobwebs, and the dust of a haunted house or other scary gray things that have spooked you since childhood.

COLORS
FOR
YOUR
EVERY
MOOD

132

CHAPTER 13

White
Clean and Pure

White. The purest of the pure. Billowy clouds. The white dove of peace and freedom. Celestial light emanating from the heavens. A choir of angels with filmy white wings. The beard and robes of deity and wisdom. What child doesn't imagine God with a long white beard? White is unsullied, divine, pristine.

White through Time

In Greek mythology, the great gods lived on the snowcapped mountains. White horses drew the chariot of Zeus, and priests in white robes sacrificed white animals.

In Rome, on the first day of the new year, the consul wore a white robe as he rode to the capitol on a white horse to celebrate the triumph of Jupiter, the god of light over the powers of darkness. All the priests of Jupiter wore white robes.

The Romans marked auspicious days on the calendar with white chalk and inauspicious days with black chalk. When a Roman general was received in triumph, he was carried on a chariot drawn by four white horses. In Greek and Roman cultures as well as Celtic and Germanic folklore the sacred horses that had knowledge of the spiritual world "beyond" were white.

In the Christian church, white represents heavenly joy, purity, and truth as well as Easter and the Resurrection. Since Vatican II, white has become a favored color for funeral vestments at "masses of the Resurrection."

The Egyptians saw white as a blazing color—the lightgiver for life—and referred to it as "a lady of strength." The great god Osiris wore a white crown. The milk of the white cow was used for magical purposes, and a sacred white storehouse was written about in the ancient *Book of the Dead*.

The clothing of the average Egyptian was white and generally made of linen. The art of spinning and weaving became very advanced early in the history of Egypt. Only the pharaoh wore color until the 18th dynasty when princes, priests, and high court officials were given the privilege of wearing colors other than white.

In Indian paintings the noblemen of the highest caste always wore white, while the warriors wore symbolic red. In Indian folklore, as well as many other cultures, paradise was a white island. To the Japanese, white (*haku*) is the color of the gods, reflecting the existence of a sacred glory and exaltations. In the Shinto religion, sacred white paper ornaments marked the boundaries of sanctified territory.

J. B. Hutchings, the past chairman of the Colour Group in Great Britain, tells of some interesting folklore involving white birds:

> In many cultures white birds carry the soul to heaven . . . White seems to equal "pure" so only a white bird would be *persona grata* in heaven . . . A Yorkshire belief is that if a dying man sees anything white, he will go to

Continues on page 136

PHOTO: HOWARD MILLARD

TRAVEL MOODS

Maine Light

Maine light is pure Americana. The "Down East" colors of Maine include: quaint fishing villages with their nautical clear blues, sturdy barn reds, the shining beacon of a flashing amber light on a white lighthouse, a patch of green in summer's vegetable garden, the solid grays of the craggy coastline.

COMBO 134-A

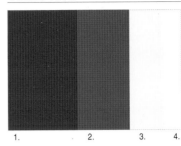

1. American Beauty
2. Patriot Blue
3. Buttercup
4. Bright White

1.   2.   3.   4.

COMBO 134-B

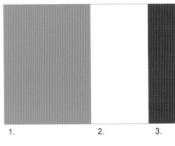

1. Regatta
2. Star White
3. Cardinal

1.   2.   3.

COMBO 134-C

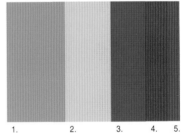

1. Deep Grass
2. Amber
3. Deep Ultramarine
4. Barn Red
5. Breen

1.   2.   3.   4.   5.

COMBO 134-D

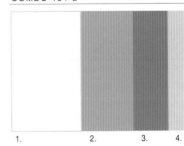

1. Sunshine
2. Marina
3. Artichoke Green
4. Pebble

1.   2.   3.   4.

COMBO 134-E

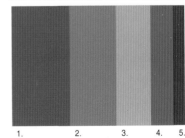

1. Dark Gull Gray
2. Captains Blue
3. Tan
4. Garden Green
5. Barberry

1.   2.   3.   4.   5.

TRAVEL MOODS

New England Foliage

The colors that carry us from the heat of summer to the cold of winter—nature's most transitional color schemes inspire glorious and often complex combinations. More warm than cool, these colors intrigue us with their complexity, with their mid to dark tones of forest greens, russet browns, flaming reds and golds, frequently and fantastically dabbed with reddened-violets.

COMBO 135-A

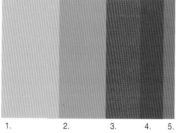

1. Willow Green
2. Forest Green
3. Grenadine
4. Burnt Russet
5. Harvest Pumpkin

1.   2.   3.   4.   5.

COMBO 135-B

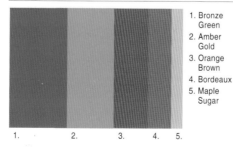

1. Bronze Green
2. Amber Gold
3. Orange Brown
4. Bordeaux
5. Maple Sugar

1.   2.   3.   4.   5.

COMBO 135-C

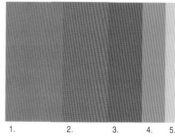

1. Brown Sugar
2. Red Violet
3. Autumn Glaze
4. Hedge Green
5. Old Gold

1.   2.   3.   4.   5.

COMBO 135-D

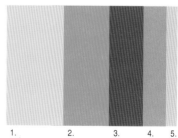

1. Sunset Gold
2. Butterum
3. Barn Red
4. Tawny Orange
5. Mustard Gold

1.   2.   3.   4.   5.

heaven, anything brown, to purgatory, anything black, he goes to hell. The belief does not, in some areas only apply to birds; white moths also carry souls.

In many African countries white is associated with the deities, peace, spirits of the dead, the afterlife, and especially worship. In some communities, the white garments worn by the leader signify a close relationship to the supernatural, and whitened figures guarded the religious relics of the community. The Ashantis don white clothes to mark the dead person's arrival into the spirit world. In Zaire, sculptured white wooden grave figures are used as memorials to the dead. In Mauritania, windows and doors are trimmed in white to keep the evil spirits away.

Unlike most of the world, in China and some other countries of southeast Asia, white is the color of bereavement and mourning because it is considered the proper color to escort the dead to a perfect state of purity and perfection. So the philosophy deals more with the future life of the deceased than the dark grief of those who are left to mourn. Symbolism and traditions are changing, however, especially with the younger generations who are emulating what they see in American TV shows, films, and the sports or music scene. Young Chinese brides are following the Western tradition of dressing in white gowns and veils, and students throughout Asia are wearing white T-shirts emblazoned with Harvard, UCLA, or the Chicago Bulls logos!

Innocent White

There is an innocence to white, a christening-dress kind of chasteness, an unsullied childlike naivete. It is traditionally the color of babies or brides. Baptismal and confirmation dresses are white, and some orders of nuns are married ceremonially to the church in a white gown. The ancient Greeks started the tradition of white at weddings, which they saw as a bridal symbol of joy. On the eve of her wedding ceremony, the Greek bride painted her body white, and on her wedding day she wore white flowers in her hair and a flowing white gown. For thousands of years, the Japanese have seen white as pure, innocent, and virginal. The ladies of the court and shrine maidens, however, wore their white kimonos over red pantaloons! In the United States, white did not become the standard color for wedding dresses until the 1800s, and colonial brides wore a variety of pastel colors.

In a fragile fabric, white creates a certain delicacy, refinement and daintiness —a "Southern Belle" quality reminiscent of magnolias, gardenias and fluttering eyelet parasols. A white suit on a man evokes the image of Mark Twain or a Tennessee Williams character, plantation porches, colonial English outposts, the Great Gatsby. It is the ultimate impracticality—a bit eccentric, but very cultivated and idyllic. These rather old-fashioned but charming and quaint qualities extend into the home as reflected by white wicker, lace curtains at the window, fine bone china, and a vase of romantic white roses gracing the tabletop.

Sterile White

At the opposite extreme, white can mean complete and absolute minimalism— "whiting out" the environment so that there is a totally blank canvas. It is rare to see this kind of approach to decorating because of its impracticality and completely cold effect. White is more often complemented by other colors or used as the "yin" to the "yang" of black.

COLORS
FOR
YOUR
EVERY
MOOD

136

The purity of white as the symbol of perfection has been used extensively in literature and drama. In the classic English film, *The Man in the White Suit,* Sir Alec Guiness portrays a scientist who creates the perfect white fabric in a suit that never needs cleaning and never wears out. He is hailed as a hero to the masses—it marks the supposed end of cleaning bills, laundering, and the need to replenish the wardrobe and ultimately, upholstery fabric, window coverings, carpets, linens, and so forth. The hero eventually becomes a villain when the reality of thousands of lost jobs and expendable industries becomes apparent!

The medical profession started to wear white in the early 20th century when it was discovered that dirt and grime so easily hidden on dark colors could spread infection. Superclean, stiff-as-a-board white has in many medical facilities given way to softer pastels. Nurses in particular are finding that patients view them as more approachable in soft pastel tints rather than sanitary starched white, and sterile pure white walls have given way to friendlier, softened tints. Glacier white was the rule in most hospitals for many years, but more recently experts have made a case against white—not only in hospital settings, but in the workplace as well.

Faber Birren reflected in his book *Color Psychology and Color Therapy* that although some lighting engineers may recommend white for working environments (to gain as much light as possible per watt consumed): " . . . the bright environment is quite objectionable. White walls may close the pupil opening, make seeing difficult, and set up annoying distractions. For the sake of a 5 or 10 percent increase in lighting efficiency, there may be a drop of 25 percent or more in human efficiency." He felt that a working environment of dark floors, material, or equipment must have soft colors on the wall in order to have the best viewing conditions.

Weird White

In spite of the association of white to the spirit world in many cultures, the filmy white of gliding ghosts is surreal and sheer—not quite as scary or as "heavy" as black to most people. But in a study done at a medical facility, to older subjects with impaired vision or a confused mental state, white uniforms worn at night took on a ghost-like appearance in semi-darkened rooms—causing an increase in a disturbed behavior just after nursing rounds. Many professionals (including myself) are encouraging a movement away from pure white particularly in hospitals and old age or convalescent homes where people are confined indoors a great deal. Monotony can bring boredom, the enemy of the sick, anxious, infirm, or aged.

This is certainly true if the white is too pure. The human eye sees pure white as a brilliant color, so it can create glare, which in turn can cause headaches and eyestrain. White walls need some visual stimulation—they will work as a background for large colorful works of art because there is so much attention focused on the art that the background almost disappears.

Pure white can exacerbate the phenomena commonly called "after-image." If you gaze at a color for a period of just a few seconds and look away at a white surface, you will see the complementary (or opposite) color. If you focus on red, you will see the complementary green. If you train your eye on blue and look away to a blank white surface, you will see orange, and so on around the color wheel, as explained in the next chapter.

Continues on page 140

TRAVEL MOODS

Parisian Cafe

Think Paris and what instantly comes to mind: the sense of style, of graceful architecture, marvelous museums, tree-lined boulevards, chic sidewalk cafes, and, of course, the food and wine. All of these elements make for the most sophisticated color combinations, some very subtle and others a paradox, but always in the best of taste: wine reds and wrought iron grays, steely-blues and softened roses.

COMBO 138-A

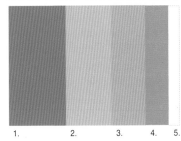

1. Bluesteel
2. Drab Gray
3. Opal Gray
4. Polignac
5. Ivory

1.　　2.　　3.　　4. 5.

COMBO 138-B

1. Fog
2. Arona
3. Dry Rose
4. Beige

1.　　2.　　3.　　4.

COMBO 138-C

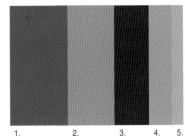

1. Gargoyle
2. Parisian Blue
3. Burgundy
4. Deauville Mauve
5. Elm

1.　　2.　　3.　　4. 5.

COMBO 138-D

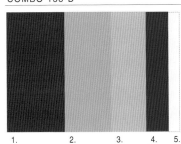

1. Deep Claret
2. Wrought Iron
3. Rattan
4. Ombre Blue
5. French Vanilla

1.　　2.　　3.　　4. 5.

San Miguel de Allende

Walk down the gray cobblestone streets of San Miguel de Allende and the artful building facades reveal the colorful history of colonial Mexico. A city brimming with artisans who strive to keep San Miguel's past true to its original colors: muted tones, both sun-warmed and chalky cool, juxtaposed against tinted neutrals and orange ochres.

COMBO 139-A

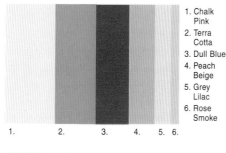

1. Chalk Pink
2. Terra Cotta
3. Dull Blue
4. Peach Beige
5. Grey Lilac
6. Rose Smoke

1.   2.   3.   4.   5. 6.

COMBO 139-B

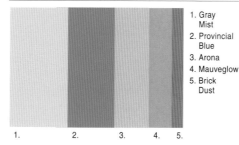

1. Gray Mist
2. Provincial Blue
3. Arona
4. Mauveglow
5. Brick Dust

1.   2.   3.   4.   5.

COMBO 139-C

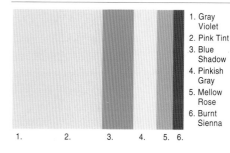

1. Gray Violet
2. Pink Tint
3. Blue Shadow
4. Pinkish Gray
5. Mellow Rose
6. Burnt Sienna

1.   2.   3.   4.   5. 6.

COMBO 139-D

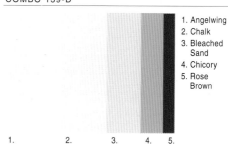

1. Angelwing
2. Chalk
3. Bleached Sand
4. Chicory
5. Rose Brown

1.   2.   3.   4.   5.

Although this exercise may seem like a fun little color trivia game, it can have broader repercussions in the environment sometimes causing bizarre color effects. There is less opportunity to experience after-image in the home because there are many more visual distractions, especially on the walls. And not all whites create the problem—off-whites, even the subtle, ever so slightly off-whites are a better choice. Not only are they easier on the eyes, but they are infinitely more friendly, especially if they have warmer undertones. They will give the illusion of utter simplicity without the harshness and unwelcoming attitude of totally pure white.

The Language of White

Is white actually a color? In pigment or dye form, white is referred to as achromatic, which literally means "without color." But if we think in terms of light, white contains all color. Remember what Sir Isaac Newton did with his spectrum. The purest "whitest" light is composed of all colors, the famous and fictitious mnemonic Roy G. Biv that every art student knows and loves: red, orange, yellow, green, blue, indigo, and violet!

When we say things are as different as black and white, we may be surprised to find that in the earliest formation of language, both black and white were associated with the absence of color; so that in some languages, the words for black and white are closely intertwined.

In the Anglo-Saxon language black is *blaec* and white is *blac*. The English word for bleach comes from the Anglo-Saxon *blaecan* (to make white), and *bleak* meaning pale. From the French *blanc* comes *blanch, blank,* and *blanket.* In other languages, white is related to wheat, as in the German *weiss*, the Dutch *wit*, the old Norse *hvitr*, the Swedish *vit* and the English *white*.

The ancient Egyptian word for white also meant "bright," "metal," "silver," and "milk." In some languages, the word for white is connected to the concept of light. The Greek word *leukos* means white or light. In Latin, *candidus* was the word for light, which was derived from the Sanskrit *candra* meaning light. So if we think in terms of light, as Sir Isaac Newton discovered, white light is caused by the reflection of all the colors of the spectrum.

Walter Sargeant stated in his classic *The Enjoyment and Use of Color:*

White is the most vital thing in nature. When it passes through the prism it is separated into colors the waves of which are constant and regular in their motion, but the waves of white light are irregular and do not repeat themselves. Its stream is tumultuous. The colors which compose it seem hardly to be held in leash or concealed. Their energies are all visible. It pours on ebullient and effervescing, possibilities of hue. . . .The quality varies with the texture of the surface which reflects it. It reverberates from silk differently than from snow.

While it is true that white light contains all colors and pure white is perceived as brilliant, there is also the association of silence to white. Think of the absolute quiet of a white snowfall. The term "white noise" is actually no noise at all—it is complete and total stillness. There were several methods for making the very important white lead pigments in the Middle Ages, most of them laborious, noxious, and obnoxious. One particular recipe called for lead to be hung over strong vinegar in a pot secured tightly (very tightly) and buried (yet again) in hot dung!

COLORS
FOR
YOUR
EVERY
MOOD

140

The grinding process that followed could cause incurable lead poisoning by breathing in the dust. Writers of Medieval times warned against the risks of apoplexy, epilepsy, and paralysis. Pigments were used on the face as well as on the walls or in paintings. Upper-middle-class Englishwomen in the Middle Ages thought it most fashionable to be wan and pale. They obtained their makeup pigments from itinerant merchants or from the workshops of cosmetics-makers, a budding cottage industry (Stratford-on-Avon Ladies?). Frequently the paint (and it was paint) that they applied to their faces was made from a dry pigment mixed with water. The pigments were usually made with white lead that would often turn gray—not a pretty sight!

Egg shells, oyster shells, and calcified bones were also ground into white pigment. The legs and wings of fowl or capon (the older the better) were recommended by Cennino, a Medieval artist: "Just as you find them under the dining table, put them into the fire. And when you see that they have turned whiter than ashes then draw them out and grind them well." In Africa the calcified bones of human skeletons were dug from paupers' graves to make the whitewash used on dwellings of important persons, in particular the king's dwelling.

The Movement to White

In the 1920s there was a strong movement away from heavy, dark furnishing to all-white rooms. In London, decorator Syrie Maugham, the wife of Somerset Maugham, created a living room for herself done in various creamy whites—even the fresh flowers were white. Ms. Maugham was inspired by the wife of a wealthy coal merchant who also did her home in all white —a symbolic repudiation of the sooty black stuff that had made her a very rich lady indeed! Furnishings done in white were a sign of affluence, a flagrant symbol that one did not have to be concerned about such mundane matters as soiling; one had servants to handle one's dirt!

This white wave of decorating continued into the 1930s. Doctors extolled suntans for health, white bathing suits and evening dresses were "of the moment." This extended into interiors with lacquered "moderne" furniture, textured wallpaper in off-white, and creamy white upholstery. Today, many big-city dwellers opt for white as a clean refuge from the polluted air and grimy streets. Luckily, advanced technology has made white more practical. Of all paint colors, white remains the number one bestseller.

But which white to choose? SNOW WHITE, BONE WHITE, IVORY, or PARCHMENT? The pink-tinged white of delicate roses? The delicious greenish-white of a sliced pear? Warm, creamy whites or the cool blue-white of luxurious marble? The choice may be predictable, but still highly personal.

Decorating with White

Obviously, for many, white is the color of choice for every room in the house. Consumer studies show that people choose it not because of any great passion for white, but simply because it is safe and "neutral." But it is not neutral if it is a bright white. Remember that the human eye sees pure white as a brilliant color, and the glare factor can become a problem if used in large areas.

Wherever pure white is used on the walls, floor, or sofa, it will jump out at you just as any other bright does. It is far from neutral! The range of whites from slightly off-white to rich-and-creamy are a better choice.

Continues on page 144

PHOTO:HOWARD MILLARD

TRAVEL MOODS

Marrakech

Marrakech—the name instantly conjures up a mystical city shimmering in the sun, a city of minarets and sheltering arcades made for quiet reflection and prayer, of subtle colorations and combinations reflected in the simple yet intricately woven pastels and muted midtone colors blending one into another.

COMBO 142-A

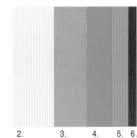

1. Antique White
2. Soft Pink
3. Coral Almond
4. Smoky Grape
5. Malachite Green
6. Autumn Glaze

1.   2.   3.   4. 5. 6.

COMBO 142-B

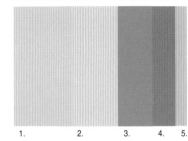

1. Gray Sand
2. Pale Blush
3. Orchid Haze
4. Desert Sand
5. Desert Mist

1.   2.   3.   4.   5.

COMBO 142-C

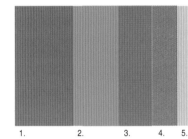

1. Brick Dust
2. Oil Blue
3. Dusty Lavender
4. Purple Dusk
5. Almond Apricot

1.   2.   3.   4.   5.

COMBO 142-D

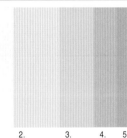

1. Sheer Pink
2. Bisque
3. Lavender Blue
4. Mellow Rose
5. Orchid Smoke

1.   2.   3.   4.   5.

COMBO 142-E

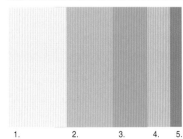

1. Lamb's Wool
2. Orchid Haze
3. Camel
4. Pink Sand
5. Dusk

1.   2.   3.   4.   5.

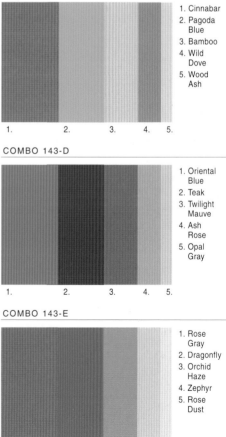

PHOTOS: NEIL HUGHES

Hong Kong Courtyard

These colors from Asia offer us places to ponder the mysteries of the past. Note the mid to deeper tones of the graceful plumed bird. Then there are the complex neutral grays of the aged tree rooted in the ancient courtyard colored in shadowy striations of mauve and deepened blue-greens. These Asian designs charm us with their complex colors used in artful simplicity.

COMBO 143-C

1. Cinnabar
2. Pagoda Blue
3. Bamboo
4. Wild Dove
5. Wood Ash

COMBO 143-A

1. Ocher
2. Pheasant
3. Blue Haze
4. Cocoon
5. Alabaster

COMBO 143-D

1. Oriental Blue
2. Teak
3. Twilight Mauve
4. Ash Rose
5. Opal Gray

COMBO 143-B

1. Mineral Blue
2. Wild Dove
3. Swamp
4. Carnelian
5. Chinese Yellow

COMBO 143-E

1. Rose Gray
2. Dragonfly
3. Orchid Haze
4. Zephyr
5. Rose Dust

The very best room in the house for white is the kitchen, especially if the cabinetry has glass doors. So many other colors can come into play in a kitchen, that the eye is distracted from the abundance of white. If the kitchen is very minimal and sleek, pure white can appear very inhospitable and cold, so that introducing another element of color—especially a warm color can change the reaction from cold to warm.

There are times when pure white can work. One is for trim, both indoors and out, because it adds a crisp finishing touch or accent and does not occupy a major space. White trim helps to define space (moldings, window trim, doors, baseboards, and so forth). Use pure white in areas where glare and light bouncing off surfaces is a visual advantage, such as low ceilings or cramped dark spaces like hallways and closets.

Personality and White

If You Love White: White can recall the rather docile days of youth, simplicity, and innocence, a longing to be young again. But it can also signify a certain self-sufficiency and uncompromising spirit. As white symbolizes cleanliness and purity, those who prefer it are neat and immaculate in their clothing and their homes. You are inclined to be cautious buyers and shrewd traders, but a bit critical and fussy. When a guest spills something on the spanking new tablecloth, you will smile and say graciously that it's nothing to be concerned about, but the minute everyone leaves, if not sooner, you'll be scrubbing it out!

If You Dislike White: As white represents cleanliness and purity, to dislike white does not exactly mean that you are a messy person; but it does mean that you have never been obsessed with order. You are not fussy. Things that are a little off-center are much more interesting to you that those that are perfectly in line. A little dust on the shelves, or on yourself, doesn't throw you into a spasm of cleaning. You are not very uptight and are easy to be with. You may see white as antiseptic and cold (remembrances of childhood visits to the dentist?).

COLORS
FOR
YOUR
EVERY
MOOD

144

CHAPTER 14

Color Replay

Now that you know more about all the Color Moods and the meaning of each color family, let's go back and re-visit the Color Word Association Quiz and your responses.

This will be an interesting exercise in self-analysis, and the end result should be a better understanding of why you react positively or negatively or indifferently to each color. Just as in any therapeutic process, when you examine the reasons why a color can literally turn you on or turn you off, you may find your attitude changing.

As you look at your responses to each color, your choices of Color Moods, and what you pictured during the guided imagery exercise, is it now apparent to you why you made these decisions? Perhaps, you now realize that some experience is so memorable that it pops right into your consciousness—but now it's in full color. Perhaps it is something as simple as "Daddy's eyes" when you've chosen sky blue. If you had a loving relationship with your father and you checked the positive column, it is fairly obvious that your response to that color will be forever associated in your mind with loving thoughts. And if you inherited your Dad's blue eyes, chances are that your reaction to blue will be even further reinforced if you got compliments whenever you wore that color as a child (and still do!)

Blue (or any other color, for that matter) can also hold some deeply rooted cultural associations. For example, in some societies, blue is viewed as a protective color. In the Middle East front doors are painted blue to keep the evil spirits from entering the house while many Native Americans paint the front doors of their dwellings blue for the same reason

These are diverse cultures, yet if you were raised with these cultural beliefs, you'll feel safe in a blue environment. Long after you've moved into new environments and become absorbed into other cultures, you may still carry these cultural color connections yet not be consciously aware of why you feel the way you do about a specific color.

The perception of color, like beauty, is in the eye of the beholder. Regardless of anything that you have learned about color through societal or cultural influences, the emotional aspect of color is ultimately a personal experience. Very often, reactions to colors have roots in childhood experiences. Some are instantly remembered, particularly those that are associated with happy or exciting times, but some are buried deeply in the psyche—too painful or frightening to want to recall.

Drs. Shulamith and Hans Krietler, in their book, the Psychology of the Arts (Duke University Press, 1972) state:

> Psychotherapeutic reports contain many examples of the origination of a specific attitude towards a color in a forgotten or repressed association of the color with a certain experience . . . associations of colors with experiences lying far back in one's life are probably more constant than associations with more recent or topical events.

That wondrous tape recorder in your head often turns to instant replay when you view a particular color. We may not be overtly aware of the experience it recalls but the message still comes through in our reactions. It is not possible to separate the "seeing" of color from the "feeling" because so much of what you see is based on what you feel. You never really forget anything you have experienced, you simply deposit it in your memory bank for future withdrawal.

Colors do evoke long-forgotten emotions—some positive, and some negative, and some simply evoke no feelings at all (or so you think). Was black the color of your very first cuddly, lovable puppy, or was it the color of scary witches and goblins that went bump in the night? Was green the color of your favorite flavor of delicious pistachio triple decker ice cream cone, or the color of your complexion after eating the whole thing? Your reaction to a color will definitely be influenced by your personal experiences, especially those that were very happy, very sad, or traumatic.

Purple Problems

Two such experiences illustrating deeply rooted reactions to the purple family come to mind as examples of how powerful personal experiences rooted in childhood can be.

Several years ago, I had a client who was about to embark on a glamorous new career as a consultant in the beauty business. She was moving to Paris and asked me to suggest two colors that she could use for decorating her company headquarters as well as in the logos, brochures, business cards, letterhead, and so forth. As she had silvery ash blonde hair and deep blue eyes that were almost violet, I chose aubergine (a deep plum) and silver gray in order to establish her own personal and unique "signature" colors. The image this combination projected was very sophisticated, elegant and appropriate in a European market, most especially in Paris where aubergine is a classic fashion shade.

When I showed her the selected colors, she got very upset and told me that she could not possibly consider anything remotely purple because the shade made her feel depressed and sad. Because her reaction was so negative and unexpected (to both of us), we decided to wait a week before meeting again. When we did meet, my client said that she had thought of nothing but aubergine for seven days. What she eventually uncovered was a touching memory of her early childhood.

She had lived with a loving aunt whose favorite color was plum. But her aunt died when my client was very young. She was deeply traumatized and in a state of shock. She remembered purple flowers, the aubergine dress her aunt was buried in, and the purple touches in the funeral home. Funerals are often associated with purple, and in many cultures purple is the color of mourning.

She had pushed the painful memory from her conscious mind—but the color remained an unconscious reminder. There was no way to convince her to use deep plum, so we went with claret and silver gray. The ambiance was similar and she was more comfortable with the choice.

Another client had a similar experience involving a purpled tint, this time lavender. Her husband had encouraged her to decorate their new living room in variations of purple: violets, mauves, and grape. For some reason that she couldn't understand, she had an aversion to them. (I guessed correctly that her husband was an artist. It is very unusual for men to favor the purple family unless they are very creative.)

COLORS
FOR
YOUR
EVERY
MOOD

146

In this client's case, the significant person in her childhood was a grandmother. As a little girl, my client would take sprigs of lavender to her grandmother and they would spend hours together making potpourris. When she was eight, her grandmother died—again, memories of a lavender dress, violet flowers, and a purple wreath on the front door. The memories of that difficult day faded, but her grandmother's favorite color had become associated with a deep sense of loss.

Once she discovered why she had bad feelings for purple, however, she was able to come to terms with this rich color. In fact, because she began to associate purple with happy times with her grandmother, she now was able to use the color family that her grandmother so loved. We chose pretty accents of grape and soft mauve combined with apricot, an appropriate background for her art Nouveau Antiques, and of course, lots of lavender accents. Surrounded by her "new" colors, poignant and happy thoughts came flooding back.

By rediscovering and using the purple palette, she had opened up a whole Pandora's box of memories long buried and is now able to share her early childhood recollections with her own grandchildren. If she had not allowed herself to experience the color, those important years with her grandmother might have remained hidden forever.

Of course, many memories can bring back pleasant sensations. Lavender might be a special color because it was the shade of a really soft and puffy quilt that felt so comfy and warm on cold winter nights. A particular shade of lilac might reawaken the scent of the wonderful fragrant flowers on a sunny summer day. Periwinkle blue might rekindle fond memories of a kindly and maternal kindergarten teacher who always wore that color (both in her clothing and her hair color!)

Broadening Your Color Horizons

As you look at each of your responses, think about the positive, negative and indifferent responses. Your mental tape recorder may not rewind to instant recall; it may take days, weeks or months before you can unearth the reasons for your reactions, and perhaps you never will. You don't have to force yourself to use a color that you dislike. If you truly want to open yourself up to trying "new" colors, however, or if you want to peacefully co-exist with a spouse or roommate whose color preferences are very different from yours, and you really want to make your home the comfort zone you deserve, it does help to ask yourself the following questions:

IS THE REASON FOR YOUR NEGATIVE REACTION REALLY RELEVANT TODAY?

Chances are, it's not. If your adverse reaction to avocado came from the sea of avocado shag carpeting you're remembering in your family's 1970s living room, dining room, den or bedroom (as well as the avocado refrigerator, dishwasher and upholstery), that was yesterday's yellow-green. Today's AVOCADO can be spiked with CHILI or a splash of BLUE CURACAO. It's definitely not yesterday's guacamole!! Look at some of the combinations listed under specific moods in the previous chapters. You'll see some interesting and beautiful ways to add sophistication to the deep yellow-greens.

DO OTHER PEOPLE INFLUENCE YOUR CHOICE OF COLOR?

Do you let other people make color choices for you? Do you lack the confidence to make the choices or get "steam-rolled" by a stronger and more vocal partner?

It's often easier to let someone else make the decisions and avoid all responsibility for the choices. It is helpful to seek opinions from others, especially those whose taste you admire; but when you get unsolicited opinions, always consider the source. You could wind up regretting that you did not follow your own instincts and resenting the advice-giver as well.

If you stifle your own creativity and basic feelings about colors, you will eventually regret it because the room or rooms just won't "feel right." So don't allow yourself to become intimidated. . . it's your life and your living space.

If you are like most people, you probably didn't have a problem choosing your favorite or least favorite color—it's the combinations that are perplexing. I've developed the concept of Color Moods to help you get in touch with your feelings about color and give you greater confidence in making your choices. And if you opt to go with professional help, you can use this book for inspiration and ideas and will instantly see how these combinations work in the illustrations throughout the book.

It is possible for two people with very different color reactions to find a happy compromise. A solution might be to use different color combinations in the rooms most frequently used by each partner—your den, his office, your sewing room, his kitchen, and so forth.

The best decorating help will always come from a professional, one who is trained to give you an objective opinion. A qualified (and caring) designer will always ask you about your feelings concerning color and will not be judgmental about your likes and dislikes. He or she will always try to work your favorites into a color scheme.

WHERE WERE YOU AND YOUR PARENTS RAISED?

If you were brought up in an area where social pressures, traditions, and rigid color rules were enforced, it may be difficult to shake those old dictums or clichés. For instance, one of the oldest of those dictatorial color taboos was that blue and green should never be used in combination; and, until the 1960s, they rarely were. This was an especially ludicrous dictum since blue and green are so beautifully combined in natural settings—a beautiful blue sky providing a background for a lush green meadow or reflected over tropical turquoise waters. Some of the most fabulous combinations appear together in natural scenes and we never challenge Mother Nature's ability to use color harmony.

Although questioning where your parents grew up might seem irrelevant, it truly is not. Your parents and their parents and all of the generations before you are the products of cultures whose beliefs and color traditions, no matter how subtle, have been passed on to you. A second or third generation Japanese American might consider themselves part of the melting pot mainstream culture, yet there may still be the vestiges of traditional beliefs. They may be drawn to the same quiet neutrals with accents of rich reds, teals, and golds of their family furnishings.

A man of Spanish descent might have difficulty wearing pink even in a casual tee shirt because in that culture, from earliest infancy, pink is strictly for females. It takes a strong will, a rebellious nature or a very open mind to defy tradition. Interestingly, most men of any culture don't have a problem snuggling under a cushy pink blanket or looking especially healthy in the reflected rosy glow of a pink bathroom, just as long as a woman has done the decorating and shares the space.

COLORS
FOR
YOUR
EVERY
MOOD

148

Women are more likely than men to have pleasant color associations and men are more apt to be indifferent to many colors. Why? Color is rarely part of a man's education; they simply haven't spent enough time involved with color. Maybe now that there are more girls than ever sliding into home plate and boys learning to cook, this will change. But it is still the case that girls spend more time dressing and coordinating their doll's wardrobe or decorating their doll house, while boys are involved in more active pursuits that are generally less artistic. Little girls shop with Mom, observe her making color choices and emulate her as their primary role model, while boys are busy pummeling each other in sports activities. If you are a man with many pleasant color associations, you probably have an eye for color or were encouraged (fortunately) by parents or teachers to exercise your "right brain" activities. Lucky you! Your life will certainly be enhanced by a greater appreciation of the colorful world around you, not to mention the unleashing of that creative urge that lies deep within you, as it does in every human being, male or female.

ARE YOUR CHOICES INFLUENCED BY TRENDS?

When a color trend takes hold, the magazines and store windows are full of it, used alone or combined with another "now" color. It's hard to ignore trends when they are so pervasive; they can be really unusual or fun and introduce unique combinations that haven't been seen before (like our blue and green in 1968), but the downside is that they can become passé very quickly.

One good way to use trendy colors is as accessories. Use that new color to be creative and freshen up your color scheme. Pillows in a new trend color can be wonderful for sprucing up a tired green sofa; new placemats can certainly add spice to the tabletop. Bathrooms and bedrooms are ideal for novel colors or mixes because it is far less expensive to change towels and bedspreads than it is to re-do the living room carpeting. Eventually, when that "new" color starts to look dated or you tire of it, it can be changed easily.

It is fun to experiment with trend colors, especially those to which you reacted very positively in the Color Word Association Quiz. They are stimulating and the novelty can help to give you an emotional "lift." They can provide instant gratification, without a lot of expense. The question is: Are you ready for a change? If the answer is a resounding "Yes!" then now is the time to go for it.

There is something to be said for staying with familiar colors: they're like old friends that give you a feeling of comfort and security because of their familiarity. But you shouldn't just stay with them out of habit. Do it because it truly feels good to you regardless of outside pressures to change. If you make choices simply because it's what everyone else is doing, you'll become a color clone and never be happy with the end result. It isn't really a reflection of you.

The purpose of the Color Word Association Quiz is to get you to analyze your feelings, get rid of old color prejudices and open your mind to new color possibilities. If you still find that there are colors you detest, you certainly don't have to use them. In fact, you shouldn't. Color should soothe or inspire or make you happy, not depress you. Color deprivation is not terminal: it's just tiresome!

YES, NO OR WHATEVER!?

At this point, look back at your answers to the Color Word Association Quiz. Add up the checks under the "Pleasant," "Unpleasant," and "Indifferent" categories.

Which column were most of your checks in? Were most of them in the "Pleasant" column? If they were, you obviously have a very positive attitude to color. You are most likely an enthusiastic, flexible, well-adjusted person, one who enjoys using many colors and is open to trying new combinations. As a child, you were probably encouraged to play with paint and crayons and your mother didn't get upset if your colors were scattered all over the kitchen table!

If more of your checks were in the "Unpleasant" category, I'm glad you found this book. You need encouragement to start trying new colors and combinations. You've probably had a hard time expressing yourself with color. Did someone criticize you when your colors didn't stay within the lines? Did you get punished for scribbling on the walls? Were you teased when you wanted to draw instead of run around outside?

One of the saddest stories I ever heard was told to me by a student who was punished severely for her scribbles. Her mother actually took her crayons and paints away and she was never allowed to have them in the house again! That's a form of child abuse that is hard to imagine, especially to those of us who love color. But there was a happy ending because the little girl grew up to be a successful interior designer—her experience strengthened her resolve to do something creative with color as an adult.

Although it may not be obvious to you why you reacted to certain colors negatively, associations are never accidental. There is always an explanation. If you think about your unpleasant associations and examine where they came from, you might find that your responses are based on such ancient history that you can't even remember the cause. Maybe now you can get rid of that old baggage and learn to enjoy color.

When you do recall an incident that provoked a negative reaction, you can often overcome your prejudice by recalling a balancing positive memory. When the client with the unpleasant reaction to lavender recalled the trauma of her grandmother's death, she also uncovered special happy memories that had long been submerged.

If most of your answers were in the "Indifferent" category, you've probably not had the opportunity to experience the creative use of color. You may be indecisive about color choices simply from lack of experience. It's never too late to learn and the Color Moods will give you a chance to get in touch with your color feelings now.

If your answers were equally divided between "Pleasant" and "Unpleasant," with few or no "Indifferents," you just need to extend your customary confidence into more colorful areas. You share that great middle ground with a lot of others. Again, the Color Moods can help you to move on to the next level of creativity.

It may take days, weeks or months for you to rewind your mental tape recorder so that you can reexamine your attitudes about color and open yourself to (literally) bringing more balance into your life through the creative use of color. So let's start finding out more about that balance and how we can attain it.

COLORS
FOR
YOUR
EVERY
MOOD

150

CHAPTER 15

Living with Your Color Moods

We've all been there. We visit the stylish displays in home furnishing stores, and if one of them appeals to us both emotionally and visually, we want it. We pore through our "wish books," the decorating magazines, and if we see the home of our dreams, we yearn to step into that setting and live in those surroundings—right now, not later. We want our homes to be the visual symbol of our dreams and fantasies.

It's been said that decorating is ten percent inspiration and 90 percent perspiration! Perhaps the percentages aren't quite that unbalanced, but the point is that while it's fun to fantasize, it takes hard work, determination, and above all, some knowledge of the really important "how-to's" before we can create that special place called home.

Now you've learned about the meaning of each color family and your own personal reactions to these colors. At this point, you either have a clear sense of the Personal, Nature, or Travel mood that is most appealing to you, noted several options that you like or may have invented one of your own. If you are like most people, you've probably identified at least two moods, possibly as many as three or four. Your final decision as to the number of moods you use in your home will be based on your living space and your personal history, but the mood you use is strictly your decision. If you reacted positively to the mood after reading the description, it "said" something that made you respond emotionally.

How "Color Moody" Can Your Home Be?

You may be wondering how many moods you can include in your decorating scheme. That depends on the size of your space. From a purely practical standpoint, if your home is small or if several rooms are visible from one central area, such as a kitchen extending into the family room, a dining room and living room combination, or all of those areas combined into one "great room," then it is best to choose one mood and utilize that theme and its accompanying colors throughout the entire area.

But bedrooms, bathrooms, and powder rooms are more private enclosed spaces and they can be done in completely different moods. We are accustomed, certainly, to children's rooms having their own colorful personalities and the same could extend into adults' private rooms as well. For instance, a Romantic setting could work in the living room and dining room, a Tranquil mood in the adult bedrooms and baths, a cheery Whimsical feeling in the children's bedrooms and baths, and warm sandy tones and cooler blue-greens from Beach Scenes in the powder room.

A hallway, a second story, or other levels can also provide a buffer zone between living spaces and resting spaces, so it is not necessary for all rooms to be identical in mood or color. Trim color such as windows and baseboards, floor covering, or floor treatments (often in neutral tile, carpet, or wood shades) can provide the common linkage that threads through adjoining areas (see chapters on white, gray, brown and black colors).

If your house is larger, it's even easier to change moods for each area. A gazebo gracing an outdoor pool might provide a cooling green oasis in varying tones from Foraging the Forest, the living and sleeping rooms might be expressing Mom's

LIVING

WITH

YOUR

COLOR

MOODS

151

COLORS

FOR

YOUR

EVERY

MOOD

152

passion for gardening, drawing her imagery and colors from the Wildflowers palette, the older kids' room and the kitchen might be Whimsical, the nursery Nurturing, while the den in the basement where dad spends a great deal of time at his computer, might be Rustic.

If you are an adventurous person with a broad range of tastes, it is fun to vary the mood for a change of scenery. But if you're the conservative type who was raised with very structured rules about using the same colors throughout the entire house, then you need to pick a dominant mood and stay with it. It's often a generational thing. If you're an older boomer or senior, then it's sometimes difficult to shake the rigid rules of the past, while the younger generations are more experimental and open to change.

If you really love a challenge or have quite a collection of furnishings left over from various decorating periods, then you might want different moods within the same room. Is this possible? The answer is "Yes," and color becomes an even more important element of this eclectic look. To keep the differing furnishing styles from becoming too confusing and busy, however, the color statement must be very distinctive and obvious. For example, a Romantic golden oak turn-of-the-century carved buffet could co-exist happily with a simple Rustic oak table of a similar finish, or sad old Duncan Phyfe chairs can go from a tired Traditional to a happy Whimsical when painted a bright lemony yellow. To keep this color compatible with the other furnishings, this vivid yellow should be utilized in another area of the room.

Why is the bright yellow chair any happier than any other color that might have been used? Well, it's obvious you might say—everyone knows that yellow is a happy color! But why is it any happier than green or blue or purple? To successfully utilize color's emotional meanings, it's important to explore the "why-is-it's" as well as the "how-to's." In previous chapters you delved into each color family's past as well as learning about its inherent meanings, messages and moods. Now let's explore some of the all-important basics that will help you to understand why and how colors harmonize.

Back to the Basics—The Color Wheel

The color wheel (see page 9) is the basis of all color combinations. This circular arrangement of the spectrum visually illustrates the basic principles of color. The primary hues of yellow, red, and blue; the secondary hues of green, orange, and purple (often called violet); and the tertiary colors of yellow-green, blue-green, blue-violet, red-orange, and yellow-orange are placed strategically around the wheel to demonstrate the important ideas of warm colors opposite to cool colors; how families of color blend, harmonize, or contrast; color schemes that are monotones, monochromatic, analogous, and complementary. A knowledge of the color wheel and its workings will make it easier for you to express the moods you want to create.

Monotones

A color scheme involving monotones uses one single neutral in varying tints (the same color with white added) and shades (the same color with black added). In some ways, these are the most difficult combinations to make appealing because distinctions between neutrals in the same color family are so subtle. An effective monotone combination of neutrals, for example, would be a room done in deeper CHARCOAL GRAY, mid-tone GULL GRAY, and a light DOVE. Other classic neutrals are those in the taupe family such as SIMPLY TAUPE (also called *greige*, a combination of beige and gray) as well as tinted whites, beiges, and grays.

Monotones can express a zen-like quality, simple and unadorned; but they can get boring unless there is a variety of textures to make up for the lack of color. They are used most effectively in the Contemplative mood, accented with a splash of dramatic color so that the atmosphere does not get too quiet and boring.

Monochromatic

Monochromatic color schemes use only one hue in varying shades or tints. Take, for example, primary blue from the color wheel. A monochromatic color scheme would use blue and its variations, ranging from the softest baby blue to the richest, deepest indigo. Monochromatic colors express a Contemplative quality; but, just as with the monotones, a variety of textures and contrasts and a dash of vivid color are essential to provide some visual interest.

Analogous

Analogous, or neighboring colors, are those that adjoin each other on the color wheel. They are "safe" to use together because they are closely related—literally flowing from one to another—such as the warm reds, oranges, and yellows. Because these colors share the same undertones, they will please the eye and bring a sense of harmony. Because they are such good neighbors and blend so nicely, analogous schemes evoke a Tranquil mood in the soft blues, muted greens, watery aquas, and cool lavenders or a Nurturing mood with its predominately warm and tender yellows, peach, and rose tones. Analogous color schemes also work well in the midtone combinations of the Romantic palette.

An analogous scheme can be expanded by adding yet another adjoining color from the color wheel. The friendly reds, oranges, and yellows can embrace a yellow-green or lean to the opposite side of red and introduce a touch of red-violet. This brings a fresh, unique sparkle, a Whimsical slant to the combination and, as you will learn in the next section, a sense of balance to the group.

To offer even more variety to the analogous scheme, a wide range of lightness, darkness, and intensities can be used, such as PERSIMMON, PEACH, and BUTTERSCOTCH—all from the neighboring families and looking very much like a nosegay of happy hues taken from Nature's Wildflowers or Summer's Gentle Petals. Add a sprig of MINT GREEN, to visually garnish the effect, making it delectable.

A Traditional setting using a Navy sofa with a plaid chair of NAVY, BILLIARD GREEN, and FAIR AQUA will not offend the eye because these colors are so closely related, but adding a touch of ROSE VIOLET to the combination brings a balancing warmth and visual excitement.

Complementary Colors

Complementary colors are those that are directly opposite to each other on the color wheel. The literal meaning of complement is that which completes or makes perfect. In a psychological or physiological sense, colors coupled as complementaries exhibit a natural balance. Every pair contains both a warm and cool hue. This need for balance carries over into every phase of our lives and particularly into our homes. There are times when the use of complementary colors can make us feel less stressed and more "in sync" with our surroundings.

When equal amounts of bright complementary hues are used together, however, the effect can be anything but relaxing. Strong contrasts such as VIBRANT YELLOW and RADIANT ORCHID scream for attention. Using these brights together creates a very bold and oscillating effect, with each complement intensifying the brilliance of its opposites, so that they seem to vibrate along the borders where they meet.

LIVING
WITH
YOUR
COLOR
MOODS

153

The term for this visual phenomena is "simultaneous contrast" because each color is reacting to the other. As you see in the color combination examples for each Color Mood, there are opportunities for using vivid complementaries together for specific effects in Dynamic, Whimsical, Contemplative, and some of the more exotic Travel moods.

The impact of complementaries is softened when one member is dominant and the other is used as an accent; or the value of each is reduced to soft pastels like the BARELY PINK and CELERY GREEN of the Nurturing palette, the deepened intensities of each like HUNTER GREEN and BURGUNDY RED of a typical Traditional scheme or the Romantic mood's BALLAD BLUE contrasted with PEACH MELBA. The complementary combinations can be used in many different mood settings.

Color Temperature—Warm or Cool?

Now that we've looked at the basic principles of the color wheel, let's get a bit more personal. Try to look at your home with an objective eye. After what you have read and learned so far, do you think your colors reflect who you are? Are you comfortable and content with your choices?

If you're like most people, your answer will be "yes" and "no"—some rooms seem very pleasant and comfortable, others simply just don't make it. Something is missing. If you feel slightly uneasy or uncomfortable in a particular room, more than likely it is the colors that are disturbing; you and even more importantly, it's the color "temperatures" that aren't quite right. Too many cool colors can make a home (and its inhabitants) seem unfriendly and aloof. Warm colors are instantly hospitable. If the colors get too warm or hot, the atmosphere can be stifling.

To better understand color temperature, let's take another look at the color wheel. Colors are seen as warm or cool because of longheld beliefs that are imprinted on our psyches. Red, yellow, and orange are considered warm colors because they are universally associated with the warmth of sun and fire. Blue, green, and purple are considered cool because they are associated with the coolness of sea, sky, the outer reaches, and sheltering foliage. But changing an undertone can change the temperature. Blue-reds are cooler than yellow-reds. The redder the purple, the hotter it gets. Blue-greens are cool; but the closer to yellow, the warmer green gets.

Both green and purple are the most adaptable to a change in temperature because they are a bridge between the warm and cool colors on the wheel. Perceptually, orange is seen as the hottest color; blue the coolest.

As colors are rarely used alone, there are other influences such as lighting, atmosphere, texture, shape, preconceived associations, and surrounding colors that affect the perception of color temperature. Warm and cool are relative terms. In the case of true red, for example, an equal mix of warm and cool undertones will appear to be more blue-red against a yellow-red, while true red will appear more yellow-red when compared to a blue-red.

The Balancing Act

When combining warm and cool colors, you can carry the balancing act too far—a combination of half warm and half cool simply doesn't work because the message is not clear as to the presiding temperature or mood. Does it feel warm, or does it feel cool? To get a real sense of the mood, one color must dominate so that the feeling is predominantly warm or cool.

Put two bright warm colors together and you're hot. Soften or deepen those colors and they're not quite as hot, but still toasty and warm. Two icy colors like GLACIER blue and FROST GREEN are refreshing, but can be perceived as

WARM
Red
Yellow
Orange

WARMEST
Orange

COOL
Blue
Green
Purple

COOLEST
Blue

WITH OTHER
COLORS
CAN APPEAR
WARM OR COOL
Green
Purple

COLOR WHEEL
Page 9

COLORS
FOR
YOUR
EVERY
MOOD

154

psychologically cold. But some cool shades should be invited into a very warm environment (like Sunset and Fire, page 118) just to dampen some of the heat.

One of the most important and fundamental guidelines in interior design is: cool colors are best balanced by a touch of warmth and warm colors by a touch of coolness. If you were to use only vibrant warm colors in a room, your eye would start to search for something cool for balance; in a cool room, your eye starts to search for a touch of warmth.

Aesthetically and psychologically, it is far more pleasing and the Color Mood much clearer in a room when you keep the cool colors dominant and the warm colors subordinate, or vice versa.

Seeking Equilibrium: Homeostasis

Throughout our lives, we seek balance on many levels: spiritually, aesthetically, emotionally, and physically (the ancient Chinese called it the balance of yang and yin). Today our lifestyles and attitudes require a perpetual balancing act between work and play, practicality and fantasy, technology and humanism; seeking what is new while treasuring the old.

Above all, our homes are critical to our sense of equilibrium. For increasing numbers of people, it is both work place and living space. Now, more than ever, there is a need for home to be a safe haven; a place where we can feel secure, nurtured, connected, and comfortable; a place to regroup, refresh, and replenish. Color can be an instant equalizer and a "quick fix" in helping us to achieve that ever-important balance in our busy, often hectic lives.

Although we have no conscious awareness of it, our eyes search for balance in our immediate environments. Having someone tell you that your home is warm is always taken as a compliment because warm colors are perceived as cheerful and welcoming. Excessive warmth, unrelieved by a cool touch, however, can be too much of a good thing. Too many cool colors with no suggestion of warmth can have a chilling effect on our moods as well as on others entering our home. And being told that your home is cold would definitely not be taken as a compliment!

Perhaps you have had your colors "done," and you were told to decorate your home in the same colors that you wear. If you were placed in a warm palette, you might have been told to decorate exclusively in warm colors. If cool colors were chosen for you, then you might have been told to decorate only in cool colors. This is not necessarily good advice especially if it came from a color analyst who got her certification from a home-maintenance product company after an "intensive" one-hour training session!

As far as color is concerned, beware of the words exclusively, only, never, and always. These are very judgmental and may be outmoded, at least as far as you are concerned. If you prefer either warm colors or cool colors for your clothing as well as your living space, then by all means use what pleases you. But remember that using warm colors exclusively can make you feel uncomfortably overheated, and using only cool colors can make you feel that the atmosphere is uninviting and sterile.

Our innate longing for balance welcomes the soothing touch of green plants in a warm room, just as a large vase of red tulips brings a cheering warmth to a too-cool interior. This need to maintain internal equilibrium or a sense of balance (called homeostasis) is a natural phenomenon that is inborn, a purely physiological reaction. To prove this to yourself try the following experiment:

Concentrate on a fixed red object for about ten seconds. Look away at a piece

AVOID

WARM
WARM
WARM
WARM

COOL
COOL
COOL
COOL

BETTER OPTIONS

COOL
WARM
WARM
WARM

WARM
COOL
COOL
COOL

of plain white paper, and you will see the complementary shade of green. This is homeostasis in action—our body's ability to provide relief to our eyes and restore our sense of balance. We need only to take a cue from our own restorative powers by turning the color temperature up or down, allowing one color to dominate and the other to support.

Dominance

If you study a well-decorated room, you will notice one of the most important aspects of interior design: one color family will always dominate. This major color sets the stage and helps to create the mood—it's the star player. There may be several other supporting colors in the color scheme, but they shouldn't upstage the star.

The dominant color not only sets the mood, but it is generally the color that occupies the greatest amount of space. This is usually the color of the walls, ceiling, or floor. There are exceptions, however, especially in the Contemplative or Dynamic mood. For example, ivory walls and carpet may occupy the major space of a Contemplative living room, but the boldly colored abstract art on the walls will definitely set the tone for the room. The same would hold true for a Dynamic black-and-white master bath with a bright red tile treatment on the vanity.

Dominance (often referred to as tonality) gives visual importance to one color family and enables the viewer to experience the ambiance of the entire area. A sweeping glance across the room should give an instant impression of the mood of that space. If one color family does not dominate the scene, the area gets too busy and disconnected and the messages confused. The colors will fight for attention, and the result is disconcerting, if not disastrous!

This is especially true in an eclectic setting where furniture styles are mixed. To make one mood prevail in a natural setting such as the Beach mood, for example, it is important to utilize both sea (cool) and sand (warm) colors. But one of those color families must dominate, such as a dominant blue or turquoise with a subordinate soft beige or taupe. The reverse could also be true, with the warm beige family predominating over the cooler blues. The choice of temperature is based on your personal preferences.

In some of the Color Moods, the dominant temperature is a given. In the Sunset and Fire mood, for example, there is no question that the dominant colors will be warm because that's what sunset and fire are all about. But too much fire may be overkill, and that's where a splash of CERULEAN BLUE could help to contain the blaze. In a room inspired by the Winter Frost, cool colors will dominate, of course. But that coolness may come across as stark and uninviting, especially on a really cold day, so a bit of sunlit yellow, if only in the floral arrangements or on the tabletop, can make the atmosphere far less frigid.

Symmetry vs. Asymmetry

Not too many years ago, symmetrical balance was the only way to decorate. A "suite" of furniture consisted of a sofa that was always flanked by matching tables of identical finishes with identically styled and colored lamps and smack in the center was a coffee table that matched the end tables. Moods were very limited; and if a mood was thought about at all, it came straight out of the furniture store setting with very little personal input.

Today we have learned from either the decorating disaster or dullness of the past that it's not necessary to have perfect symmetrical balance. In fact, it is far more interesting to use asymmetrical balance where colors do not have to be repeated in exactly the same patterns, proportions, or placement. Patterns can be mixed, and

COLORS

FOR

YOUR

EVERY

MOOD

furniture from different periods can be used together. This eclectic approach to decorating allows you to mix many styles—it's the color that can make it all cohesive.

We now know that color balance cannot be attained if the hues are used together in equal proportions. If one hue is to dominate, then the other color should be subordinate. The proportion might be 75 percent to 25 percent or 80 percent to 20 percent but never 50-50. When a third color is introduced into the scheme, it then becomes subordinate to the other two and is often used as an accessory or trim color. The first color is dominant, the second is subordinate, and the third member provides an accent, a "touch" of color and sometimes, when you are cooking up a color scheme, only a "pinch" of color.

The use of four or more solid colors in any of the Color Mood palettes gets a bit more complex and a little more challenging. A multicolored pattern, however, can actually be easier to work with because it becomes the source of inspiration for accessory or accent colors. In the 1960s, equality was often the rule. Hot pink and neon orange were often used in equal amounts with "revolutionary" results. Equal amounts of those two noisy brights together boggles the eye (and the mind). Where to look first?

Many people tried that particular combination—it was different and fun and had never really been done before and the 1960s were a time for experimentation, after all. So, up went the neon orange and hot pink cabbage roses (in equal amounts) on the powder room walls. And within six months, everyone who put it up was ready to claw it off! So that color scheme never made it into the 1970s. Instead of orange and pink, there was avocado and harvest gold!

We got much smarter about decorating in the 1980s. This was an era when it was all right to wear short skirts or long skirts, to mix a patterned tie with a patterned shirt, to experiment with new color combinations that had been rigidly prohibited prior to that time. People became far more open to change in both personal and business attire, and that couldn't help but influence home and business decor.

Decorating Steps

There are five basic steps in putting together your decorating plan once you've taken the Color Word Association Quiz, have considered all Color Moods and their color combinations, and know your favorite colors and your least favorite colors. If you live alone, you are ready to proceed, but if you live with significant others, you must take their feelings into account as well, especially in rooms where you all gather together. Perhaps, everyone who lives with you should take the Color Word Association Quiz in chapter 1 and look at the suggested color combinations with you.

STEP ONE

The first step in decorating your home, if you haven't already done so, is to choose the Color Mood for each room you wish to decorate. This might involve some discussion with your housemates. But make your mood choices—whether they are Personal, Nature's, or Travel. All of the Color Moods are based on emotional reaction to colors, but use different means to get there. Just as you have collected various types of artifacts, posters, artwork and other kinds of mementos on your travels, or might choose a much-different motif, colors, and furniture styles for a child's room than you would for your bedroom, you can mix types of moods in your home. For instance, you might choose Tranquil for your bedroom and Beach Scene for your living room, Whimsical for the kitchen, and New England Foliage for your dining room.

AVOID

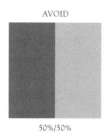

50%/50%

BETTER OPTIONS

20%/80%

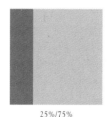

25%/75%

COLORS

FOR

YOUR

EVERY

MOOD

STEP TWO

Step two is to review the furnishings and accessories you have and want to use in the room: architectural details, such as the wood tones in the floor and woodwork, other floor coverings that you wish to retain, plaster moldings or other details you want to emphasize. Or you may have a favorite piece of furniture, an Oriental or patterned rug, a fabulous decorative item from one of your travels, a piece of artwork, even a needlepoint pillow made by your great aunt that you want to feature in the room. Note the colors in what you have and want to use in the room.

If you must decorate around existing colors, such as carpet or tile or wood tones that cannot be changed, then those colors must be included in your scheme, and you must proceed from there. For instance, if you are decorating the living room of an old Victorian house and the paneling in the room is a golden oak, don't ignore that wonderfully warm honey undertone. Use it to create a Romantic or floral-inspired mood including a honey yellow or apricot that "connects" to the warm oak paneling.

Perhaps that old Victorian had been fairly well gutted over the years and there is little left of the original interior except for the unique fretwork with all of its swivels, scrolls, and curlicues that have been painted a bright white. Perhaps the original dark wood flooring of unknown origin has been painted over many times and stripping the wood surfaces will be a laborious and expensive task. Perhaps instead this dark-light contrast could be a very dramatic backdrop for a Dynamic setting—unexpected in a Victorian, especially if the accent colors are jewel tones such as GARNET or AMETHYST.

In a wonderful old home built in 1947 that we bought facing Puget Sound, we inherited the tile treatments in four of the bathrooms. The colors were all vintage late 1940s: aqua, a deep CLARET RED, a dark DUSTY ROSE, and an AZURE BLUE. Almost 50 years later, they were still in perfect condition and the colors were wonderful, so much so that I decorated around each of the tile shades, making them the focal point of the rooms. My favorites were the powder rooms. In the larger of the two, the AQUA tile was enhanced by deep TURQUOISE walls, and in the second, we extended the CLARET RED tile color onto the wall and ceiling color. The colors stayed true to the history of the home and truly inspired the moods of the rooms. And I know that the lady who built the house and was gone but—who was rumored to roam around the house at night (although she never bothered us)—was probably pleased with our faithfulness to the original colors.

STEP THREE

Step three is to look at the color combinations for each Color Mood. Now is the time to let your own very definite color preferences and your inventory of furnishings and accessories for each room influence your choice of color combinations as much as the particular Color Mood you've selected. For example, let's say your favorite color is blue, you want to create a Tranquil mood in the living room, you're not enthusiastic about yellows or oranges, but your new house has warm pine wide-planked floors. What can you do to marry the two temperatures? You have the perfect solution if you already own or plan on purchasing an Aubusson carpet that combines both warm and cool colors, like WEDGWOOD, PEONY, ROSE DAWN, and ANTIQUE WHITE. The warmish pinks, rose, and off-white flatter the warm tones of the pine floor, but you can really play up the blue in the carpet by using it on large areas like the walls, upholstered pieces, and window coverings, for instance, so that it becomes your dominant color. The remaining colors in the carpet should be connected to other furnishing elements, but they will be subordinate to the blue.

STEP FOUR

Step four is to decide which are your dominant, secondary, and accessory colors for each room—using the combination you've selected.

In formulating your color picture, consider:

1. The major or dominant area of walls, ceiling, and floor;
2. The secondary area of window treatments and larger upholstered pieces;
3. Additional pieces such as tables, lamps, occasional chairs, accent pieces, and other accessories you want to keep in the room.

The colors of the walls and ceiling (including windows and doors) are critical to the success of any room. They set the stage for the room's atmosphere and often account for more than two-thirds of the available space.

Your biggest wall-treatment decision will be: Do you want the walls to remain in the background, or do you want them to be a major element of the decor mood?

Generally the more colorful the other furnishings are, the less color you need on the walls. Your paint brush can become a magic wand to change Color Moods, with a fresh coat of paint instantly transforming your room with a clean, new look. If you are stretching your budget, it is the least expensive way to redecorate. The more coats of paint you use, the truer the color will be. If you have chosen the softer colors from the Nurturing or Tranquil moods or were inspired by the Summer's Gentle Petals palette, you especially need to know that yellows and pastel pinks often need three coats; two coats will do for most other colors. Remember that color intensifies and becomes darker than the paint chip when applied to the wall.

Now indicate in your decorating chart which colors are dominant, secondary, and accent for each room.

STEP FIVE

Step five is to make sure of your color choices before making a big financial commitment. One of the most important aspects of gaining color confidence is to work with color swatches or samples for every decorating project. This is the most efficient way to check the harmony of your color scheme and fit the mood that you are trying to achieve.

The size of the swatches should relate to the way the colors will be used in the actual room. Make your dominant color the largest swatch, the subordinate color a little more than half that size, and your accent colors a scant one-fourth of the largest swatch. Put them all against a white poster board. Use double-sided cellophane tape or Velcro for easy removal in case you change your mind. It's so much easier to work this way than with bits of tattered wallpaper and unraveling fabric pinned to paint chips!

After you have selected your paint color, apply it to a plain piece of canvas purchased from a fabric store. You can cut this into smaller pieces and take it with you for color-matching purposes when you are shopping for upholstery fabric, carpeting, accessories, and so forth.

When you have completed these five steps, you are ready to develop your own decorating plan based on Color Mood combinations for each room you plan to decorate. Starting with a color combination makes many of the other decorating decisions much easier. But in case you are still feeling a little unsure, the next

LIVING
WITH
YOUR
COLOR
MOODS

159

chapter will give you the answers to some of the most frequently asked questions I've received in talking to consumers and professionals concerning color choices.

Below is a form to help you develop your color ideas and organize the color information you'll need to decorate a room. Use this or copy it and fill it out.

Room Planner

ROOM: _____

MOOD: _____

COLOR COMBINATION AND ITS USE:

	COLOR	SURFACES / FURNISHING IN THIS COLOR
DOMINANT:	_____	_____
		_____
		_____
		_____
		_____
SECONDARY:	_____	_____
		_____
		_____
		_____
		_____
ACCENT:	_____	_____
		_____
		_____
		_____
		_____

PASTE CHIP AND SWATCHES HERE

COLORS
FOR
YOUR
EVERY
MOOD

160

CHAPTER 16

Color Questions

When I meet people for the first time at a social function or on a plane during one of my frequent flights to conduct seminars, they are fascinated by what I do. They will eventually tell me what their most favorite and their least favorite colors are, and then they always ask for advice about how to use colors in their surroundings. Here are some of the most frequently asked questions regarding color in decorating.

Q: *Why does the paint chip I choose in the paint store never look quite the same when I paint it on the walls?*

Color is intensified when it is applied to a large area like a wall, and it can look darker (or brighter) than what you thought you were choosing. A cool blue in a tiny chip, for example, might turn icy cold on a wall and a rosy pink can expand into a bubble-gum wrapper color. When in doubt, it's always best to go a bit lighter than your initial choice and to do a "color sampling." Buy a small can of the paint color you have chosen, apply it to a small section of the wall (or a piece of heavy poster board available in art material stores) and let it dry overnight in order to judge the color truly.

Look at it at various times of day in both natural and artificial light because the lighting will change the effects of the color. The investment in that small can of paint will be well worth it, certainly better than having to repaint the whole room, or worse than that, living with a color that makes you feel uncomfortable. Your environment should be aesthetically pleasing to yourself and to those who share it with you, comfortable, and above all, comforting.

Q: *When I purchased my living room sofa, I was given a choice of upholstery fabrics and colors. I chose a small floral print of red and blue. From just a few feet away, the sofa appears to turn purple. Why and what can I do about it?*

Early in my career, I remember a client who had that very same experience prior to hiring me. While awaiting delivery of a new red and blue sectional sofa for her rather large den, she carefully purchased accessories, carpeting, wallcovering, everything, to go with it. On the day her sofa arrived, she almost suffered cardiac arrest—it looked purple! She had selected the fabric based on a smallish swatch. At a distance the colors in the small print appeared to merge on the large sofa surface! Remember the first time you put a small wet dot of red paint into the little tin of blue paint, and a whole new color magically appeared: purple.

The answer to this dilemma is to be sure to get a large piece of the fabric or, better yet, a pillow of the print being considered. Take it home, and place it on a chair. View it from a distance of at least three feet to see what happens to the color. If the colors appear to meld into another color that does not work with the other room furnishings, you will need to get a larger, well-defined pattern or a solid color.

If the offending item is non-returnable, don't despair; there are some solutions. The first one is to pull a color out of the pattern that you really do like, and make it the dominant theme in some large solid-color pillows. A large throw draped across the back of the sofa can also serve as a distraction, especially if it occupies a lot of space. The sofa will become the background and the pillows or throws will become the focal point. Be certain that the color you choose is a favorite because it will have the most impact and help to set the mood of the room. If, for example, the sofa's main pattern colors are BRICK RED and CURRY, which have melded into rust when viewed from a distance, you would want to use either BRICK RED or CURRY as the dominant accessory color.

If the pattern is a floral, it will more than likely be embellished with green leaves, and this could provide yet another solution. As I pointed out in chapter 8, this is nature's neutral—the color of foliage that blends with every other color in the spectrum. If you haven't used green anywhere else in the room, bring in a friendly green plant, and that will help to "connect" the accessories to something else in the room.

I live on an island near Seattle where green is ubiquitous in the landscape— every room in the house has a window that frames the greenery. If you look out to grass, trees, or any other kind of foliage, then green becomes an inevitable part of your color scheme. And if you don't have any greenery outside, you can certainly create your own "garden" with indoor plants.

Q: *Does white really "go with everything"?*

There are many nuances of white such as ANTIQUE WHITE, WINTER WHITE, or WHISPER WHITE that function better as neutral colors than pure white. The human eye sees pure white as a brilliant color, so it is dazzling and obtrusive and does not blend well as efficiently as an off-white. Mixing different shades of white should be avoided. Off-white will look dull and dingy next to pure white. Beautifully aged antique lace curtains will look yellow and faded next to pure white louvers.

Undertones are key in choosing the proper white. Cooler shades will look best with whites that have a slightly cool undertone, whereas whites with a warmer undertone will look best with other warm shades. Cream is often a better option that white as a neutral accent for warm shades.

Snowy whites can certainly be very effective in evoking a very dramatic or pristine look, as in the Contemplative, Dynamic, or Winter Frost moods, but they are best used with some colored accents in order to avoid too cold a look. Remember, too, that pure whites enlarge any area in which they are used, so when decorating your bed or your body, remember that anything amply upholstered will look larger in white!

Q: *Do I have to paint the interior of my home white when I place it on the market?*

Occasionally you will hear real estate agents make that suggestion. Since most people buy a home based on "emotional appeal," however, and the colors are very much a part of that emotion, you might strip the house of its personality if you strip the walls of their colors.

A rental property is different. Most people do not see rentals as permanent and generally want a blank canvas that won't interfere with their furnishings. As much as I dislike suggesting neutrals or off-white throughout the entire space because of their boring sameness, it's probably a good thing if you are the landlord.

COLORS
FOR
YOUR
EVERY
MOOD

162

Q. *Are there certain colors that seem the most versatile in interiors?*

Yes, there are certain color I call "Crossover Colors" because they occur frequently in nature and our eyes are accustomed to seeing them used as background, or in combination with other color in much the same way a neutral color might be used. There are 15 Crossovers and they can be used successfully in any color mood—if not in large amounts—then certainly in small touches, especially when there is a need to bring color balance into play.

See page 59 for a list and illustrations of these colors.

Q: *I'm the type who likes change and want to alter my look every few years.*
Are there any Color Moods that are easier to change than others?

Any scheme can be changed easily with slipcovers, new area rugs, paint, tabletop items, bed linens, towels, and other accessories. It's much more problematic (and expensive) to change wall-to-wall carpeting, tile or other permanent installations. If you're unable to change those elements, then you can change a room's Color Mood. For instance, in a room with PEACH tiles, change your towels from CREAM to AQUA, and you go from Nurturing to Beach Scenes. So if your dominant color is still a favorite and you used that color for the permanent items you can't change, look at the color combinations listed under each Color Mood. Perhaps you can change the secondary and accessory colors and inspire that change of Color Mood you are yearning for.

Another solution could be to utilize a Color Mood that is close in feeling to your preferred mood. If you like the concept of the Tranquil palette but are not comfortable with predominantly cool colors, you may opt to use the Nurturing palette with its soft, warm colors. The tender, safe feelings that the Nurturing palette evokes may bring a certain serenity and calm to you, so the ultimate effects may be very similar. This is a very personal reaction, after all.

Do remember that every dominant color scheme should have some touch of its balancing opposite, so a predominantly Tranquil mood of cool colors should have some warmth, and this could be enough to satisfy you. The blue wall-to-wall carpeting that you cannot afford to change sets the emotional tone (because it occupies so much space), but it certainly can be balanced by the lesser accents of an APRICOT/PLACID BLUE/CORNSILK print sofa and/or CORNSILK accessories.

Q: *Why do I feel the need for brighter color after years of decorating*
with safe neutrals?

Your needs are easily diagnosed. After living in such bland surroundings, you are suffering from "color deprivation," and the only thing that will cure you is a shot of some stimulating color. In each of us there is the needy child, the dominating parent, and the well-balanced adult, all with opinions about how we should react to any given situation. The demanding child says: "I really want a red sofa." The autocratic parent says: "You can't have a red sofa. It's too bright and impractical." But the reasonable adult can come to the rescue with a solution like, "How about a big squishy red pillow sitting on the beige sofa?" Of course, there's nothing wrong with a red sofa if you want to express the playful child within you, but in order to unleash your creativity, you'll need to muzzle the finger-wagging parent with the no-no's and must-not's!

Q: *What about wooden furniture and woodwork? Can wood colors clash? How many woods can you use in a room?*

There was a time when combining wood tones was considered a decorating faux pas. If a matched suite of mahogany furniture was used in the dining room, another wood surface was generally not recommended, with the possible exception of another equally dark and similar wood floor. Today, there are no hard and fast rules, and it's more about mood than it is about matching.

Most people, if starting from scratch, will opt to buy matching wood tones. That does make the decision-making process easier, for example: a light pine hutch, table, and chairs in a Romantic kitchen, or a dark oak buffet, china cabinet, table and chairs in the Traditional dining room. It works in the setting, fits the mood, and everything coordinates—the eye "connects" all of the pieces because of their similar finishes and "feel."

But what if you inherited your grandmother's dark mahogany sideboard, and your dining room floors, table, and chairs are all done in a light blonde ash? Your tastes run to cool and Contemplative while Grandma was definitely in the deeper Traditional mode. But that sideboard stores more than platters and plates; it holds some precious memories as well. Stripping that charming antique would be downright sacrilegious, and darkening that sleek Danish blonde wood is not an option you'd want to live with. What to do?

The key is to keep the wood finishes "color-connected" in some way so that the eye can pick up on the continuity or flow from one area to another, from furniture to floor, paneling, paint, accessories, wall covering, window covering—all of the other decorating elements.

This is truly an easy solution and one that you might have already done by instinct. For example, in the dark and light dilemma mentioned above, the chair pads, placemats, centerpiece, wall or window coverings could contain both darker and lighter elements (just like the furniture and floor)—perhaps a combination taken from the Nurturing mood of TOFFEE BROWN, VANILLA CREAM, CANDLELIGHT PEACH, and SMOKE GREEN.

The question of pine is always a knotty one as it is such a popular wood. What if you purchased a home that is exactly the right size, price, and location, but the only drawback (in your mind) is that the floors and wall paneling are a golden honey pine and your wood furnishings are primarily a bluish-red cherry wood?

You have three options. One is to paint the paneling and change the flooring. The second is to stain the paneling and the floor a deeper tone that will complement the furnishings. The last solution is more expedient and less expensive and that is to bring warmer accents into the room to pick up the warmth of the wood tones in the floor and paneling. As previously mentioned, there are always opportunities to coordinate colors that are somewhat "off" by giving the eye something else to light on that will provide a connecting link to the colors in question.

Another possible solution is to look to the undertones of the honey pine floor/paneling in question. In addition to the obvious honey, tan, or ochre tones, look at the knots in the wood—what colors are they? The darker tones in the knots that are always present in pine might offer even more possibilities—they will provide some burgundy-brown tones to connect with the cherry wood.

In my own home, we have a small powder room where I display my collection of antique evening bags on the walls. The flooring I inherited was a

COLORS
FOR
YOUR
EVERY
MOOD

164

honey pine that has a country feel, the evening bags are rather elegant and formal. I opted to paint the walls and ceiling a color that was inspired by the knots—a very deep PORT WINE shade in a shiny reflective enamel. The marble countertop has elements of both the purplish wine and honeyed shades running through it. Although the floor was very casual and the decorative elements very dressy, the color pulled it all together.

Look beyond the obvious. This is what decorators know how to do. It really is a very creative exercise that will help you expand your color sense. You can also look to nature for inspiration: there's an infinite variety of bark, stems, and twigs surrounding us, and our eyes are accustomed to seeing these blends within the context of nature. This can work in your environment as well, if you, like the proverbial willow, are willing to bend and shake off some of the outmoded and rigid restrictions of the past.

Q: *What about wall coverings?*

Wall coverings can add a wonderful dimension to any room, as the pattern can combine all of the colors in your room, giving an instant appearance of coordination. Wall coverings can also provide color inspiration that is ready-made—all you have to do is to pull color out of the pattern to use in other elements of the room.

As to the number of colors that may be present in the pattern—that will vary depending on how complex the Color Mood you've selected. A beautiful undulating paisley pattern chosen for a Sensuous powder room might be unique and contain as many as six shades, whereas a super simple bathroom inspired by your memories of a Cape Cod Fourth of July weekend vacation might contain just three colors—red, white, and blue!

Wall coverings can provide instant gratification. Whatever the feeling you want to convey—cozy, informal, glamorous—there are always wall coverings to express a mood. This choice should be based on that emotional tug. If the scene or pattern says something to you, evokes some special memory, or draws you to it for no apparent reason, remember: There is always a reason. We simply may not remember why it is so appealing.

As to the purely practical considerations, wall coverings can add effective optical illusions: striped papers with contrasting values can create height or width in a room. The way color is placed in a design can also create a rhythmic pattern to draw the eye vertically or horizontally to affect how large a room seems. Large designs and deep dark colors will make a room appear smaller, but light solid colors and small designs make a room seem larger.

Again, it's a matter of personal choice. You might enjoy a small, dark, den-like room or you may prefer the open, airy feeling of a large, light room. And if you like variety, there is a place in the house for both. Glossy foil and faux treatments can brighten a space as they add depth and interest. They will also visually increase the size because of their mirror-like effect.

Q: *I have a teen-age son who wants his room painted black (or some other bizarre color request). What should I do?*

As difficult as it may be to allow a child to do something that is so different from the rest of the house, I have to say yes to this not-so-unusual request. Just as you let him play with his crayons when he was very small, you need to let him decorate his own space in his own way. Color is a very personal choice, and no matter how bizarre it may seem to you, he feels this is his private space. If he is like most adolescents, his doors are usually closed (a good thing considering the music that is generally blasting and the dirty clothes all over the floor) and there are posters all over the walls that obscure most of the color. But do negotiate with him prior to the painting. When he tires of the black (and fortunately, he will), then he gets to repaint it!

Q: *What can I do with an overbright green chair that I bought (on sale, of course!) It looked much darker in the store than it does in my apartment.*

This is a common problem that we can blame on lighting. The lights in the store are very different than those in your home. This shift of color caused by differing light sources is called "metamerism," and we have all experienced it with a variety of products.

The best solution for the future is to have the store provide you with an actual color sample (they might let you "sign out" a pillow or a large swatch with the promise of bringing it back the next day and/or charging it to your account).

When it's too late for returns, or you've decided to live with it, place an analogous color next to it or on it. A color that seems too loud can be quieted with an adjacent hue. A bright green chair, for instance, can be "quieted" with a soft blue-green pillow or throw.

Q: *What happens if two or more people living together prefer different colors for decorating?*

Often the person with the strongest personality has the strongest color preferences. It used to be that men would defer to women when it came to decorating because it was traditionally her role to decorate their home. But traditional roles have changed, and men's moods will be equally affected by color. Preferences will probably vary within a family, but there are several solutions. If each person has his or her own bedroom, obviously that room can be done according to the occupant's preferred Color Mood. When rooms are shared, however, such as bedrooms or mutual living areas, the people involved must try to reach a compromise.

It's a really good idea to have everyone involved take both the Color Word Association Quiz as well as circling his or her favorite moods and discussing personal reactions. You'll come out of the experience with a better understanding of your own feelings as well as everyone else's and you'll share some special moments. At the very least, perhaps you'll get some reactions like: "I never knew why those colors and/or moods were so important to you and now I know why you need to use them!"

Q: *What are the secrets of professional designers—how do they manage to get it so "right"?*

The answer is that there are no "secrets." Designers are trained professionals experienced in the process of decorating and design. They have honed their skills in school while most people have spent just a comparative fraction of their time decorating their homes.

They read everything they can get their hands on, attend trade shows, continuously shop for and with clients, attend seminars, and, if they are licensed or certified, must pass rigorous tests to qualify for licensing. I have personally witnessed the dedication and interest of hundreds of interior designers in the

COLORS
FOR
YOUR
EVERY
MOOD

166

continuing education courses in color I teach in venues all over the United States, Mexico, and Canada.

They get it right because they work hard at it. They also have this unique talent that has probably been evident since they were tiny tots. As children, they learned to paint, draw, and fix up their rooms. They were astute observers, and their friends, no doubt, came to them for their decorating and/or color advice (which they were always happy to dispense)!

If this sounds like a description of you, then you might have made an excellent interior designer, but you chose another career path instead. Fortunately, your creative urges can be satisfied by following the very same color guidelines utilized by professionals, which you have learned in this book. Above all, most interior designers pay close attention to color and mood. Now you can use the information in this book and determine the Color Moods you want to attain in your home with the color combinations that will make those moods work for you.

Q: *I am a devout do-it-yourselfer. How do I know when and if I need the help of a professional?*

You know that you need help when decorating is no longer fun or creatively satisfying and you're getting so anxious or uptight that you keep procrastinating. Another important consideration is time and energy. If you're running short of both, then look for help. Interior designers and color consultants are out there all the time looking for new fabrics, trends, and colors because it's an integral part of their service.

You don't have to give up "creative control" entirely, nor should you. Working with a designer is a collaborative effort where your input is welcome. A designer would find both the Color Word Association Quiz and the "moods definers" in this book are a tremendous help in better understanding your needs and reactions to color.

Q: *If color is so personal, how do professional decorators separate their personal notions of desirable color from their clients' personal wishes?*

Even those decorators who have a distinctive "look" will opt to bring your personality into the picture. Your responsibility is to communicate your feelings to them. And designers do like new challenges and will experiment with different looks. Mario Buatta, known as the "Prince of Chintz" for his elegant decorating style once said: "If I see another faux finish, I think I'll faux up!"

It would obviously be best for you to choose a designer with somewhat similar color sensibilities. Choosing someone who leans toward a Dynamic use of monotones with brights is obviously not the best person if your tastes run to the muted colors of Dawn and Dew. If a designer has a great track record doing very subtle colors, and that is your preferred mood, then he or she is obviously on the same wavelength as you.

Most designers integrate their clients' needs and desired moods into their homes. Famed interior designer Vicente Wolf is best known for his quiet monotone/monochromatic understatements, but he sometimes infuses his otherwise neutral schemes into a Dynamic mood with the bold contrast of a color like POMPEIAN RED.

Q: *Are there rules professionals use in choosing a color combination?*

The operative word here is "rule" and the answer is "no." There are no absolutes. Designers are trained in the usage of the color wheel as a fundamental guideline, just as you have been in this book. But some designers will push beyond the usual color clichés. For example, as a designer, I might tweak the Traditional NAVY and a HUNTER GREEN combination by changing the navy to a more Dynamic COBALT or the HUNTER GREEN to CHARTREUSE.

Roy G. Biv is the mythical memory tweaker that professionals learn about in design school. His name represents the scant seven rainbow colors of **r**ed, **o**range, **y**ellow, **g**reen, **b**lue, **i**ndigo, and **v**iolet. But there are millions of nuances between. The combinations in the color mood chapter will help you to expand your own color "barriers," just as professionals do.

Q: *Are there certain color combinations that professionals avoid?*

It depends upon the professional. But they are not trained to avoid certain color combinations at all costs. Generally speaking, the combinations that do not veer too far away from those mentioned previously—monotone, monochromatic, analogous, complementary, and some variations on the complementary—will always work. Color harmony is very subjective, often dependent on cultural connotations, and it is based on the individual view of what is pleasing to the eye. As far as designers are concerned, much of their final decision is very innate. It just comes from something within—that "eye" for color and sense of mood.

There may be certain colors that are not recommended for purely practical and obvious reasons. A suggested mixture of both the Traditional and Tranquil moods in the very creative combination of a powdery blue sofa against a rich plum colored wall may work beautifully, but it is not a good idea if Spots, the client's dalmatian, makes his home in that room and lives up to his name!

Q: *What are the most frequent color mistakes?*

The most frequent color mistake is a lack of cohesion—not enough dominance of a particular mood or color scheme that tells you from the moment you enter the room what the message is. Your personality (and that of your significant others) should be immediately apparent, and the only way to achieve this is to follow the guidelines in this book.

After reviewing your answers to the quiz, review the decorating steps in chapter 15 (page 151). Utilizing the charts after each Color Mood section, you are then ready to start decorating. It will take some time and effort, but it will pay off in the end because you will feel more comfortable in your surroundings and so will your friends and family.

Q: *What about trend colors? Should I use them?*

Using trend colors is the fastest way to add a fresh new look to your surroundings. But— they will date your surroundings when the trend is over. If you love to redecorate or money is no object and your friends describe you as a "trendy" type (and you consider that a compliment), then you can have fun with the changes.

But in the real world, faced with budget constraints, it is best to use trend colors as refreshers, knowing that you may grow very tired of them very quickly.

COLORS
FOR
YOUR
EVERY
MOOD

168

My best advice is not to use a hot trend color on a big-ticket item—save the trends for the easily changeable areas like tabletops, bedspreads, towels, accessories, and most all, wall paint. This covers a large area; but dollar for dollar, especially if you do the grunt work yourself, this will change a look faster and cost less than anything else.

And paint isn't used exclusively on the walls. It can be used very effectively on the furniture. I have wicker pieces that have been reborn approximately every seven to ten years, and it's such fun because it's instant gratification for the price of a few cans of spray paint.

Old and preferably beat-up furniture, especially when bought at a yard sale for practically nothing, can be the most fun of all to paint, and it's the fastest way to change a mood. A sturdy willow chair that seems like it's destined to remain in a Rustic setting can be rendered more Romantic when painted a mauvey rose. And nothing will make a stodgy but scratched Traditional table more Whimsical than a coat of PERIWINKLE paint.

Q: *Can color create optical illusions in a room?*

Painted surfaces can work magic though optical illusions. Walls may appear to retreat or come forward without benefit of sledgehammers. You can raise the roof or shrink a sofa simply by using color wisely. Nooks and crannies seem to disappear simply by blending into the background color, or an interesting object can be dramatically emphasized with a background of its complementary color.

It is best to use a light background in a small room and to keep the window treatment light and airy so that the area is not too cut up. A small, dark space like a hallway, alcove, entry, or powder room, however, can be dramatized by making the area colors intense or sparkly. Bright colors that would be overwhelming in rooms in which you spend a lot of time can be really energizing in small doses.

Dark or intense colors can be very effective in a passageway when it leads to a large lighted area. The effect is that of a light at the end of a tunnel. If you want to lengthen a short hallway or passage, paint the walls a deep tone and keep the floor and ceiling light. Place pictures along the wall in frames to match the ceiling or floor color. This forms a horizontal pattern that the eye will follow to create more length.

To open up a cramped space, lighten the hue on the wall you want to expand. For example, if a sofa must be placed on a short wall, lighten both the wall behind it and the wall immediately opposite. The two remaining walls may be darkened to a medium or deeper tone. This same technique works for a narrow room. Paint the narrow walls lighter than the wider wall.

To make a square room less box-like, do one wall in a deeper tone than the other three walls. Dark or warm colors seem to enclose a room, while light or cool colors open it up.

Monochromatic and neutral schemes unify the space in a small room and give it the illusion of greater size. A ceiling will appear higher if it is painted white or a shade lighter than the walls. White or pale colors will also give the greatest light reflection. Simply add white to your wall color and use it on the ceiling.

If you want to lower the ceiling, paint it one tone deeper than the walls. Painting a wide band of ceiling color around the top part of the walls will also give the illusion of a lower ceiling, as will molding that is the same color as the ceiling.

To enlarge small windows, use the same shadings as the walls in your window treatment. Blinds and shutters all have built-in vertical or horizontal lines that act as excellent expanders. Avoid using anything too heavy or dark on small windows and allow as much as light to come in as possible.

In smaller rooms, it's best to keep the woodwork the same color as the walls. Contrasting colors will break the wall into sections. In larger rooms, woodwork can be used as an interesting contrast, especially if it is embellished. Indeed, it can become a charming focal point. In a dull entry or hallway, brightly colored doors can add some cheer and entice the viewer to enter. It can certainly do the same on the front door and shutters.

Q. *What are the effects of color under your feet?*

Color underfoot is equally as important as color used on the walls, ceilings, windows, and furnishings And it may be even more important if the room is fairly simple: a Contemplative room that is done in varying shades of blue, for example. If there is no outstanding art or wall hangings that serve as a focal point, then a large carpet on the floor might provide just the right amount of balancing warmth by incorporating, in this particular space, a pattern of CHINESE RED surrounded by graceful tendrils of CYPRESS and interspersed with accents of DELFT and CREAM PEARL—a dramatic focus that, although underfoot, is definitely not understated.

Q. *Should I consider value or intensity of color more than hue?*

Hue (the color family: blue, red, yellow, orange, purple, and green), value (light to dark) and intensity (degree of brightness) should all be considered in planning an interior, as they are of equal importance.

A hue must be chosen to establish the dominant mood of a room, but the value or intensity of the hue ultimately helps to define the message. For example: in a Forest mood, a monochromatic setting of various greens can be chosen to depict a sense of the outdoors. A variety of "natural" greens, in a variety of values from ELM, SPRUCE, ASPEN GREEN, and SAGE might be selected, but a really strident bright LIME GREEN will look too restless among the more quiet tones. They are all shades of the same color family, but some relatives are noisier than others and seem to disrupt the harmony. It would be far better to reach out of the family and choose an analogous neighbor such as DUSKY BLUE GREEN that would better suit the mood. Just a hint of BUFF YELLOW would bring a touch of sunshine into the forest and provide the necessary color balance.

Q. *How does texture affect color?*

Color can be greatly altered by texture because of light absorption and light reflection. The best example of this is one of the most obvious: a newly vacuumed soft pile carpet. It appears to change color slightly depending on the direction of the pile. Rougher textured woven fabrics will deepen a hue while shiny surfaces intensify color. The same color will appear brighter in velvet than it does in a nubby wool.

Matte, or flat, surfaces absorb light and appear darker than glossy, light-reflecting surfaces. Colors appear lighter and more lustrous on smooth surfaces that have a sheen. WEDGWOOD blue on a satin pillow will seem much brighter than the WEDGWOOD blue cotton bedspread it sits on. A nappy or shiny texture is more versatile than a dull texture and is less apt to call attention to a color match that is not "right on." For example, if a chenille throw draped across a leather loveseat

COLORS
FOR
YOUR
EVERY
MOOD

170

is not exactly the same color as the leather, the pile surface of the chenille allows for some flexibility and a variation of color. The changeability of the texture will "fool" the eye.

Q. *How does pattern affect color?*

There are several primary considerations in combining patterns. The first is: If patterns are not similar, such as a bargello (flamestitched) needlepoint pillow on a floral chair, but they contain the same colors, they will work together. Color is the common thread that links them. Similar patterns will also work together, but are more interesting if the scale is different. For example, a large plaid den sofa done in a CRUSHED BERRY shade could be used with a small houndstooth checked chair done in the same colors.

When combining colors, the "weight" of a fabric should be taken into consideration as well. Patterns always appear heavier than plain fabrics, so if you are choosing a pattern for a petite loveseat or a small bed, for example, a pattern especially should be used sparingly (if it is large) so that it does not overwhelm the piece.

Remember that the colors of small-patterned fabrics and tweeds tend to blend. Seen from up close, a small floral pattern in yellow and pink will optically turn to peach from just a few feet away.

Q. *How are metallic finishes affected by color?*

Metals are actually more versatile than painted surfaces because of their reflective qualities. Shiny surfaces often pick up and reflect surrounding colors. For example, a glass and chrome table from the Dynamic palette is usually thought of as rather cool and "slick." If this table is sitting on a carpet of BRICK RED, however, some of that warmth will be reflected on to the table.

In general, high gloss in cool tones of silver, chrome, anodized aluminum, and stainless steel works best with a predominantly cool palette; while burnished copper, gold, bronze, and brass look best with predominantly warmer tones. Pewter and antiqued surfaces will work with either. Always think in terms of the surrounding colors, however, and how they will reflect on the metallic surfaces. Some antiqued or matte-finished metals reflect very little, if any, of their surroundings. Deep coppers will pick up very little of the coldest blues and purples. In fact, using the principle of complementary color, the cool blues will intensify copper because they are opposites on the color wheel.

Q. *What is the most beautiful room you've ever seen? Why?*

The most beautiful room I ever saw was in a home in Foggy Bottom, in Washington, D.C., near the U.S. State Department. The owner was a world traveler in the diplomatic service, and she had a marvelous eye for color. She was not a trained interior designer, but self-taught.

As she had collected so many interesting artifacts in her travels, her tastes leaned to Travel moods: A Parisian guest room with marvelous and colorful French posters, an African safari inspired den done in earthy reds and accented with dark wood carvings and ornamental masks. The bedroom was a study in cool meditative shades inspired by an antique prayer shawl. A master bath mirrored the PERSIAN VIOLET and rosy TERRA COTTA in handmade tiles.

But it was the living room that captured my eye as soon as I entered the house. First there was the magnificent Oriental carpet of a warm luscious wine and a deep green-blue, accented by a DUSTY ROSE and a very LIGHT TAUPE. The walls were painted in a LIGHT TAUPE and all of the furnishings were highly polished mahogany and cherry woods. Everything else in the room echoed the shades in the rug. The adjoining foyer and powder room were painted in the deep wine color. The accents, too, were inspired by the carpet.

The house was very small, but there was a definite sense of drama in this Contemplative setting that greeted you as you opened the door. As it was so small, my talented friend utilized similar, although not identical, colors in every room, common threads that linked everything visually.

Another of the most memorable homes I've ever seen belonged to a famous film and TV star. Her family life is very important to her, and that was evident from the moment you walked into the entry. This beautiful light-filled home in the Hollywood Hills reflected a Nurturing palette throughout much of the space with a background of eggshell and light beiges in walls and sofas. Tender pastels were sprinkled against the neutral backdrop: in pale melons, lilacs, and misty grayed-green. The dining room was a peachy tone called CARAMEL CREAM combined with POWDER BLUE, TERRA COTTA tile and natural wood tones.

The children's rooms were the colors that most parents choose, especially as their children reach the toddler stage: whimsical LOLLIPOP red, POPCORN YELLOW, EASTER EGG blue, and CLOUD CREAM. This was not a make-believe set. It was a comfortable, livable and very real home that truly reflected a sense of the family who lived there.

I hope this book has given you a sense of your own true decorating colors and put you in touch with your personal feelings about the various colors that have touched your life and may "color" it in the future.

I know you'll find the many Color Moods a handy way to organize your decorating plans for each room and each person who inhabits your personal space with you.

Use them not only to decorate your spaces with color but also to bring the balance, harmony, confidence and fun you crave into the place you go to rest and reflect and enjoy your loved ones—or just your own great thoughts.

L.E.

COLORS
FOR
YOUR
EVERY
MOOD

172

Color Name and Specification Cross-Reference

These are color names used in *Colors for Your Every Mood*. While every effort has been made to show the colors accurately, their representation is subject to the limitations of printing. If you would like to see the actual colors chosen by the author, this list gives the color name and its corresponding color specification number in the PANTONE® TEXTILE Color System®. PANTONE® colors cited are from the PANTONE® TEXTILE Color System® Paper Edition. For more information on this System, contact Pantone at (201) 935-5500.

COLOR NAME / PANTONE SPECIFICATION / (PAGE-COMBO NO.) *if any*

Abyss PANTONE® 16-4404 (115-C)
Acorn PANTONE® 18-1314 (99-C)
Afterglow PANTONE® 11-0510 (71-F)
Air Blue PANTONE® 15-4319 (71-D, 111-A)
Alabaster PANTONE® 12-0812 (83-A, 143-A)
Alaskan Blue PANTONE® 14-4225 (111-F)
Almond Apricot PANTONE® 15-1319 (142-C)
Almond Blossom PANTONE® 13-2006 (127-B)
Almost Aqua PANTONE® 13-6006 (115-A)
Almost Mauve PANTONE® 12-2103 (115-F)
Aloe Wash PANTONE® 13-0608 (71-B, 91-B)
Alpine PANTONE® 18-4018 (111-E)
Amber PANTONE® 14-1045 (95-F, 135-C)
Amber Gold PANTONE® 16-1139 (135-B)
Amber Green PANTONE® 17-0840 (79-C)
Amberglow PANTONE® 16-1350 (119-B)
American Beauty PANTONE® 19-1759 (135-A)
Amethyst PANTONE® 18-3015 (87-G)
Amparo Blue PANTONE® 18-3945 (119-D, 123-D)
Andorra PANTONE® 19-1327 (131-B)
Angel Blue PANTONE® 14-4814 (71-A)
Angelwing PANTONE® 11-1305 (143-D)
Angora PANTONE® 12-0605 (83-B)
Antelope PANTONE® 16-1126 (99-C)
Antique Bronze PANTONE® 17-1028
Antique Gold PANTONE® 16-0730 (87-G)
Antique White PANTONE® 11-0105 (91-A)(142-A)
Antler PANTONE® 17-1510 (115-I)
Apricot PANTONE® 15-1153
Apricot Cream PANTONE® 13-1027
Apricot Ice PANTONE® 13-1020
Apricot Illusion PANTONE® 14-1120 (71-H, 91-A)
Apricot Nectar PANTONE® 14-1133
Apricot Sherbet PANTONE® 13-1031 (75-E)
Aqua PANTONE® 15-4717 (71-H)
Aqua: Cabbage PANTONE® 13-5714 (12-H)
Aqua Green PANTONE® 15-5421 (130-D)
Aqua Sky PANTONE® 14-4811 (71-C)
Aquamarine PANTONE® 14-4312 (107-D)
Arabesque PANTONE® 16-1441 (95-D)
Aragon PANTONE® 17-1532 (95-B)
Arctic Ice PANTONE® 13-4110 (111-D)
Arona PANTONE® 16-4109 (115-E, 138-B, 143-B)
Artichoke Green PANTONE® 18-0125 (135-D)
Aruba Blue PANTONE® 13-5313 (107-A)
Ash PANTONE® 16-3802 (115-A)
Ash Rose PANTONE® 17-1322 (143-D)
Aspen Gold PANTONE® 13-0850 (67-E)
Aspen Green PANTONE® 17-0215 (99-B)
Atmosphere PANTONE® 14-1406 (115-D)
Aubergine: Eggplant PANTONE® 19-2311 (59)
Aurora Pink PANTONE® 15-2217
Aurora Red PANTONE® 18-1550 (95-A, 103-A)
Autumn Glaze PANTONE® 18-1451 (135-C, 142-A)
Autumn Sunset PANTONE® 16-1343
Avocado PANTONE® 18-0430
Azalea PANTONE® 17-1842 (123-I)
Azalea Pink PANTONE® 16-2126 (123-G)
Ballad Blue PANTONE® 14-4304
Bamboo PANTONE® 14-0740 (143-C)
Banana PANTONE® 13-0947
Barberry PANTONE® 18-1760 (135-E)
Barely Pink PANTONE® 12-2906
Bark PANTONE® 16-1506 (79-D, 83-E)
Barn Red PANTONE® 18-1531 (79-G, 135-C, 135-D)
Basil PANTONE® 16-6216 (71-C, 127-E)
Beach Sand PANTONE® 14-1225 (107-E)
Beaver Fur PANTONE® 17-1417 (103-E)
Beetroot Purple PANTONE® 18-2143
Beige PANTONE® 14-1118 (13-E, 138-B)

Billiard Green PANTONE® 16-5427 (67-E)
Billowing Sail PANTONE® 11-4604 (107-F)
Birch PANTONE® 13-0905
Biscuit PANTONE® 16-1336 (83-C)
Bison PANTONE® 18-1027 (99-E)
Bisque PANTONE® 13-1109 (75-A, 142-D)
Bit of Blue PANTONE® 11-4601 (107-B)
Bitter Chocolate PANTONE® 19-1317
Black: Phantom PANTONE® 19-4205 (15-G)
Black Ink PANTONE® 19-0506 (87-D)
Black Olive PANTONE® 19-0608 (87-E, 131-C)
Blarney Green PANTONE® 16-5942
Bleached Denim PANTONE® 18-3930 (103-A, 107-C)
Bleached Sand PANTONE® 13-1008 (59, 83-E, 143-D)
Blue Bonnet PANTONE® 17-3936 (123-B)
Blue Curacao PANTONE® 15-4826
Blue Graphite PANTONE® 19-4015 (119-B)
Blue Grass PANTONE® 12-5206 (75-B)
Blue Gray PANTONE® 15-4703 (83-F, 107-A)
Blue Haze PANTONE® 15-4707 (71-G, 143-A)
Blue Iris PANTONE® 18-3943 (95-E)
Blue Moon PANTONE® 17-4328 (71-A)
Blue Nights PANTONE® 19-4023 (95-G)
Blue Shadow PANTONE® 14-4205 (143-C)
Blue Spruce PANTONE® 18-5308 (123-A)
Blue Ribbon PANTONE® 19-3839 (79-C, 83-A)
Bluebell PANTONE® 18-4141 (123-A)
Bluesteel PANTONE® 18-4222 (138-A)
Bluewash PANTONE® 12-4304 (67-B)
Bluish Lavender PANTONE® 18-3737 (67-G)
Blush PANTONE® 15-1614 (91-B)
Bone White PANTONE® 12-0105 (67-C, 71-I, 79-F)
Bordeaux PANTONE® 17-1710 (15-B)
Boysenberry PANTONE® 19-2431 (99-F)
Brandied Melon PANTONE® 16-1340
Breen PANTONE® 19-1034 (135-C)
Brick Dust PANTONE® 17-1424 (142-C, 143-B)
Brick Red PANTONE® 19-1543 (14-F)
Bridal Blush PANTONE® 11-1005 (127-A, 127-D)
Bridal Rose PANTONE® 15-1611
Bright Chartreuse: Tender Shoots PANTONE® 14-0446 (12-D)
Bright Cobalt PANTONE® 19-4037 (67-B, 67-D)
Bright Gold PANTONE® 16-0947 (87-I)
Bright Green PANTONE® 15-5534 (12-E)
Bright Pink: Azalea Pink PANTONE® 16-2126 (14-C)
Bright Red Violet PANTONE® 18-3339 (67-B, 83-D)
Bright Rose PANTONE® 18-1945
Bright White PANTONE® 11-0601 (67-H, 123-I, 135-B)
Bright Yellow: Vibrant Yellow PANTONE® 13-0858 (12-A)
Brilliant Blue PANTONE® 18-4247 (87-C)
Bronze Green PANTONE® 18-0317 (131-C, 135-B)
Brown Patina PANTONE® 18-1242 (131-E)
Brown Stone PANTONE® 19-1322
Brown Sugar PANTONE® 17-1134 (135-C)
Buckskin PANTONE® 16-1442 (103-B)
Buff PANTONE® 13-1024
Buff Orange PANTONE® 14-1128 (95-E, 127-F)
Buff Yellow PANTONE® 14-0847
Burgundy: Cerise PANTONE® 19-1955 (14-G)
Burgundy PANTONE® 19-1617 (79-E, 138-C)
Burnished Lilac PANTONE® 15-1905 (115-A, 115-F)
Burnt Henna PANTONE® 19-1540 (95-F)
Burnt Orange PANTONE® 16-1448 (67-A)
Burnt Russet PANTONE® 19-1530 (99-B, 103-F, 135-A)
Burnt Sienna PANTONE® 17-1544 (119-A, 143-C)
Burro PANTONE® 17-1322 (103-C)
Buttercup PANTONE® 12-0752 (123-F, 135-A)
Butternut PANTONE® 18-0830 (99-C)
Butterscotch PANTONE® 15-1147
Butterum PANTONE® 16-1341 (135-D)
Byzantium PANTONE® 19-3138 (83-C, 87-B)
Cactus Flower PANTONE® 18-2326 (103-E)
Cadet PANTONE® 18-3812
Cadmium Orange PANTONE® 15-1340 (83-C)
Cadmium Yellow PANTONE® 15-1054 (95-G)
Cafe Creme PANTONE® 16-1220
Calypso Coral PANTONE® 17-1744 (67-H, 119-C, 130-B)
Camel PANTONE® 17-1224 (142-E)
Camellia PANTONE® 16-1541
Cameo Blue PANTONE® 16-4414 (91-F)
Cameo Green PANTONE® 14-6312 (75-E, 91-D)
Canary Yellow PANTONE® 12-0633
Candlelight Peach PANTONE® 15-1621 (127-E)
Candy Pink PANTONE® 14-1911
Cantaloupe PANTONE® 15-1239
Cappuccino PANTONE® 19-1220
Capri Blue PANTONE® 17-4735 (107-B, 130-C)
Captains Blue PANTONE® 18-4020 (135-E)
Caramel Cream PANTONE® 13-1022

Cardinal PANTONE® 18-1643 (79-H, 135-B)
Carmine PANTONE® 17-1831 (87-I, 119-F)
Carnelian PANTONE® 16-1435 (95-C, 143-B)
Catchup PANTONE® 18-1449
Cedar Green PANTONE® 18-0328 (123-G)
Celadon PANTONE® 13-6108 (71-H, 83-G)
Celadon Green PANTONE® 14-0114
Celadon Tint PANTONE® 13-6105
Celery Green PANTONE® 13-0532
Celestial PANTONE® 18-4530
Cerulean PANTONE® 15-4020
Chalk PANTONE® 12-2902 (143-D)
Chalk Pink PANTONE® 13-1904 (143-A)
Charcoal Gray PANTONE® 18-0601 (83-F)
Charcoal Gray: Gunmetal PANTONE® 18-0306 (15-D)
Chartreuse PANTONE® 15-0751
Cherry PANTONE® 17-1563
Chicory PANTONE® 16-4013 (143-D)
Chili PANTONE® 18-1448 (119-E)
China Blue PANTONE® 18-3918
Chinchilla PANTONE® 17-1109 (95-D)
Chinese Red PANTONE® 15-0948
Chinese Yellow PANTONE® 15-0948 (143-B)
Chintz Rose PANTONE® 13-1408
Chocolate Chip PANTONE® 19-0809 (67-D)
Chrysanthemum PANTONE® 17-1641 (99-C)
Cinder PANTONE® 17-1506 (115-D)
Cinnabar PANTONE® 18-1540 (83-B, 95-C, 143-C)
Claret Red PANTONE® 17-1740
Classic Blue: Palace Blue PANTONE® 18-4043 (13-C)
Cloud Blue PANTONE® 14-4306 (75-E)
Cloud Cream PANTONE® 12-0804 (91-B)
Cloud Pink PANTONE® 13-1406
Clover PANTONE® 18-2320 (67-C, 123-A)
Cobalt PANTONE® 16-4127
Cobblestone PANTONE® 16-1407
Cocoa Brown PANTONE® 18-1222
Cocoon PANTONE® 14-1025 (91-D, 143-A)
Coffee PANTONE® 19-0812
Colonial Blue PANTONE® 18-4522 (79-C)
Conch Shell PANTONE® 15-1624 (107-E, 130-C)
Confetti PANTONE® 16-1723
Coral Almond PANTONE® 16-1434 (142-A)
Coral Haze PANTONE® 16-1329 (83-G)
Coral Pink PANTONE® 14-1318
Coral Sands PANTONE® 14-1224
Cornflower Blue PANTONE® 16-4031 (123-G, 127-A)
Cornhusk PANTONE® 12-0714
Cornsilk PANTONE® 13-0932
Coronet Blue PANTONE® 18-3929 (79-B)
Corsican Blue PANTONE® 18-3828 (95-D, 119-C)
Covert Green PANTONE® 18-0617
Cowhide PANTONE® 19-1533 (103-B)
Crabapple PANTONE® 16-1532
Cranberry PANTONE® 17-1545 (79-A, 99-F)
Cream PANTONE® 12-0817 (13-H)
Cream Pearl PANTONE® 12-1006 (71-E)
Cream Puff PANTONE® 13-1026 (75-F)
Crimson PANTONE® 19-1762
Crushed Berry PANTONE® 18-1418
Crystal Blue PANTONE® 13-4411 (111-B)
Curry PANTONE® 16-0928
Cypress PANTONE® 18-0322 (99-F, 123-H)
Daffodil PANTONE® 14-0850
Dahlia PANTONE® 18-3324 (123-H)
Dahlia Purple PANTONE® 17-3834 (123-E)
Dandelion PANTONE® 13-0758
Dark Brown PANTONE® 19-1012 (13-G)
Dark Denim PANTONE® 19-4118 (79-G)
Dark Earth PANTONE® 19-1020 (59)
Dark Green: Shady Glade PANTONE® 18-5624 (12-G)
Dark Green PANTONE® 19-5513 (135-E)
Dark Gull Gray PANTONE® 18-0403 (135-E)
Dark Red Brown PANTONE® 19-1526 (59)
Dawn Blue PANTONE® 13-4303 (115-F)
Dawn Pink PANTONE® 15-2205 (115-B)
Deauville Mauve PANTONE® 16-1707 (91-E, 115-I, 138-C)
Deep Blue PANTONE® 19-3847 (83-B)
Deep Claret PANTONE® 19-1840 (59, 79-D, 138-D)
Deep Grass PANTONE® 17-6219 (135-C)
Deep Lichen Green PANTONE® 18-0312
Deep Peacock Blue PANTONE® 17-5029 (67-D, 83-F)
Deep Periwinkle PANTONE® 17-3932 (83-E)
Deep Purple PANTONE® 19-3323
Deep Purple: Gentian Violet PANTONE® 19-3730 (15-B)
Deep Taupe PANTONE® 18-1312 (83-B)
Deep Ultramarine PANTONE® 19-3950 (119-E, 135-C)
Deep Water PANTONE® 18-4032
Delft PANTONE® 19-4039

Desert Dust PANTONE® 13-1018 (95-B)
Desert Flower PANTONE® 15-1435 (123-G)
Desert Mist PANTONE® 14-1127 (142-B)
Desert Sand PANTONE® 17-1524 (142-B)
Directoire Blue PANTONE® 18-4244 (83-F)
Double Cream PANTONE® 12-0715 (75-A)
Dove PANTONE® 15-0000
Drab Gray PANTONE® 15-1119 (138-A)
Dragonfly PANTONE® 19-4826 (143-E)
Dream Blue PANTONE® 15-4005 (71-C, 91-C)
Dresden Blue PANTONE® 17-4433
Dry Rose PANTONE® 18-1725 (138-B)
Duck Green PANTONE® 18-6011 (79-I, 115-I)
Dull Blue PANTONE® 17-4320 (143-A)
Dusk PANTONE® 17-3812 (71-I, 103-E, 142-E)
Dusk Blue PANTONE® 16-4120
Dusky Citron PANTONE® 14-0827
Dusky Green-Blue PANTONE® 18-5112 (103-A)
Dusty Cedar PANTONE® 18-1630
Dusty Lavender PANTONE® 17-3313 (142-C)
Dusty Pink: Blush PANTONE® 15-1614 (14-B)
Dusty Rose PANTONE® 17-1718 (91-F)
Dusty Turquoise PANTONE® 16-5114 (87-H)
Easter Egg PANTONE® 16-3925
Ebony PANTONE® 19-4104 (131-A)
Ecru PANTONE® 11-0809
Eggplant PANTONE® 19-2311 (79-B)
Eggshell Blue PANTONE® 14-4809 (71-B)
Elm PANTONE® (91-E, 83-G, 138-C)
Elm Green PANTONE® 18-0121 (99-B)
Emberglow PANTONE® 17-1547 (119-A)
Emerald PANTONE® 17-5641
Empire Yellow PANTONE® 14-0756
English Ivy PANTONE® 18-0110 (79-G, 127-D)
English Rose PANTONE® 13-1310 (75-B)
Ether PANTONE® 14-4506 (115-H)
Ethereal Green PANTONE® 11-0609 (83-B)
Eucalyptus PANTONE® 15-0513 (83-G, 103-A, 115-C)
Evening Sand PANTONE® 14-1311 (91-E, 107-F)
Faded Denim PANTONE® 17-4021 (103-C)
Faience PANTONE® 18-4232
Fair Aqua PANTONE® 12-5409
Fandango Pink PANTONE® 17-2033 (67-G, 130-C)
Fawn PANTONE® 16-1510 (99-D)
Feather Gray PANTONE® 15-1305
Feldspar PANTONE® 16-5815 (99-D)
Fiesta PANTONE® 17-1564
Fir PANTONE® 18-5621 (99-D)
Firecracker PANTONE® 16-1452 (67-G)
Flame PANTONE® 17-1462 (119-B)
Flame Orange PANTONE® 15-1157 (95-G)
Flame Scarlet PANTONE® 18-1662 (119-E)
Flamingo PANTONE® 16-1450
Flax PANTONE® 13-0935
Fog PANTONE® 13-0607 (138-B)
Foggy Dew PANTONE® 13-4305 (87-B)
Foliage PANTONE® 16-0237 (123-C)
Forest Green PANTONE® 17-0230 (135-A)
Forget Me Not PANTONE® 15-4312 (91-D, 127-E)
Four Leaf Clover PANTONE® 18-0420 (79-E)
Freesia PANTONE® 14-0852 (123-D)
French Vanilla PANTONE® 12-0722 (138-D)
Frost PANTONE® 12-6207 (111-F)
Frosty Green PANTONE® 15-5706
Frosty Spruce PANTONE® 18-5622 (111-A, 111-E)
Fuchsia: Fuchsia Red PANTONE® 18-2328 (14-D)
Fuchsia Purple PANTONE® 18-2436 (130-D)
Garden Glade PANTONE® 13-0614 (71-E, 75-D)
Garden Green PANTONE® 19-0230 (75-D, 123-F, 135-E)
Gargoyle PANTONE® 18-0503 (138-C)
Garnet PANTONE® 19-1655 (87-H)
Georgia Peach PANTONE® 16-1641 (123-E)
Geranium PANTONE® 17-1753 (123-A)
Geranium Pink PANTONE® 15-1922 (127-C)
Ginger PANTONE® 17-1444 (95-E)
Ginger Bread PANTONE® 18-1244
Ginger Spice PANTONE® 18-1535 (131-E)
Glacier PANTONE® 12-5505
Gobelin Blue PANTONE® 18-4011 (75-A)
Gold Earth PANTONE® 15-1234 (131-D)
Golden Apricot PANTONE® 14-1041 (95-A)
Golden Fleece PANTONE® 12-0822 (127-C)
Golden Glow PANTONE® 15-1050 (131-C)
Golden Mist PANTONE® 13-0643 (83-D)
Golden Nugget PANTONE® 16-1142 (103-D)
Golden Straw PANTONE® 12-0921
Golden Yellow PANTONE® 15-0953 (99-F)
Golden Yellow: Banana Cream PANTONE® 13-0941 (12-C)
Golden Rod PANTONE® 14-0951 (123-H)

Granite Green PANTONE® 16-5907 (115-A)
Grape PANTONE® 19-3728
Grape Royal PANTONE® 19-3518 (79-F)
Grass Green PANTONE® 15-6437
Gray Dawn PANTONE® 14-4106 (115-H)
Gray Mist PANTONE® 15-4706 (91-B, 143-B)
Gray Morn PANTONE® 13-0403 (115-C)
Gray Sand PANTONE® 13-1010 (142-B)
Gray Violet PANTONE® 14-4103
    (83-D, 71-C, 115-H, 143-C)
Grayish Lavender PANTONE® 16-3310 (91-F)
Green Banana PANTONE® 14-0434 (130-D)
Green Eyes PANTONE® 16-0224 (95-C)
Green Essence PANTONE® 12-0607 (111-C)
Green Haze PANTONE® 14-0615 (83-A, 115-E)
Green Tea PANTONE® 15-6428
Grenadine PANTONE® 17-1558 (67-A, 135-A)
Grey Lilac PANTONE® 13-3804 (143-A)
Greyish Purple PANTONE® 18-3513 (95-D)
Gull Gray PANTONE® 16-3803
Gun Metal PANTONE® 18-0306 (87-A)
Harvest Pumpkin PANTONE® 16-1260 (135-A)
Heather PANTONE® 14-4110 (75-C, 127-B)
Heather Rose PANTONE® 17-1608 (99-E)
Heavenly Pink PANTONE® 12-1305
Hedge Green PANTONE® 17-6323 (135-C)
Hibiscus PANTONE® 18-1762 (119-B, 123-F)
Honey Gold PANTONE® 15-1142 (67-G)
Hot Pink PANTONE® 17-1937 (67-I, 119-G)
Hunter Green PANTONE® 19-5511 (79-A)
Hushed Violet PANTONE® 14-3803 (71-C, 75-C, 115-C)
Hyacinth PANTONE® 17-3619 (123-F)
Ice PANTONE® 11-4803 (111-D)
Ice Flow PANTONE® 13-4404 (111-B)
Impala PANTONE® 13-1025 (127-B)
Impatiens Pink PANTONE® 13-1510 (127-E)
Imperial Blue PANTONE® 19-4245 (83-D)
Indigo PANTONE® 19-3215 (131-E)
Insignia Blue PANTONE® 19-4028 (79-H)
Iris Orchid PANTONE® 17-3323 (130-D)
Italian Plum PANTONE® 19-2514
Italian Straw PANTONE® 13-0917 (75-E)
Ivory PANTONE® 11-0907 (131-E, 138-A)
Ivy PANTONE® 18-5620
Jacaranda PANTONE® 17-3930 (67-I, 127-A)
Jade Green PANTONE® 16-0228 (67-A, 87-I)
Jade Grey PANTONE® 14-6011 (99-D)
Jade Lime PANTONE® 14-0232 (67-B)
Jaffa Orange PANTONE® 16-1454
Jasper PANTONE® 19-5413 (83-A)
Juniper PANTONE® 18-6330 (131-B)
Kashmir PANTONE® 17-6319 (95-A)
Kelly Green PANTONE® 16-6138 (67-I)
Khaki PANTONE® 14-0726 (105-D)
Lamb's Wool PANTONE® 12-0910 (103-B, 142-E)
Languid Lavender PANTONE® 15-3910 (91-F)
Lapis PANTONE® 17-5034 (67-F)
Lavender PANTONE® 15-3817 (14-H)
Lavender Blue PANTONE® 14-3905 (71-C, 142-D)
Lavender Gray PANTONE® 17-3910 (115-H)
Leaf Green PANTONE® 15-0332 (127-F)
Lemon Chrome PANTONE® 13-0859 (67-F, 87-E)
Lemonade PANTONE® 12-0721
Leprechaun PANTONE® 18-6022 (67-B)
Light Gray PANTONE® 12-0404 (87-D)
Lilac Gray PANTONE® 14-3903 (71-F, 75-C, 91-C)
Light Pink: Candy Pink PANTONE® 14-1911 (14-A)
Light Taupe PANTONE® 16-1210 (59, 71-G, 83-B)
Light Yellow: Sunshine Yellow PANTONE® 12-0727 (12-B)
Lilac Hint PANTONE® 13-4105 (71-B, 111-B)
Lilac Sachet PANTONE® 14-2710
Lilac Snow PANTONE® 13-3405 (75-D)
Lily White PANTONE® 11-4301 (123-D)
Lime Green PANTONE® 14-0452
Limestone PANTONE® 14-4702 (83-F)
Limoges PANTONE® 19-4044
Lion PANTONE® 17-1330 (131-B)
Lipstick Red PANTONE® 19-1764 (119-G)
Living Coral PANTONE® 16-1546 (67-D)
Loden Frost PANTONE® 17-0210 (99-E, 111-C)
Loganberry PANTONE® 19-3622 (79-D)
Lollipop PANTONE® 18-1764 (67-E)
Lotus PANTONE® 14-1905
Lupine PANTONE® 16-3521 (127-A)
Magenta PANTONE® 17-2036
Magenta Haze PANTONE® 18-2525 (103-D)
Mahogany PANTONE® 18-1425 (79-A, 67-I)
Malachite Green PANTONE® 16-5917 (115-G, 142-A)
Mallard Blue PANTONE® 19-4318

Mallard Green PANTONE® 19-4818 (79-F)
Mandarin Orange PANTONE® 16-1459 (95-G)
Mandarin Red PANTONE® 17-1459
Mango PANTONE® 17-1446
Maple Sugar PANTONE® 15-1316 (115-G, 135-B)
Marina PANTONE® 17-4041 (135-D)
Marine Blue PANTONE® 15-4712 (107-F)
Marine Green PANTONE® 16-5721 (107-A)
Maroon PANTONE® 18-1619
Mars Red PANTONE® 18-1655 (87-A)
Marsala PANTONE® 18-1436 (95-E)
Mauve: Mauve Mist PANTONE® 15-3207 (14-J)
Mauve Morn PANTONE® 12-2102
Mauveglow PANTONE® 16-1617 (143-B, 111-F)
Meadow Green PANTONE® 16-0233 (123-E)
Mediterranean Blue PANTONE® 18-4334 (107-B)
Mellow Rose PANTONE® 15-1515 (91-A, 142-D, 143-C)
Mellow Yellow PANTONE® 12-0720
Midnight PANTONE® 19-4127
Midnight Navy PANTONE® 19-4110 (59)
Mineral Blue PANTONE® 16-4712 (143-B)
Mineral Red PANTONE® 17-1537 (99-A, 103-D)
Ming Green PANTONE® 16-5930
Mint Green PANTONE® 17-6333 (123-D)
Misted Yellow PANTONE® 14-0837 (79-E, 99-C)
Mistletoe PANTONE® 16-0220 (111-D)
Misty Lilac PANTONE® 15-3807 (115-E)
Moonbeam PANTONE® 13-0000 (115-B)
Moonlight PANTONE® 15-1309 (75-A)
Moonlight Mauve PANTONE® 16-2614 (99-D)
Morning Glory PANTONE® 15-1920 (127-D)
Morning Mist PANTONE® 12-5204
Mosstone PANTONE® 17-0525 (99-A)
Moth PANTONE® 13-0611 (71-G)
Mulberry PANTONE® 17-3014
Murmur PANTONE® 12-5203 (71-D)
Muskmelon PANTONE® 15-1242
Mustard Gold PANTONE® 16-1133 (135-D)
Nasturtium PANTONE® 16-1451 (123-A)
Natural PANTONE® 16-1310 (71-A, 83-C)
Nautical Blue PANTONE® 19-4050 (67-F, 130-A)
Navy PANTONE® 19-3714
Navy Blue: Patriot Blue PANTONE® 19-3925 (13-D)
Neutral Gray PANTONE® 17-4402 (15-C, 59, 83-F, 87-A)
Nile Blue PANTONE® 15-5210 (71-B)
Norse Blue PANTONE® 15-4427 (111-C)
Nude PANTONE® 12-0911
Nugget Gold PANTONE® 16-1142
Oak Bluff PANTONE® 16-1144 (99-A)
Ocher PANTONE® 14-1036 (103-F, 143-A)
Oil Blue PANTONE® 17-5111 (142-C)
Old Gold PANTONE® 15-0955 (135-C)
Olive Green PANTONE® 17-0929 (12-F)
Olympian Blue PANTONE® 19-4056 (131-D)
Ombre Blue PANTONE® 19-4014 (138-D)
Opal Gray PANTONE® 16-3801 (138-A, 143-D)
Opaline Green PANTONE® 14-0226 (87-F)
Orange: Vermillion Orange PANTONE® 16-1362 (13-J)
Orange Brown PANTONE® 18-1346 (135-B)
Orange Ochre PANTONE® 14-1036
Orchid PANTONE® 15-3214 (107-E)
Orchid: Radiant Orchid PANTONE® 18-3224 (14-I)
Orchid Bloom PANTONE® 14-3612 (107-C, 119-G)
Orchid Bouquet PANTONE® 15-3412 (127-F)
Orchid Haze PANTONE® 16-2107 (143-E)
Orchid Ice PANTONE® 13-3406
Orchid Pink PANTONE® 13-2010 (107-D)
Orchid Smoke PANTONE® 15-2210 (142-D)
Oriental Blue PANTONE® 19-4535 (143-D)
Otter PANTONE® 18-1018 (103-B)
Oyster Gray PANTONE® 14-1107 (79-B)
Oyster White PANTONE® 13-1007 (107-C)
Pagoda Blue PANTONE® 17-4724 (143-C)
Pale Banana PANTONE® 12-0824 (75-F)
Pale Blush PANTONE® 14-1312 (142-B)
Pale Gray Green PANTONE® 14-0108 (83-G)
Pale Gold PANTONE® 15-0927 (79-A, 83-A)
Pansy PANTONE® 19-3542 (127-A)
Papaya Punch PANTONE® 15-1433 (107-C)
Paprika PANTONE® 17-1533
Papyrus PANTONE® 11-0107 (75-F, 131-D)
Paradise Pink PANTONE® 17-1755 (119-D, 130-A)
Parchment PANTONE® 13-0908 (79-I)
Parisian Blue PANTONE® 18-4036 (138-C)
Parrot Green PANTONE® 15-0341 (130-A)
Partridge PANTONE® 18-1124 (79-I)
Pastel Lavender PANTONE® 14-3209 (127-E)
Pastel Parchment PANTONE® 11-0603 (83-C, 91-E)
Pastel Rose Tan PANTONE® 12-1007

Index

Credits

ALEXANDER JULIAN, INC.
63 Copps Hill Road
Ridgefield, CT 06877
TEL (203) 438-3481 FAX (203) 438-6018

CARL D'AQUINO INTERIORS, INC.
180 Varick Street, 4th Floor
New York, NY 10014
TEL (212) 929-9787 FAX (212) 929-9225

CHEW & CO.
P.O. Box 382, Wayne, PA 19087

DON PAULSON PHOTOGRAPHY
9875 Miami Beach Road
Seabeck, WA 98380
TEL (360) 830-2212

DOUGLAS A. SALIN, PHOTOGRAPHER
647 Joost Avenue
San Francisco, CA 94127
TEL (415) 584-3322

EDWARD J. NORTH, PHOTOGRAPHER
102 Christopher Street
New York, NY 10014
TEL (212) 924-9404

ESTO PHOTOGRAPHICS INC.
222 Valley Place
Mamaroneck, New York 10543
TEL (914) 698-4060

GRANGE FURNITURE, INC.
200 Lexington Avenue
New York, NY 10016
TEL (212) 685-9494
TOLL FREE 1-800-GRANGE-1

HERB EISEMAN

HOWARD MILLARD, PHOTOGRAPHER
220 Sixth Avenue
Pelham, NY 10803
TEL (914) 738-6912

JAMIE DRAKE ASID
Jamie Drake Associates, Inc.
140 East 56th Street
New York, NY 10022
TEL (212) 754-3099

LYNN AUGSTEIN ASID CID
LAS Color & Design
3 Wolfback Terrace
Sausalito, CA 94965
TEL (415) 332-3323

MICHAEL LOVE ASID
Interior Options
200 Lexington Avenue
New York, NY 10016
TEL (212) 726-9708

NEIL HUGHES

OLSON SUNDBERG ARCHITECTS
108 First Avenue South, Fourth Floor
Seattle, WA 98104
TEL (206) 624-5670 FAX (206) 624-3730

PETER MARGONELLI, PHOTOGRAPHER
TEL (212) 431-5494

THIBAULT JEANSON, PHOTOGRAPHER
523 W. 45th St, New York, NY 10036
TEL (212) 664-1784

Learn More about Color and Lifestyles

Use this convenient coupon to receive further information on colors and color combinations from the Eiseman Center for Color Information and Training and Capital Books, Inc.

Yes!

❏ Please send me information on Lee Eiseman's color update newsletter, "Views on Hues."

❏ Please send me information on Lee Eiseman's workshops and lecture schedule.

❏ Please send me Capital Books complete catalog of titles on business, lifestyles, travel, careers and religion.

NAME _____

ADDRESS _____

_____

CITY _____

STATE _____ ZIP _____

Send a self-addressed stamped envelope to:
Capital Books, Inc.
P.O. Box 605, Herndon, Virginia 20172-0605